The Living Past
of America

The Living Past
of America

A Pictorial Treasury of our Historic
Houses and Villages that have been
Preserved and Restored

By CORNELIUS VANDERBILT, JR.

Crown Publishers, Inc.
NEW YORK

Ninth Printing, September, 1963

Dedicated

to

My Father, General Cornelius Vanderbilt,

a true patriot, a fine man, a good soldier, without whose guiding hand and whose vision
these lines could never have been written.

Contents

INTRODUCTION   xi
PICTURE CREDITS   xiii

NEW ENGLAND

MASSACHUSETTS

Plymouth: The Landing of the Pilgrims   1
The John Alden House   2
Salem: "A New World Venice"   3
Boston: "Hub of the Universe," "Mother of Freedom"   5
Concord   8
The Saugus Ironworks   10
Adams National Historic Site   12
The Adams Birthplaces   13
Old Deerfield: An Extraordinary Village—A "Natural" Preservation   14
Old Sturbridge Village: Town of the 1800's   16
Amesbury   16
Historic Seacoast: The Cape, Martha's Vineyard, Nantucket   17

MAINE

Augusta: Trading Post, Shiretown, Capital   18
Portland: "Resurgam!"   19
Lady Pepperrell Mansion   19
The Colonel Black Mansion   19

NEW HAMPSHIRE

Portsmouth: The Old Town on the Sea   20
The Daniel Webster Memorial   22

VERMONT

The Shelburne Museum: A Typical Vermont Village   23

RHODE ISLAND

Newport: Historic Port and Last Resort   26
Governor Stephen Hopkins House   28
Carrington House   28
Gilbert Stuart Birthplace   29
Old Slater Mill   29

CONNECTICUT

Mystic Seaport: Living Museum of the Sea   30
Henry Whitfield House   32
Webb House: Scene of the Yorktown Conference   33
The Glebe House: Birthplace of American Episcopacy   34
The Tapping Reeve House   34

MIDDLE ATLANTIC

NEW YORK

Bowne House: A Shrine to Religious Freedom   35
Sagamore Hill: Home of Theodore Roosevelt   36
Fraunces Tavern   38
Cooper Union   38
The Roger Morris-Jumel Mansion   39
The Frick Collection   40
Van Cortlandt Mansion   41
Philipse Castle: Residence of the First Lord of the Manor   42
Philipse Manor   43
Sunnyside: Sleepy Hollow Land   44
Vanderbilt Mansion   45
Hyde Park: Home of Franklin Delano Roosevelt   46
Hasbrouck House   48
Senate House: Where the First State Senate Met   48
Street of the Huguenots   49
Fort Crailo   50
Schuyler Mansion   50
Mark Twain's Study: A Literary Shrine   51
Herkimer Home: "Old Honikol's House"   51
Cooperstown: The *Leatherstocking Country*   52
Old Fort Niagara   54
The George Eastman Birthplace: A Photographic Shrine   56

NEW JERSEY

Nassau Hall: Academic and Historic Shrine   57
The William Trent House   57
Morristown: A Military Capital of the American Revolution   58

PENNSYLVANIA

Independence Hall: Shrine of Liberty   60
The Betsy Ross House   61
Christ Church: The Nation's Church   62
Elfreth's Alley   63

Contents

MIDDLE ATLANTIC (*continued*)

PENNSYLVANIA (*continued*)

Fairmount Park: The Park of Mansions 64
Letitia Street House 64
Cedar Grove 65
Mount Pleasant 66
The "Colonial Chain" 67
Sweetbrier 67
Woodford 67
Belmont 67
Strawberry Mansion 68
Valley Forge: Symbol of the American Spirit 69
The Thompson-Neely House: "Where Washington Crossed the Delaware" 71
The John Morton Homestead 71
Pennsbury: The Manor House of William Penn 72
Hopewell Village 74
The Daniel Boone Homestead 74
The Drake Oil Well: The World's First Successful Oil Well 75
Ephrata Cloister: An Unusual Religious Experiment 75

DELAWARE

Winterthur: Home of 100 Period Rooms 76
Holy Trinity (Old Swedes) Church 80

MARYLAND

Great Falls Tavern: on the Chesapeake and Ohio Canal 81
Hager's Fancy 82
The Hammond-Harwood House 82
The Poe House 83
Peale Museum: A "First" in Museums 83
Hampton: One of the Great Georgian Houses of America 84

DISTRICT OF COLUMBIA

Pierce Mill 85
Joaquin Miller Cabin 85
The White House: The Executive Mansion 86

SOUTHEAST

VIRGINIA

Colonial Williamsburg: "That the Future May Learn from the Past" 91
Arlington House: The Lee Mansion 98
Mount Vernon: George Washington's Home 99
Woodlawn Plantation: George Washington's Birthplace 100
Gunston Hall 101
Stratford Hall: Birthplace of Robert E. Lee 101
Historic Fredericksburg 103
Mary Ball Washington House 103
James Monroe Law Office and Museum 104

Stonewall Jackson Shrine 105
Hugh Mercer Apothecary Shop 105
Richmond: Capital of the Confederacy 106
The Wickham-Valentine House 106
Wilton 106
Monticello: Home of Thomas Jefferson 107
Ash Lawn: Home of James Monroe 108
Michie Tavern: Boyhood Home of Patrick Henry 109
Woodrow Wilson Birthplace 109
Colonial National Historical Park: Jamestown Site, Cape Henry Memorial and Yorktown 110
Berkeley 111
Appomattox Court House 111
Lee Chapel and President's House 112

WEST VIRGINIA

The Washington Homes of Jefferson County 113
Harewood 113
Happy Retreat 113
Claymont Court 113
Blakeley 113
Shepherd Hall 114
Mansion House 114

KENTUCKY

Abraham Lincoln National Historic Park 115
Ashland: Home of Henry Clay 116
Harrodsburg: Cradle of Kentucky 118
William Whitley House 119
Duncan Tavern 119
Federal Hill: "My Old Kentucky Home" 120
Wickland: Home of Three Governors 120
The Ephraim McDowell Memorial: A Medical Shrine 121
The Rob Morris Memorial 121

TENNESSEE

The Hermitage: Home of Andrew Jackson 122
Ancestral Home of James K. Polk 124
Belle Meade: Home of Thoroughbreds 124
The Governor William Blount Mansion 126

NORTH CAROLINA

Andrew Johnson Birthplace 126
Old Salem 127
Biltmore 128
The Duke Homestead 130
Oconaluftee Indian Village 130

SOUTH CAROLINA

Fort Hill: Home of John C. Calhoun 131
Historic Charleston: Seat of Old Southern Culture 132

Contents

SOUTHEAST (*continued*)

GEORGIA

Picturesque Savannah: Historic Waterfront
City   136
The Little White House   138
Fort Frederica   139
Midway Church   139

ALABAMA

Ivy Green: Birthplace of Helen Keller   140
Rosemount Mansion   140
Arlington Historical Shrine   141

FLORIDA

Old St. Augustine: Oldest City in the
Country   142
Vizcaya: Palace of a Merchant Prince   146

NORTH CENTRAL

OHIO

The Rufus Putnam House   148
U. S. Grant Birthplace   148
Thomas Edison Birthplace   148
Adena   149
Zoar Village State Memorial: A Typically
Unique Religious Community   150
Schoenbrunn Village   151
The Pioneer Home   151
Hawthorn Hill, Home of Orville Wright   152
Rubicon Homestead, The Patterson Memo-
rial   152

INDIANA

Territorial Capitol   153
Harrison ("Tippecanoe") Mansion   153
Lincoln Pioneer Village   154
The Lanier Home   154
James Whitcomb Riley Birthplace   154
New Harmony: Scene of Two Utopian Ven-
tures   156

MICHIGAN

Greenfield Village: The Henry Ford Museum   157

ILLINOIS

New Salem State Park: "The Lincoln Vil-
lage"   162
Abraham Lincoln's Home: The Lincoln
Country   164
Ulysses S. Grant Home   165

WISCONSIN

Pendarvis: The Cornish Restoration   166
Waelderhaus   167
Lincoln-Tallman House   168
Milton House   168
Kilbourntown House   169
The Dewey Homestead   169

MINNESOTA

Grand Portage   170
Fort Snelling   170

IOWA

Herbert Hoover Birthplace   171

MISSOURI AND SOUTH CENTRAL

MISSOURI

Ste. Genevieve: Missouri's Oldest City   172
Mark Twain's Boyhood Home   173
St. Louis: Gateway to the West   174
The Eugene Field House   174
Campbell House   175
Hardscrabble House   175
Fort Osage   176

ARKANSAS

Arkansas Territorial Capitol   177

MISSISSIPPI

Natchez: The Pilgrimage City   178

LOUISIANA

New Orleans: America's Old World Capital   182
The Acadian Country   186
Oakley Plantation House: Audubon Me-
morial Park   186

SOUTHWEST, CENTRAL AND MOUNTAIN

TEXAS

Sam Houston Memorial   187
The Alamo   188
San Jose Mission   189
Judge Roy Bean's Court   189

KANSAS

Eisenhower Home   190
Fort Leavenworth   190

SOUTH DAKOTA

The Gordon Stockade and the Way Museum   191

Contents

SOUTHWEST, CENTRAL AND MOUNTAIN
(*continued*)

WYOMING

Fort Laramie: Historic Fur Trade and Military Post   192

COLORADO

The Healy House and The Dexter Cabin   193

UTAH

Lion House: Mount Vernon of the Mormons   194

NEW MEXICO

Old Santa Fe   196
Taos Pueblo   196

ARIZONA

Mission San Xavier del Bac   198
Pipe Spring National Monument   198
Tombstone   199

NEVADA

Virginia City   199

THE PACIFIC COAST

CALIFORNIA

Sutter's Mill and Sutter's Fort: The Gold Discovery Memorials   201
The California Missions: "The Camino Real"   202
Columbia Historic State Park   207
Fort Ross   207

OREGON

McLoughlin House   208

WASHINGTON

Old Fort Nisqually   209

DIRECTORY OF NATIONAL HISTORIC PRESERVATIONS   211

Introduction

WHEN I was a boy my parents took me all over the country—and all over the world—with them. My father, General Cornelius Vanderbilt, had a deep sense of history and almost always, wherever we were in the United States, he would take me to some historic place and tell me about the happenings that made it historic.

"You remember what I told you about those icebergs we saw last spring. You see the high point only, but you know there's much more under the surface and if you put your mind on it you can visualize the whole thing. It's the same way with these historic houses. Take this house—Thomas Jefferson's home. There's where one hundred years ago Jefferson sat and worked on the many great projects that helped to make our country great. These old things help you to think of how it was in those days. You can visualize the men and women who walked through these halls and you can re-create for yourself the scene of our past and make it live. When Thomas Jefferson was a young man—"

I am sure that my father was not the only one who thought like that, for the idea of looking back that way over our history has spread throughout the country. Perhaps also the uncertainties and confusions that troubled us beginning with the turbulent twenties made us search our past for the assurance of strength. But in any case, the last thirty years or so have been a wonderful Age of Restoration and Preservation. What has been preserved, in the process of restoring birthplaces and homes and shops and mills, is fundamentally the American tradition.

My journeyings did not stop when I was a boy. I have traveled extensively all my life, not only on trains and ships, but chiefly by automobile and in recent years in my trailer. The way you can really see the country, know the out-of-the-way spots as well as the important city places, is "on the road!" There's really no part of this country that I don't know from first-hand knowledge, hardly a town I haven't visited. And always in the course of my newspaper, lecture and pleasure tours I went to see the local landmarks. Probably because of my family tradition and training, the historic places of America have been more than a hobby with me, they have been a major interest.

Two years ago it occurred to me that the restoration activity had arrived at such a point that almost every facet of the American past was represented in some way, through the efforts of John Q. Citizen and John D. Rockefeller, informal local groups, town newspapers, State Historical Societies, the National Park Service, the National Trust for Historic Preservation. I decided it would be a good idea to make a book that would show America's past living today, a book that could be a new kind of American history. I set to work on it and this is it—a comprehensive, panoramic view of the country's historic places, representative of the thousands of such shrines, landmarks, early homes, buildings and villages that Americans treasure.

In my selection I have included only such places as may be considered to be "living," that is, preserved or restored to its state when history was made there. By this standard monuments and museums per se are excluded. I confess, however, that I could not and did not attempt to draw an exact line as to museums. In fact, I have not wanted to draw *any* exact lines. I have visited personally most of the places described and pictured here, but not all. In every case, of course, I checked the data and did not rely only on my notes, some of which are many years old. I have included not only major shrines but also a number of minor ones, chiefly because that's how history is, but also because I have considered local history as well as national, and I have tried to give this book *focus*.

Thus, I have included not only places associated with great men or great events but also "way-of-life" places which show how Americans lived and worked in earlier days, and, in addition, early American homes notable for their beauty, for their decorative or architectural features.

There are many other places I would like to have shown, many other pictures I would like to have used. But I didn't want *The Living Past of America* to be "text-booky" or encyclopedic. I wanted it to be warm with the emotion of history as I have felt it in these historic places.

I thought it useful, however, to provide a directory of historic places and to make it as nearly complete as possible. You will find this directory, listing the primary information a prospective visitor might want, compiled with the aid of the publisher's staff, in the back of the book. It contains practically all the important places (with the exceptions—museums, monuments, etc.—noted above) on which data were available and most of those that have appreciable significance.

Introduction

This book which bears my name is the product of thousands of people. In the course of its preparation some ten thousand communications requesting information went out from my own office or that of the publisher to national, state, county and city organizations and historical societies, to friends and acquaintances, to curators and superintendents, to periodicals, to photographers, to every possible source of facts or pictures. And it was one of the most gratifying experiences of my newspaper, writing and lecturing career to see the way people responded and went to great lengths to supply the material we required. I am deeply grateful to those who helped and I want to acknowledge my great indebtedness to all of them. My thankfulness extends equally to those whose material was not used. I was terribly sorry each time a decision had to be made not to include some interesting place or some fine picture.

I have listed picture credits and I hereby express my appreciation of the helpfulness of Anne Needham, David L. Brown and members of the publisher's staff, including Ferris Scott Billyou for ideas and suggestions, Helen Staeuble, Bertha Krantz, Virginia Soskin Ellison, Carolyn Wood and Ruth Popofsky.

Among the many organizations which contributed information and assistance were almost every state, city and county historical society in America, the National Trust for Historic Preservation, National Park Service, Daughters of the American Revolution, Society of Colonial Dames in America, Society for the Preservation of New England Antiquities, Society for the Preservation of Virginia Antiquities, Colonial Williamsburg, Greenfield Village and the Henry Ford Museum, Old Salem, Inc., the Shelburne Museum, etc. etc. To these organizations and to the many, many others who cooperated, my sincerest thanks.

CORNELIUS VANDERBILT, JR.

Vanderbilt Ranch, Reno, Nevada
May 23, 1955.

Picture Credits

PAGE

1. The Dicksons
2. top, The Dicksons
   bottom, Massachusetts Department of Commerce
3. top and bottom, National Park Service
   center, Essex Institute
4. Essex Institute
5, 6, 7. Massachusetts Department of Commerce
8. Fogg Art Museum
9. Margaret M. Lothrop
10, 11. American Iron and Steel Institute
12, 13. Massachusetts Department of Commerce
14, 15. Samuel Chamberlain
16. top across, U.S. Forest Service
    upper right, Old Sturbridge Village
    center right, Stan and Maryjane Bean
17. top right, Massachusetts Department of Commerce
    center right, *Vineyard Gazette*
    bottom right, Massachusetts Department of Commerce
    top left, *Vineyard Gazette*
    center left, *Vineyard Gazette*
    bottom left, *Vineyard Gazette*
18, 19. Maine Development Commission
20. top, center, Douglas Armsden
21. top, G. W. Patch
23, 24, 25. Taylor & Dull, courtesy *Antiques*
29. Rhode Island Development Council
30, 31. Louis S. Martel, courtesy Mystic Seaport
32. top center, Schlegel from *Vision*
33. Meyers Studio
34. top and center, Peter R. Lucas
35. Bowne House Historical Society
36, 37. NYSPIX-Commerce
38. top, courtesy, Sons of the Revolution
39. Louis H. Frohman, courtesy, Jumel Mansion
40. The Frick Collection
41. top, The Frick Collection
42. Lawrence D. Thornton
43. top, Lawrence D. Thornton
    bottom, University of State of New York
44. Lawrence D. Thornton
45. National Park Service
46. Park Pictures, Hyde Park, N. Y.
47. National Park Service
48. top, University of State of New York
49. top right, Dr. William J. Johoda
    center right, courtesy, Huguenot Historical Society
    bottom left and right, Erma R. De Witt
50. University of State of New York
51. top, Elmira College
    bottom, University of State of New York
52. New York Historical Assn.
53. National Baseball Hall of Fame and Museum, Inc.
54. S. Grove McClellan
55. top, S. Grove McClellan
56. George Eastman House
57. top, Princeton University
58, 59. Morristown National Historical Park
60. top, Pennsylvania Department of Commerce
    bottom, National Park Service

PAGE

61. top, National Park Service
    bottom, Pennsylvania Department of Commerce
63. Courtesy, Elfreth's Alley Assn., Inc.
64, 65, 66. Philadelphia Museum of Art
67. center bottom, Philadelphia Museum of Art
68. Philadelphia Museum of Art
69, 70. National Park Service
71. bottom right, Pennsylvania Historical and Museum Commission
73. Pennsylvania State Department of Commerce
75. Pennsylvania State Department of Commerce
76, 77, 78, 79. Henry Francis du Pont Winterthur Museum
80. bottom, Sayborn Studio
81. National Park Service
82. top, Washington County Historical Society
    bottom, J. H. Schaefer & Son
83. top, Jack Engeman
    bottom, The Peale Museum
84. top, John Scarff
    bottom, John E. Deford
85-90. National Park Service
91-97. Colonial Williamsburg
98. National Park Service
99. Mount Vernon Ladies Assn.
101. top, Virginia State Chamber
     bottom, Thomas F. Scott
102. Thomas F. Scott
103. Judson Smith Studios
105. top, National Park Service
     bottom, Judson Smith Studios
108. top right, William Edwin Booth
     top left, Dementi Studio
     bottom, William Edwin Booth
110. National Park Service
113. West Virginia Industrial and Publicity Commission
115-117. John E. Thierman
118. Kentucky Division of Publicity
119. top, left, John E. Thierman
     top right and bottom, Kentucky Division of Publicity
120. top, bottom, John E. Thierman
126. top, Paul A. Moore, Tennessee Conservation Department
     bottom, North Carolina News Bureau
127. top, North Carolina News Bureau
     center and bottom, E. T. Simons
128, 129. The Biltmore Company
130. center, Duke University, Photo by Whitley
     bottom, North Carolina News Bureau
131. center, S. E. Hartin
     bottom, Marion R. Rhea
132. Ronald Allen Riley
133-135. Charleston, South Carolina, Chamber of Commerce
136. Muncie and Malcolm Bell, Jr.
137. Andrew Bunn
138. top, Kenneth Rogers
     center and bottom, Raymond K. Martin
139. top right and left, Publicity Department, Sea Island, Georgia
140. center and bottom, William Cline Company

Picture Credits

PAGE

141. top and bottom right, A. C. Keily Studio
142. top, St. Augustine Historical Society
    bottom, F. Victor Rahmer
143. F. Victor Rahmer
144. top, St. Augustine Historical Society
    bottom, Benjamin Johnston
145. National Park Service
146, 147. Dade County Art Museum
150. Ohio Historical Society
151. top, Ohio Historical Society
157-161. The Henry Ford Museum, Dearborn, Michigan
164. Illinois Division of Department Reports
165. bottom, Rockford *Morning Star*
166. Pendarvis House
168. top and center, Rock County Historical Society
169. bottom, Wisconsin Conservation Department
170. Minnesota Historical Society

PAGE

172, 173. Massie-Missouri Resources Div.
175. bottom, Massie-Missouri Resources Div.
177. Arkansas Publicity and Information Dept.
178-181. The Pilgrimage Garden Club, the Natchez Garden Club and Mrs. Hugh Evans
182-185. Bureau of New Orleans News
188. Ford Green
190. center, U.S. Army Photograph
192. National Park Service
196, 197. New Mexico State Tourist Bureau
198. top, Western Ways Photo
    bottom, Joseph Muench
203. Santa Clara Univ.
207. California Division of Beaches and Parks
208. top, Barnett's Pictures
209. Washington State Advertising Commission

The Living Past
of America

Plymouth

The Landing Place of

the Pilgrims

PLYMOUTH, MASS.

The Pilgrim John Howland House.

WHERE did American history begin? Of course there was no one place. The Plymouth landing was in 1620, Jamestown was founded in 1607, St. Augustine in 1565, and New Mexicans claim the history of the white man in America began in their pueblo country with Cabeza de Vaca in 1536 and with Coronado in 1540. But surely it is clear that the two mainstreams of American culture started in Jamestown and in Plymouth with the Pilgrims.

The famous Rock can be seen in Plymouth today, but there is some question as to its authenticity. There is no question as to the authenticity of the *Pilgrim John Howland House*. That is the one house still standing in Plymouth where Pilgrims actually lived. It was built in 1666, acquired by Jabez Howland, son of *Mayflower* passengers John and Elizabeth Tilley How-

The 1667 living room.

land in 1667. An addition was built in 1750, and in 1912 the Pilgrim John Howland Society acquired it and began to restore it. Today the visitor can see the original house and its rooms as they looked in the seventeenth century and the addition and its rooms as they looked in the eighteenth century.

Other historic places in Plymouth worth visiting are the *Richard Sparrow House* (1636–40), *Harlow Old Fort House* (1677), *Pilgrim Hall,* which contains a collection of Pilgrim relics and memorial, and *Antiquarian House* (1809-1830). The Rock is preserved in the Waterfront State Reservation.

How to reach: On U. S. Route 44, 3A. Signs direct tourists to historic spots.
Open: May 15 through October 31, weekdays, 9:00 A.M. to 5:00 P.M.; Sundays, 10:00 A.M. to 5:00 P.M.
Admission: 25¢. Guide service available.
Administration: The Pilgrim John Howland Society.

The 1750 bedroom.

The John Alden House

"SPEAK FOR YOURSELF, JOHN"

DUXBURY, MASS.

TEN MILES from Plymouth is the home of those *Mayflower* Pilgrims whose fame was spread by their descendant Henry Wadsworth Longfellow in "The Courtship of Myles Standish." John Alden was the youngest of the *Mayflower* men and the last survivor of the signers of the compact. He and Priscilla were married in 1622, built this house, which contains many rare articles (dating back to 1500), in 1653. Only Aldens and their direct descendants have lived in it since then and the house has never been out of Alden hands. The framework and general plan of the house remain as when it was first built. Furnishing and restoration to the Pilgrim aspect were effected through the efforts of Charles L. Alden, eighth-generation descendant in direct line, with the assistance and partly under the direction of Wallace Nutting.

How to reach: Just off U. S. Route 3A, on Alden Street.
Open: April 1 to November 1, daily, 9:00 A.M. to 5:00 P.M.
Admission: 35¢.
Administration: The Alden Kindred of America.

Salem

"A New World Venice"

SALEM, MASS.

SALEM, the first town in the Colony of Massachusetts Bay, was founded by Roger Conant in 1626 as the plantation of Naumkeag. From the start its colonists engaged in maritime pursuits, and throughout the colonial period it was a great fishing and shipping center. Ships from this port ranged from the West Indies to Europe and later pioneered routes throughout the world. During the Revolution, Salem provided more men and ships for privateering than any other port in the colonies. And after the Revolution it earned the reputation of a "New World Venice" and was a leader in the first golden age of America's foreign trade. But its harbor was shallow and when, in the clipper ship days of 1850–60, vessels increased greatly in size, Salem lost out to the deep-water ports and gradually declined. *Derby Wharf,* begun soon after 1762, the *Custom House* (1819), where Nathaniel Hawthorne was employed from 1846 to 1849, and the *Derby House* still survive, preserved as the Salem Maritime National Historic Site.

Long before the Historic Site was established in 1938 by the National Park Service, other organizations, chiefly the Essex Institute, had done much to preserve historic aspects of Old Salem. Besides its museum, containing over 500 notable American portraits and collections of miniatures, costumes, silver, pewter, china,

Derby Wharf seen from the front doorway of the Salem Custom House.

Front hall, second floor of the Pingree House, built 1804, designed by Samuel McIntire and regarded as one of his best.

Southeast corner room of the Derby House (1761-62) showing portrait of Elias Hasket Derby, foremost American merchant and first American millionaire after the Revolution.

The John Ward House, built 1684, restored and furnished as a house of the period. In the lean-to are an apothecary shop of 1825, a cent shop c. 1840 and a weave room.

glass, clocks, etc., the Institute maintains and administers a number of historic houses, including the *John Ward House* (1784), the *Peirce-Nichols House* (1782) and the *Pingree House* (1804). Besides these and other houses—like the *House of Seven Gables* (1668) made famous by Hawthorne—that reveal Old Salem's way of life, there are reminders of the witchcraft delusion episode (1692-93) in the *Original Witch House* (built 1642), restored by Historic Salem, Inc., in 1948 and in

the *Old Witch Jail and Dungeon,* which is now maintained as a museum.

———

How to reach: Via Routes 1A, 107, 114.
Open: Derby House, 10:00 A.M. to 5:00 P.M.; *Custom House,* 2:00 P.M. to 5:00 P.M. weekdays, Sundays during the summer; *John Ward and Pingree Houses,* 9:00 A.M. to 11:00 A.M., 2:00 P.M. to 4:00 P.M. except Sundays and holidays.
Admission: 25¢; except *Pingree House,* 50¢.
Administration: Salem Maritime National Historic Site, National Park Service; *John Ward* and *Pingree Houses,* Essex Institute.

Kitchen of the John Ward House.

Boston

"Hub of the Universe," "Mother of Freedom"

BOSTON, MASS.

Faneuil Hall.

BOSTON was never exactly the hub of the universe but most certainly it was the hub of the Revolution. "The Boston Massacre," "The Minute Men," "The Boston Tea Party," Paul Revere, Benjamin Franklin, Lexington, Concord, Bunker Hill, Samuel Adams, John Hancock—so many of the hallowed names of our history are identified with that city that it is justifiably called "Mother of Freedom."

Boston began as an offshoot of Salem. It was settled in 1630 by colonists led by John Winthrop and it was not long before it became an important commercial center and then capital of the Massachusetts Bay Colony. It was probably the Boston Massacre in 1770, when British troops fired on a mob of citizens near the Old State House, that fanned the revolutionary ardor of the Boston patriots to a roaring blaze. But in any case Bostonians were the vigorous and violent advocates of revolution and leaders in the great fight for liberty.

Most of the historic places of Boston are downtown within walking distance of each other on a "Freedom Trail" laid out for the convenience of tourists. It starts at the corner of Park Street opposite the State House, and signs guide you all along the way.

Faneuil Hall (Faneuil Hall Square) was the "Cradle of Liberty." It was there that the patriots held their meetings during the revolutionary period, there they planned the moves and maneuvers in the great fight for freedom. Built and given to the city by Peter Faneuil in 1742 as a meeting place and market, it burned in 1761 and was rebuilt in 1763. It was enlarged in 1805 from Charles Bulfinch's plans.

How to reach: On U. S. Route 1.
Open: Monday to Friday, 9:00 A.M. to 5:00 P.M.; Saturdays, 9:00 A.M. to 12:00 M.
Admission: Free.

[5]

The Paul Revere House.

The Paul Revere House (19 North Square) is the oldest house in Boston. Built about 1670, it was purchased by Revere in 1770. Now restored, it contains furnishings of Revere's time.

Open: 10:00 A.M. to 4:00 P.M. except Sundays and holidays.
Admission: 25¢; children free; children in groups, 10¢.
Administration: Paul Revere Memorial Assoc.

Old North Church (Christ Church [P.E.], 189 Salem Street). "Hardly a man now alive" needs to be told that it was from the steeple of this church, the oldest in Boston, that Paul Revere's lanterns signaled the approach of the British. The church, designed by William Price, was built in 1723. The interior follows Christopher Wren design. The original steeple where the lanterns hung was blown down by a hurricane and a new tower was erected, 16 feet lower than the original. After all these years the steeple was blown down once again in the 1954 hurricane but it is being restored. Pew 54, owned by Paul Revere's son, was probably occupied on occasion by Paul Revere.

Open: Daily, 10:00 A.M. to 4:00 P.M. Sunday service at 10:45 A.M.
Admission: Free.

Old State House (Washington and State Streets), built in 1713, burned in 1747, then rebuilt, was the seat of the provincial government; here the early colonial courts met. The Declaration of Independence, the repeal of the Stamp Act and the declaration of peace with England were all proclaimed from the balcony. The building was restored during the nineteenth century and it is probably the oldest public building in America.

Open: May 1 to October 1, weekdays, 9:00 A.M. to 4:30 P.M.;
    Saturdays, 9:00 A.M. to 1:00 P.M. October 1 to May 1, Monday
    to Saturday, 9:00 A.M. to 4:00 P.M. Closed holidays.
Admission: Free.

"Old Ironsides," the U. S. S. Constitution, has been preserved just as it was in 1797, and is open to the public at the Boston Naval Shipyard in Charlestown at Wapping and Chelsea Streets.

Open: Daily, 9:30 A.M. to 4:30 P.M.
Admission: Free.

The Old North Church and the Paul Revere statue.

Old State House. Note the British Lion and Unicorn.

Old Ironsides at the Boston Navy Yard.

Concord

"Where the Embattled Farmers Stood"

CONCORD, MASS.

The Emerson House.

Once you are across the Charles, it is not so far to Lexington, where the "shot heard round the world"—that started the shooting in the Revolutionary War—was fired. It's not so far from that to the "rude bridge that arched the flood" at Concord where a little group of American Minute Men, determined but untrained, defeated and routed British troops in the first battle of the Revolutionary War.

The man who wrote the immortal lines about those unforgettable events at Lexington and Concord was the Concord poet Ralph Waldo Emerson. His house in Concord where he lived for almost half a century is still standing.

The *Emerson House* was built some years before Ralph Waldo Emerson acquired it in 1835, when he and his newlywed wife Lydia Jackson moved in. They lived there until 1872 when the house was burned down. But most of the contents were saved. The house was rebuilt, made over and improved when the Emersons, having toured Europe, returned to it in 1873. It was his home until his death in 1882. Except for the removal of books, manuscripts and the furniture from the study, the house is now very much as it was in 1882.

How to reach: On State Route 126.
Open: April 19 to November 16, daily except Mondays, 10:00 A.M. to 11:30 A.M., 1:30 P.M. to 5:30 P.M.; Sundays, 2:30 P.M. to 5:30 P.M.
Admission: 35¢; children, 20¢.
Administration: Ralph Waldo Emerson Memorial Assoc.

Emerson's study.

The books and furniture from Emerson's study were removed to Concord's *Antiquarian House,* at Cambridge Turnpike and Lexington Road, which displays a reconstruction of the study just as Emerson was using it at the time of his death. There are also Thoreau, Hawthorne, Alcott and other exhibits and collections in this Concordiana museum, which is open at the same time and at approximately the same fees as *Emerson House.*

I was fascinated to learn that one house in Concord was the home of the *Little Women,* the *Five Little Peppers* and the *Tanglewood Tales* children. That house is *The Wayside,* on Lexington Road and Hawthorne Avenue, more a literary than a historical shrine.

Built in 1717, it was the home of the Alcott family, who needed to add two wings in 1845. Probably Bronson Alcott and his wife wanted more space to entertain their many friends and to give Louisa May and their other daughters more room for their imaginative activities. The Alcotts' name for this house was Hillside. In 1852 Nathaniel Hawthorne bought it—the only home he ever owned—and later added a tower study and other rooms. And then in 1883 Daniel Lothrop,

of the publishing firm now known as Lothrop, Lee and Shepard, Inc., acquired it and lived there for many years with his wife Margaret Sidney, author of *The Five Little Peppers.* The furnishings of the house as you see it today are those of the Hawthorne and Lothrop families, and Miss Margaret Lothrop still lives there.

———————

Open: July and August, daily except Mondays, 10:00 A.M. to 5:00 P.M.; Sundays, 12:00 M. to 5:30 P.M.
Admission: 40¢; 12 to 18-year-olds, 25¢; 8 to 12-year-olds, 20¢; children under 8, free.

Orchard House, on Lexington Road, was the home of the Alcotts for many years after they moved there in 1857. It was in this house that *Little Women* was written. Furnished and maintained by descendants of Anna ("Meg") Alcott Pratt, it is open to the public weekdays from 10:00 A.M. to 5:00 P.M. (except Mondays until after June 15) and Sundays, 2:00 A.M. to 6:00 P.M.

———————

Admission: 50¢; children, 20¢.

The Wayside.

The Saugus Ironworks

The "Birthplace" of the American Iron and Steel Industry

SAUGUS, MASS.

The rolling and slitting mill. Wrought iron bars were reheated and run through rollers operated by two huge water wheels.

THE FIRST successful ironworks in America, dating back to 1646, has been restored, including all the major units—blast furnace, forge, rolling and slitting mill, wharf, warehouse, ironmaster's house, and a museum. It is a complete and authentic replica built, at a cost of over a million dollars, by the American Iron and Steel Institute.

John Winthrop, Jr., son of the founder of Boston, and Richard Leader, an English merchant, were instrumental in setting up at Saugus the "Company of Undertakers for the Iron Workes in New England," and the plant was soon producing cast iron at the rate of a little over a ton a day, supplying hammers, nails, axes, saws and other iron tools so vitally needed. Articles of wrought iron as well as cast iron were made.

The *Ironmaster's House,* built probably in 1636, was restored by Wallace Nutting in 1915. Furnishings are representative of the colonial period. The *Ironworks' Museum* houses relics of the early days and exhibits tracing the growth of the steel industry.

How to reach: U. S. Route 1, then east on Route 129 (10 miles north of Boston) .
Open: April 15 to December 1, Tuesday to Sunday, 10:00 A.M. to 5:00 P.M.
Admission: 50¢; children, 25¢. Guide service if requested by group in advance.
Administration: First Iron Works Assoc., Inc.

Nearby, but not part of this integrated restoration, is the *"Scotch"-Boardman House,* Howard Street, built in 1651 to house the Covenanter prisoners captured by Oliver Cromwell at Dunbar, Scotland, and brought to the Massachusetts Bay Colony to operate the ironworks. The original sheathing, staircase and sponge painting may be seen.

Open: June to September, by appointment.
Admission: 15¢.
Administration: Society for the Preservation of New England Antiquities.

A guide in seventeenth-century dress demonstrates the operation of the forge hammer.

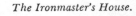

The Ironmaster's House.

The upper front chamber in the Ironmaster's House at Saugus, Mass.; when not in use, the bed could be folded up against the wall—the forerunner of the Murphy bed.

Adams National Historic Site

A Living Monument to Four Generations of a Famous American Family

QUINCY, MASS.

THE ADAMS family of Quincy has played a uniquely distinguished and extraordinarily important role in shaping the destiny of America from the seventeenth century to our own day. Beginning in 1640, generation after generation, the Adamses left their stamp on American history. Harvard was their college; the law and letters, their pursuit; government, their field. Of John Adams, first Vice-President and second President of the United States, Herbert A. L. Fisher said, "The best mind of Massachusetts, at this, the greatest hour in her history, is to be found in the writings of this rigorous, uncompromising, far-sighted man." He was, Thomas Jefferson said, "as disinterested as the Being who made him. His deep conceptions . . . and undaunted firmness made him truly our bulwark in debate . . . and to him more than to any other man is the country indebted for our independence." Besides being the "Architect of American Constitutions," John was the father of the American Navy. As President he brought about the creation of a separate department of the Navy. The final act of his public career was to appoint John Marshall Chief Justice of the Supreme Court of the United States.

John Adams' son was John Quincy Adams. Sixth President of the United States, 1825-29, he filled many other offices in the service of his country. He was, at various times, Minister to the Netherlands, Prussia, Russia, England; he was a United States Senator, President Monroe's Secretary of State, and after his presidency he served as a Representative in Congress, the only ex-president to do so. He was a Congressman for seventeen years and literally died at his post, being stricken at the age of eighty-one on the floor of the House.

The women, too, were unusual (three were named Abigail). Abigail Adams, wife of the second President, was the only woman to be the wife of one president and the mother of another. Her lively letters, which give a picture of the family and of life in eighteenth-century New England, have delighted several generations of Americans.

The Old House.

There are three Adams houses, the most important of which is the Adams home from 1788 to 1927—the mansion known to the family as the "Old House." When Brooks Adams died in 1927, the Adams descendants, as the Adams Memorial Society, decided to preserve the "Old House" and library just as Brooks Adams left it. It was maintained as a memorial until 1946 when the National Park Service acquired it for a National Historic Site.

The oldest portion of the Adams mansion or "Old House" was built in 1731 by Major Leonard Vassall, wealthy West Indian planter. His grandson sold it to John Adams who took possession in 1788 and named it Peacefield, but it was never widely known by that name. John, John Quincy, Charles Francis and Brooks each made additions to the house and of course the furniture in the house tells a story in itself. Each member who went abroad on a diplomatic mission brought back prized pieces. The furnishings in general show the continuity of life in the house. Each generation contributed something and each generation is remembered by what it left. The house is not a "period piece" but a house which was lived in and which changed from 1788 to 1927.

How to reach: On State Route 135, near State Route 3, about 8 miles south of Boston. 135 Adams Street.
Open: May 10 to November 10, daily, 9:00 A.M. to 5:15 P.M.
Admission: Adults, 30¢; children under 12, free when accompanied by adults. Guide service available.
Administration: National Park Service.

The Adams Birthplaces

QUINCY, MASS.

IN 1720 Deacon John Adams purchased the six-room frame "salt-box" house that William Needham, one of the earliest settlers, had built sometime in the seventeenth century. The deacon's first son John, later to become the second President of the United States, was born in that house, October, 1735. In 1744 the deacon purchased the adjoining house, which had been built about 1663, and when he died in 1761 he willed it to his oldest son John, and it was in this house that John's son, John Quincy, was born in 1767. The John Adams family lived there until 1783 when the family went to Europe. In 1774 John Adams had acquired the Needham house, in which he was born, and this house as well as the Adams home were rented out for many years, until 1896-97, when both houses were restored. They are now the property of the city of Quincy, administered by the Quincy Historical Society, which owns the furnishings.

In the John Adams birthplace the former kitchen used by John Adams as a law office prior to and during the Revolution is exactly the same with original furnishings today. A number of other original items are to be seen in both houses, including a front door knocker from Paul Revere's foundry. Other furnishings are authentically of the period.

The John Adams Birthplace.

The John Quincy Adams Birthplace.

How to reach: 129-139 Franklin Street.
Open: April 19 to October 31, daily except Mondays, 10:00 A.M. to 5:00 P.M.
Admission: For both houses, 50¢; children, 30¢. Guide service available.
Administration: Quincy Historical Society.

The street.

Old Deerfield

An Extraordinary Village—A "Natural" Preservation

DEERFIELD, MASS.

WHEN you walk down Old Deerfield Street you do actually feel that you are in the eighteenth century. It is not only the fine old elms and fine old homes that line that quiet street, not only that the atmosphere is peaceful and tranquil—to me, thinking about it, after my first visit, it seemed that the most important factor was that I did not feel that I was in an exhibit, that I was seeing a sight. For Old Deerfield is not, in the sense that Williamsburg or Dearborn or other restored or preserved "villages" are, a formal organized historic site. No National Park Service, no historical society, no wealthy individual or organization assembled, restored or preserved it, and yet Old Deerfield, because it retained its village life relatively unchanged from its eighteenth-century way, stands as a living monument to the early Americans.

I say that Old Deerfield is a "natural" preservation because quite obviously it was the nature of Old Deerfield's location that made it possible and helped to keep it unchanged. It is off the main highway, a little spot in the rich agricultural valley of the Connecticut River, surrounded by woods and hills, protected from the invasion of modernism, undesired by industrialists, developers, commuters. Other villages have had these or similar advantages, but they may not have

considered them advantages, especially if they did not have the additional important advantage of prosperity.

The Sheldon Homestead.

For another great factor in Old Deerfield's history is that its eighteenth-century citizens were prosperous. Their farmlands were fertile, their beef cattle traders, their tanners and leather dealers, their craftsmen and their merchants did especially well when Deerfield was a trading center during and after the Revolutionary War.

Having the means for it, these Deerfield people also had the good taste, the judgment and the faith in the future to build beautifully designed and well-constructed houses and to furnish them with the finest and best materials available in furniture, fabrics, china, glassware, silver and pewter. You can see these houses and these furnishings today, essentially as they were in the late 1700's. For many of the houses, preserved or restored—for the most part by their owners—are open to the public.

Old Deerfield now is devoted particularly to education. It is the home of historic Deerfield Academy, established in 1797 by an act of the Massachusetts legislature, and formally opened on January 1, 1799, when Deerfield already had a dramatic, honorable 130-year-long history. The land, 8,000 acres in the western wilderness of Massachusetts, was bought in 1666 from the Pocumtuck Indians for the relatively high price of four pence per acre. The first settler, Samuel Hinsdell, arrived in 1669, and by 1673 the village street and the house lots were laid out, essentially as they are today. On a number of occasions Indian raids created havoc. In 1675 and again in 1704 they massacred the inhabitants, set fire to the buildings and virtually obliterated the village. In each case survivors carried on and the village was rebuilt. The last important foray was in 1746. After that, the town became an important wheat and cattle center, and since then prosperity and ease have marked Deerfield's history.

Among the houses in Old Deerfield notable for their historicity or beauty or both are *Ashley House, Old Indian House, Asa Stebbins House,* the *Joseph Stebbins House, Hall Tavern, Frary House,* the *Pink House, Memorial Hall, Wilson Printing House* and the *Dwight Barnard House* besides the *Old Manse* and the *John Williams House* of the Deerfield Academy.

How to reach: Via State Routes 2 and 10.

Open: The houses listed under *Administration* are open to the public weekdays and Sundays, usual hours. Some are not open on Tuesdays.

Admission: Generally, 30¢ to 50¢; 15¢ for children. $1.50 for a combination ticket to the Heritage Foundation houses.

Administration: Ashley House, Asa Stebbins House, Hall Tavern, Wilson Printing House, Dwight Barnard House, Heritage Foundation. *Frary House, Memorial Hall,* Pocumtuck Valley Memorial Assoc. *Old Indian House,* Old Indian House Assoc.

The living room of the Allen House.

The taproom of the Barnard Tavern.

Old Sturbridge Village: Town of the 1800's

STURBRIDGE, MASS.

RE-CREATED on a 200-acre tract of meadow woodland and river shore near Springfield, Old Sturbridge is a living museum and craft center of some fifty authentic early nineteenth-century buildings. Most are old houses moved to the site and reassembled there. Some are copies or adaptations of old houses. Included are homes, shops, mills, churches, a tavern and a general store. There are appropriate displays of early objects, and in the shops craftsmen work at their trade as they did one hundred and fifty years ago.

How to reach: Via Routes 15 and 20.
Open: April to November, daily, 9:30 A.M. to 5:30 P.M. December to March, weekends, 10:00 A.M. to 4:30 P.M.
Admission: Summer, adults, $1.75; children, $1.00; eleven years or under, 60¢. Winter, $1.00.
Administration: Old Sturbridge Village.

Sturbridge interior.

Amesbury

AMESBURY, MASS.

IN AMESBURY, at the northern tip of Massachusetts, are the homes of two famous Americans whose achievements were of the spirit—John Greenleaf Whittier and Mary Baker Eddy. It was in the Bagley house (right) where Mary Baker Eddy lived from 1868 to 1870 that she wrote her first manuscript of *The Science of Man.* The room from Whittier's house, where he lived from 1836 until his death in 1892, was his favorite garden room where he received his friends.

How to reach: On Route 150.
Open: Eddy House, April 1 to November 30, 2:00 P.M. to 5:00 P.M. except Sundays. *Whittier Home,* 10:00 A.M. to 5:00 P.M. except Sundays.
Admission: Eddy House, 25¢. Whittier Home, free.
Administration: Longyear Foundation. Whittier Home Assoc.

Garden Room, Whittier Home.

Bagley House. The Mary Baker Eddy Home.

The Cape,
Martha's Vineyard, Nantucket
Historic Seacoast
MASSACHUSETTS

THERE'S a spot in my heart that belongs to this old middle-of-the-sea part of New England, one of the best and most famous smallboat areas in the U. S. A. I remember fondly how in the days of my youth when I fished and sailed and cruised around the many harbors, I was impressed with the time-standing-still quality of the old places. Perhaps no one of them is truly important historically, but seen together, they re-create at least the mood of the early days.

Nantucket's Old Mill (1764). The vanes turn only when the wind is due west.

The 1721 House in Yarmouth (Cape Cod).

The Squire Thomas Cooke House (Edgartown, Martha's Vineyard, built 1765-66 of timbers hand-hewn from Vineyard trees.

Aptuxcet Trading Post (Bourne, Cape Cod) (1626).

The Stoney Brook Mill at Brewster (Cape Cod). America's first water power grist mill, more than 200 years old.

The Jethro Coffin House, built 1686. It is the oldest house in Nantucket.

Augusta

Trading Post, Shiretown, Capital

AUGUSTA, MAINE

SIR Walter Raleigh's nephew, Raleigh Gilbert, was the first white man to reach the place that is now Augusta. When he sailed up the Kennebec and landed there, he found that it was a meeting place of the Abnaki Indians, called Koussinoc. In 1629 a trading post was established there and prospered modestly through the years. In 1754 Fort Western was erected there and in 1797 the community became a town. By 1799, when it became a shiretown, the name had been changed to Augusta, and in 1827 it was chosen as the capital of Maine.

Charles Bulfinch was selected to design the State Capitol, and the Bulfinch front has been retained, though the building has been remodeled. Of Augusta's early days the only memorial standing is the restored *Fort Western*, but Down Easters are also proud of the *Blaine Mansion*, home of James G. Blaine, who was the "nearliest" to becoming President of the United States.

Fort Western, Bowman and Cony Streets, was built in 1754 by a committee of the Plymouth Company, constructed of hand-hewn logs cut and dovetailed at Topsham. The foundation was of stone, with the timbered walls twelve inches thick, and four cannon were mounted in the blockhouses. A garrison of twenty men under the command of James Howard was stationed here, but the fort was never fired upon. In 1775 General Benedict Arnold and his men stopped here during their march on Quebec. Descendants of the Howards restored the fort in 1921 and presented it to the city of Augusta. It houses an interesting collection of Americana.

How to reach: On U. S. Routes 201 and 202.
Open: May 1 to mid-September, weekdays, 9:00 A.M. to 12:00 P.M.
Admission: 25¢, children, 10¢.

The State Capitol.

The *Blaine Mansion,* State and Capitol Streets, now the residence of the Governor, was purchased in 1862 by James G. Blaine. The house, built in 1830, was presented to the State of Maine in 1920 by the Blaine family and is furnished with period antiques. Of particular interest are the Blaine Study and the silver service presented by the State of Maine to the U. S. battleship *Maine* when it was launched in 1895. After the U.S.S. *Maine* was sunk in 1898, the silver lay in Havana harbor for more than a dozen years. When the ship was raised, the silver was reprocessed and returned to Maine. It is now in the State Dining Room of the Blaine Mansion which is open to visitors on weekdays from 2:00 P.M. to 4:00 P.M.

Historic Fort Western.

Portland

"Resurgam!"

PORTLAND, MAINE

The Wadsworth-Longfellow Home.

PORTLAND, continuously settled since 1633, was destroyed twice by Indian raids, once by a British fleet and again in 1866, by fire. Each time, in accordance with its official motto, *"Resurgam, I will rise again,"* the city recovered from its disaster and re-established itself. Yet not all its historic houses were destroyed, and in the case of one of the most historic houses in Maine, we have a paradoxical man-bites-dog situation. That is the *Wadsworth-Longfellow House,* historic because it was the home of Henry Wadsworth Longfellow, paradoxical because it was the poet's father—not his son—who helped to start the Maine Historical Society that now maintains the house as an historic shrine. It was the poet's grandfather, General Peleg Wadsworth, who, in 1785, built the house at 487 Congress Street. The poet's father, Judge Stephen Longfellow, became in 1822 one of the original members of the Maine Historical Society, chartered two years after Maine separated from Massachusetts. This house where the poet lived until he was a young man is furnished with articles which belonged to the two families.

How to reach: Via U. S. Route 1.
Open: Mid-June to mid-September, weekdays except holidays, 9:30 A.M. to 4:30 P.M.
Admission: 40¢, children, 30¢.

Lady Pepperrell Mansion

KITTERY POINT, MAINE

THIS famous house on Route 103 was built in 1760 by the widow of Sir William Pepperrell, commander of the Louisburg expedition in 1745 and the first American to be knighted by the Crown. It is an outstanding example of northern colonial architecture and the interior is notable for the delicacy of proportion and detail, a magnificent background for the eighteenth-century furniture displayed here.

How to reach: Via U. S. Route 1 and State Route 103.
Open: Mid-June to mid-September, weekdays, 2:00 P.M. to 5:00 P.M.
Admission: 50¢.
Administration: Society for the Preservation of New England Antiquities.

The Colonel Black Mansion

ELLSWORTH, MAINE

"WOODLAWN," the *Black House,* on West Main Street, a modified Georgian mansion of red brick, was built about 1825 from Asher Benjamin plans. The original furniture, much of it priceless antiques at the time the house was built, may be seen. Among the notable features are a beautiful circular staircase, a French girandole mirror, a German hand organ and a Dutch wing-back chair which may be lengthened into a bed, as well as Waterford and Sandwich glass.

How to reach: Via U. S. Route 1.
Open: June 1 to November 1, daily, 10:00 A.M. to 5:00 P.M.
Admission: 50¢.
Administration: Hancock County Trustees of Public Reservations.

Portsmouth

The Old Town on the Sea

PORTSMOUTH, N. H.

THIS fine old town on the Piscataqua has remained remarkably unspoiled and unchanged. The area was first settled in 1623 by a small band from Plymouth, England, who came to provide timber and spars for the Royal Navy. Soon its magnificent harbor helped it to become a prosperous seaport and shipbuilding center, flourishing in colonial times, especially during the Revolutionary War. Many Continental Navy ships used it as a home port, and John Paul Jones lived in Portsmouth while he was outfitting the *Ranger*.

Many fine homes, chiefly in the Georgian style, were built during Portsmouth's golden age of the 1700's and quite a number of them are still standing. Probably the best preserved and one of the most beautiful is the *Warner House*, Daniel and Chapel Streets, an urban brick mansion in the Georgian style, built about 1716 by Captain Archibald Macpheadris. It was occupied later by the captain's daughter Mary and her husband, Jonathan Warner, and their collateral descendants, until 1930. A one-story ell, called the "summer kitchen," was added about 1815. Unusual murals on the walls of the staircase and some early marbleization on the wood panels of the dining room are among the interesting features. Two floors of the house are appropriately furnished.

How to reach: Via U. S. Route 1.
Open: June 15 to September 20, Monday through Saturday, 10:00 A.M. to 5:00 P.M.
Admission: 50¢. Guide service.
Administration: Warner House Assoc.

The *Thomas Bailey Aldrich Memorial*, 386 Court Street, is the house which provided the background and characters for *The Story of a Bad Boy.* The house was built in 1790 by the author's great-grandfather, Thomas Darling Bailey, who was a ship owner and a merchant of ship chandlery and hardware. It was restored with its original furnishings in 1908 after the death of Thomas Bailey Aldrich.

Open: June 15 to September 15, weekdays, 10:00 A.M. to 5:00 P.M. and by appointment.
Admission: 50¢; children, 25¢.
Administration: Thomas Bailey Aldrich Memorial.

The Warner House.

Parlor of the Warner House.

Spare room of the Aldrich House.

The *Wentworth-Gardner House*, Mechanic and Gardner Streets, built in 1760, is one of the most perfect examples of Georgian architecture in America. Among notable items in the house are the carving throughout, said to have required fourteen months to complete, the scenic wallpaper in the dining room, the original Dutch tiles on a number of fireplaces and the spinning attic on the third floor.

Open: June 15 to September 15, weekdays, 10:00 A.M. to 5:00 P.M.
Admission: 50¢.
Administration: The Wentworth-Gardner and Tobias Lear Houses Assoc.

The *Moffat-Ladd House,* 146 Market Street, was built in 1763 by John Moffatt. After his death at the age of ninety-four it was occupied by his daughter and her husband, General William Whipple, a signer of the Declaration of Independence. The front door opens upon a "hall" in the English sense, which is unique in New England. The staircase against the exterior wall is lit by a beautiful round-head window at the landing. The walls are covered with a rare wallpaper, usually known as the "Bay of Naples" series made in Paris by Joseph Dufour about 1815. The drawing room mantel has a panel of flowers delicately cut in high relief, which is thought to have been carved by Grinling Gibbons and brought from the Moffatt house in Hertfordshire. The house is now the headquarters for the National Society of the Colonial Dames of America in the State of New Hampshire.

Open: June 15 to September 15, daily, 10:00 A.M. to 5:00 P.M.
Admission: 50¢.

The Thomas Bailey Aldrich House and a view of Court Street.

The *Governor John Langdon Memorial,* 143 Pleasant Street, described by George Washington as "the handsomest house in Portsmouth," was built in 1784 by the man who was Governor of New Hampshire five times and the first President of the United States Senate. The drawing room extends the full length of the house and occupies half the first floor.

Open: June 1 to September 15, weekdays, 1:00 P.M. to 5:00 P.M.
Admission: 50¢.
Administration: Society for the Preservation of New England Antiquities.

The *Jackson House,* 76 Northwest Street, built in 1664, is the oldest frame house in New Hampshire.

Open: June 1 to November 1, weekdays, 11:00 A.M. to 5:00 P.M.
Admission: 25¢.
Administration: Society for the Preservation of New England Antiquities.

The entrance hall of the Moffat-Ladd House.

The Daniel Webster Memorial

"Black Dan with the Silver Tongue"

NEAR FRANKLIN, N. H.

NEW HAMPSHIRE'S greatest hero, one of the country's noblest statesmen and one of the world's most famous orators was Daniel Webster, nicknamed "Black Dan of the Silver Tongue." He was born January 18, 1782, on the hardscrabble pioneer farm of his brother Ebenezer Webster, in what was then Salisbury but is now in the township of Franklin. A few years later the family moved a few miles to Elms Farm, and it was here that Daniel grew up. Except for a few months at Phillips Academy in Exeter and his year at Dartmouth College, he lived here until 1807 when he moved to Portsmouth.

The 130 acres of farm and pasture land on which the Memorial is located originally comprised the Ebenezer Webster farm which had been sold by him in 1787, then reacquired by Daniel Webster in 1851. After Daniel's death the following year the property was sold again, but in 1910 a group of citizens acquired it and constructed on it a memorial house, intended to represent the Webster birthplace and home, to house the numerous mementos of his life and articles of the period. Later the property was transferred to the State.

How to reach: Route 127 between Franklin and Salisbury, N. H.
Open: Daily, June 15 to October 15, 9:00 A.M. to 5:00 P.M.
Admission: 25¢. Guide service.
Administration: New Hampshire Recreation Division.

Fireplace of the Daniel Webster Memorial House.

The Shelburne Museum

A Typical Vermont Village

SHELBURNE, VT.

I hope Vermonters will not think I am pixilated when I say that in their own peculiar independent way they don't seem to bother much about historic preservations, though no Americans can surpass the Green Mountain State people in their fidelity to old traditions and time-proven ways of life. From the days of Ethan Allen and beyond the time of Vermont's most famous son, Calvin Coolidge, Vermont has played its part in the history of the nation, and undoubtedly in the sense I mean Vermont's past is living, but not in historic houses.

Over in Castleton there are some fine houses, 100 to 150 years old, but most of them are private homes open only one day a year in August, when Castleton has its Colonial Day. In Plymouth you can see the room in which Calvin Coolidge was born, and in Sharon you can see where Joseph Smith, founder of Mormonism, was born December 23, 1805. The Vermont Guild of Old-Time Crafts and Industries is nearing completion of its restoration of a 1790 sawmill in Weston, twenty-two miles from Manchester. And there are other historic places, too.

But Vermont's living outstanding preservation of its past is at Shelburne Village. It is a unique restoration and a collection of collections, including a collection of old houses from all over Vermont that were moved, reassembled, restored and placed in the pattern of a typical Vermont village, and furnished to accord with its period. Besides, there are exhibits of

The covered bridge, through which may be seen the 1840 brick meeting-house brought from Charlotte, Vt.

A panoramic view of the village.

Interior of the Cavendish House.

all sorts of excellent samples of articles of the period, from toys, dolls, tools, trade signs, duck decoys, weather vanes and figureheads to glassware, silver, needlework, crewelwork, furniture, carriages. Among the sixteen buildings now open to the public are the *Country Store, Horseshoe Barn,* the *Red Shed,* the *Shaker Building,* the *Castleton Jail,* the *Hat and Fragrance Unit,* the *Little Stone Cottage,* the *Toy Shop,* the *Variety Unit,* the *Vergennes School,* the *Stagecoach Inn,* the *Covered Bridge,* the *Cavendish House,* the *Colchester Lighthouse* and the *Vermont House.*

How to reach: On Route 7, 7 miles south of Burlington.
Open: May 15 to October 15, daily, 9:00 A.M. to 5:00 P.M.
Admission: $1.75; children, 50¢; children under 6, free. Guide service is available.
Administration: Shelburne Museum, Inc. (Mr. and Mrs. J. Watson Webb).

Bedroom under the eaves of the ell of the Cavendish House.

Parlor of the Vermont House. Note octagonal table with "collared" legs. The magnificent paneling came from a house near Essex, Conn. Note also chair on the right, with arms terminating in parrot heads.

The kitchen of the Vermont House. Note the window chair in the corner, the pad feet of the pine table. The curtains are homespun wool. The chest is painted black and red on dull orange.

Newport

Historic Port and Last Resort

NEWPORT, R. I.

The Breakers.

THE EARLIEST recollections of my youth are of Newport, as my parents spent more time here than in any other spot in the United States. Here my sister and I grew up in our large old-fashioned house which sat high on the famed Cliff Walk. We had a cabin at exclusive Bailey's Beach; the sailing and steam yachts left from the New York Yacht Club landing in the harbor. On Sundays we attended Trinity Church where we sat in the same boxed-in pew in which George Washington worshipped when he was in Newport. Repeatedly we visited the historic spots of this beautiful old town of narrow hilly streets, white frame houses, towering horse-chestnut trees, rocky cliffs and long, wide Atlantic beaches.

It was in 1639 that colonists under the leadership of William Coddington left Portsmouth, the first settlement on Rhode Island, to found Newport. Men of many faiths were attracted by the complete religious freedom practiced by the settlement. Ships were being built by 1646, and because of the large deepwater harbor, Newport became one of the leading ports in the triangular trade in rum, slaves and molasses. After the British occupation during the Revolution, its importance as a port declined. Its climate, scenery and wide sandy beaches soon attracted numerous summer visitors, and by the 1860's the fashion of summering in Newport was well established. It became the great summer capital of "Society" and was for years the most fashionable resort of the country.

THE BREAKERS

The most magnificent of the many Newport summer residences, The Breakers, at Ochre Point and Ruggles Avenue, was built in 1895 for Cornelius Vanderbilt, the grandson of the Commodore. Richard Morris Hunt, the architect, modeled the building after the sixteenth-century Italian villas. The house measures about 250 feet by 150 feet, and around the central hall are arranged the approximately 70 rooms.

The galleried Great Hall rises over 45 feet through two full floors. One wall is almost entirely of glass, affording an unobstructed view over the terrace to the ocean. The other three walls are faced with Caen stone imported from France, and the huge pilasters are fluted and decorated with oak leaves and acorns, this design being a symbol of the Vanderbilt family.

The dining room, the most magnificent of the rooms, is two stories high. The kitchen is really fabulous. It has a floor area equal to the entire frontage of an average home, and an enormous coal-burner range occupies almost one whole side of the room.

I have to mention, of course, the children's playhouse, which has all its furniture and equipment children's size. It is a separate structure between the side gate and the main house.

How to reach: Via State Route 114 from Providence.
Open: Memorial Day to November 1, daily, 10:00 A.M. to 5:00 P.M.
Admission: $1.50; children, 6 to 16, 60¢. Combination ticket—adults, $2.00, children, $1.00—admits visitors to *Wanton-Lyman-Hazard House, Hunter House, Whitehall* and the *Breakers stables.*

Trinity Church.

The *Breakers stables,* located nearby on Coggeshall Avenue, with a large carriage room and twenty-six open stalls, have been maintained almost as they were fifty years ago. Carriage, harnesses and trophies are on display.

Open: July 1 to September 6, daily, 10:00 A.M. to 5:00 P.M.
Admission: 50¢.

Our own house, *Beaulieu,* was a mile or so east of the Breakers. My mother did the house over herself in typical Louis XIV style. There were and are many other social landmarks, but Newport's older historic buildings are more notable.

Trinity Church, 141 Spring Street, was built in 1726 by Richard Mundy. The slim spire is still tipped with the gold crown of England. A three-tiered wineglass pulpit with a sounding board above stands in the center aisle.

Touro Synagogue, the oldest synagogue building in the United States, is a National Historic Site. It has served Jewish residents of Newport since 1763, but its congregation, Jeshuat Israel, was founded in 1658 when fifteen Jewish families moved to Rhode Island in response to Roger Williams' declaration of religious freedom. The General Assembly of Rhode Island met in the synagogue in 1780, and a town meeting was held there in 1781 when George Washington was in Newport.

The architect was Peter Harrison, who designed the Brick Market and Redwood Library in Newport as well as buildings in Boston. In 1763, when the synagogue was dedicated, its spiritual leader was the Reverend Isaac Touro, father of the famed Judah Touro, one of the great philanthropists of the United States.

The *Wanton-Lyman-Hazard House,* at 17 Broadway, built about 1675, is the oldest house in Newport and one of the finest Jacobean houses in New England. Its furniture and furnishings and its garden are typical of the period.

The *Nicholas-Wanton-Hunter House,* at 54 Washington Street, was built in 1748, at a time when Newport was a great port and Washington Street was lined with homes of successful merchants. Completely restored, it contains fine paneling and carved woodwork, Newport furniture.

The *Vernon House,* at 46 Clarke Street, built in 1758, served as Revolutionary War headquarters for the Count de Rochambeau while the French occupied Newport. Washington visited Newport for ten days in March, 1781, and stayed at the Vernon House. The building is owned by the Family Service Society, but visitors may see the room used by Rochambeau as his office.

Touro Synagogue.

Wanton-Lyman-Hazard House.

Vernon House.

Governor Stephen Hopkins House

PROVIDENCE, R. I.

The little north room of the Hopkins House, with tiles around the fireplace, flanked by narrow cupboards.

THE TWO-ROOM and unfinished-attic house that Stephen Hopkins bought in 1742 had been built in 1707. In the following year Hopkins added other rooms. In 1804 it was moved from its location on what is now the corner of South Main and Hopkins Streets, and in 1927 it was moved to its present location and the work was begun of restoring it to its appearance at the time of Hopkins' occupancy.

Stephen Hopkins, a member of the Society of Friends, was a first citizen of the colony. He was Chief Justice of the Superior Court, first chancellor of Brown University, ten times Governor of Rhode Island and a signer of the Declaration of Independence.

How to reach: On U. S. Routes 1, 6 and 44. At Benefit and Hopkins Streets.
Open: Wednesdays and Saturdays, 1:00 P.M. to 4:00 P.M.
Admission: Free. Guide service available.
Administration: Owned by the State of Rhode Island, administered by the Society of Colonial Dames.

Carrington House

PROVIDENCE, R. I.

A SERENE, graceful house, this has been the home since 1811 of three generations of a distinguished Rhode Island family engaged in the China trade. It was presented to the Museum of Art of the Rhode Island School of Design by a great-granddaughter in 1936. The skill of Chinese workmanship lends an air of romance to every room—from the wicker lounging chair in the office wing to the hooded cradle and tiny bathtub of Canton china in one of the bedrooms. Teakwood tables and fine porcelains blend with Chippendale chairs in the eighteenth-century front parlor, while the back parlor contrasts comfortable mid-Victorian furniture with a gold-lacquered secretary and sewing table. Except for draperies and some reproduction wallpapers, the interior is substantially in its original condition.

How to reach: Benefit Street.
Open: Daily except Mondays, 1:00 P.M. to 5:00 P.M.
Admission: Free. Guide service is available by appointment.
Administration: Museum of Art, Rhode Island School of Design.

Southeast parlor of the Carrington House.

Gilbert Stuart Birthplace

SAUNDERSTOWN, R. I.

JUST about the time this book is scheduled to make its first appearance, the two-hundredth anniversary of Gilbert Stuart's birth—June 10, 1755—will be observed with appropriate ceremonies. The house in which the great portrait painter was born was built four years earlier and has been restored together with the waterwheel and snuff mill which were part of the manufactory of the artist's father, Gilbert Stuart, snuff-grinder.

How to reach: U. S. Routes 1 and 1A.
Open: Daily, 9:00 A.M. to 5:00 P.M.
Admission: 25¢.
Administration: Gilbert Stuart Memorial, Inc.

Sitting room of the Gilbert Stuart birthplace.

Old Slater Mill

PAWTUCKET, R. I.

THE OLD Slater Mill, erected by Samuel Slater and his partners in 1793, was the first successful cotton mill in America. It has been restored to its appearance of about 1840. The mill will be opened as a museum sometime in 1955 with an exhibition of early textile mill operations showing machines of the period, or replicas of them, rooms for hand spinning and hand weaving operations, objects, paintings, diagrams and models pertaining to early cotton milling. There will be replicas of Arkwright's spinning frame, Whitney's cotton gin, Crompton's mule, Slater's carding engine, etc.

How to reach: U. S. Route 1 alternate. On Roosevelt Avenue in the center of Pawtucket.
Open: To be announced.
Admission: To be announced.
Administration: Old Slater Mill Assoc.

Mystic Seaport
Living Museum of the Sea
MYSTIC, CONN.

e Charles W. Morgan, which sailed more miles and caught more whales than any other ship of its kind.

The Counting House.

Scrimshaw (sailor-made carvings in whalebone and walrus ivory).

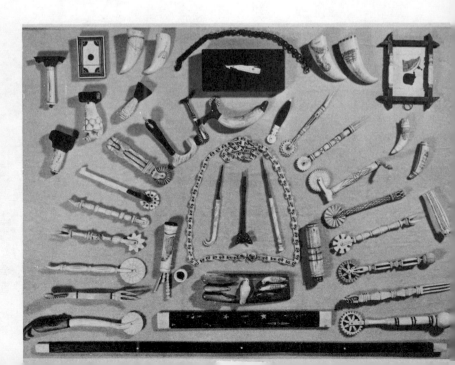

AT MYSTIC not only has a whole New England seaport town been re-created but also its memorabilia have been preserved. There is a wealth of paraphernalia, paintings, figureheads and scrimshaw, ships' models and charts, logs and histories of great and small voyages, in all sorts of vessels to all parts of the world, and actual ships themselves, all kept in a perfect state of preservation. It is one of the most important museums of the sea in the world.

Some of my earliest memories are of Mystic, when we were sailing in my father's famous steam yacht *North Star*. We used Mystic when it was too rough to go around Point Judith or too foggy to risk Block Island on our way to Newport. My father told me that my great-great-grandfather, Commodore Cornelius Vanderbilt, had had several of his famed clipper ships built in the Mystic shipyards, and it was from Mystic that he established a regular sea route via Cape Horn to San Francisco Bay. Here, too, he had developed and built a kind of fast sail and paddle-wheel vessel which he operated to the east coast of Nicaragua. From the coast he took his passengers by mule team and river steamer to clipper ships which he had sent through the Straits of Magellan. By this method he cut by half the sea voyage to the California gold fields.

The Rope Walk (built 1824).

The Rigging Loft.

From the late 1600's and for 200 years after, Mystic was the leading shipbuilding town in the country. Clippers and other types of sailing vessels, schooners, racing yachts, transports, whalers and steamships were all built here—from the *Hero* in which Captain Palmer discovered the Antarctic to the first gasoline-powered racing boat. It's interesting that the company which built the first gasoline-powered boat also built the atomic-powered submarine, *Nautilus.* Mystic clippers established sailing records which still stand unsurpassed.

How to reach: On Route 27, a connecting road between Route 1 and Route 84.

Open: Daily except Christmas and Thanksgiving, 9:00 A.M. to 5:00 P.M.

Admission: Adults, $1.00; children, 25¢. Guide service available.

Administration: The Marine Historical Assoc., Inc.

Fishtown-Chapel (1880's) and The Little Red Schoolhouse. The chapel is non-sectarian.

Henry Whitfield House

First of the Guilford Covenanters

GUILFORD, CONN.

THE Guilford Covenant is one of the most eloquent documents of the first settlers in the United States: "We whose names are here underwritten, intending by God's gracious permission to plant ourselves in New England, and if it may be in the southerly part of Quinnipiack, do faithfully promise each, for ourselves and our families . . . that we will, the Lord assisting us, sit down and join ourselves together in one entire plantation and be helpful each to the other in any common work, according to every man's ability and as need shall require, and we promise not to desert or leave each other or the plantation, but with the consent of the rest, or the greater part of the company who have entered into this engagement. . . . In witness whereof we subscribe our names, this first of June, 1639."

Few of these *first* houses built by the colonists as their first shelter on their arrival from England remain. The Reverend Henry Whitfield and a group of the younger members of his congregation in Ockley were forced to leave England because of the persecution of the clergy, the Puritans and Independents (later Congregationalists) by King Charles I between 1625 and 1640. They bought land from the Sachem squaw Shaumpishuh and settled Menuncatuck (Guilford). The first house built was the *Old Stone House* for Henry Whitfield, because it was to serve as garrison, church, inn and meeting house as well as a private residence. The house is made of local stone and mortar mixed of yellow clay and pulverized oystershells. Walls are two feet thick. The furnishings are all of the period 1640-1700, including such rare pieces as the silver Communion service of the First Congregational Church, Bible boxes, chests of all kinds, a big hooded settle, wainscot and Carver chairs and forms (benches), a rare hutch table, a six-legged folding bed fitted with linen tick filled with straw, a cradle with small patchwork quilt, four kinds of spinning wheels, a loom with all equipment. A clock made by Ebenezer Parmelee in 1726 is the earliest town clock known. It had only an hour hand and was in the tower of the North Church until 1893. The kitchen equipment includes a dough box, shoulder yokes, candle mould, flip iron, stilyard, firkins and two warming pans. A typical mid-seventeenth-century herb garden adjoins the house. Spinning and weaving are demonstrated on request.

Besides the church, there are many other old houses in Guilford. The *Kingsworth-Comfort Starr House* (1646), a private residence, is not open to the public, but the restored *Hyland House,* (1660-1720), on the old Boston Post Road, is open. Its overhang and five great fireplaces are of interest.

How to reach: On U. S. Route 1.

Open: Whitfield House, December 1 to October 31, daily except Mondays, 10:00 A.M. to 12:00 M., 1:00 P.M. to 5:00 P.M. December 1 to April 1, 1:00 P.M. to 4:00 P.M. *Hyland House,* June 15 to September 15 (or by appointment), 11:00 A.M. to 5:00 P.M. except Mondays.

Admission: Whitfield House, free. Guide service available. *Hyland House,* 25¢. Guide service available

Administration: Whitfield House, Henry Whitfield State Historical Museum. *Hyland House,* Dorothy Whitfield Historic Society.

Webb House

Scene of the Yorktown Conference

WETHERSFIELD, CONN.

Exterior view of the Webb House.

IN 1781 George Washington met with the Count de Rochambeau at Wethersfield and laid the plans which resulted in the successful termination of the Revolutionary War. Washington was quartered at the Webb House for the entire five days of the conference (known as the Yorktown Conference) which resulted in the Yorktown surrender, and the meetings were held in the room now called the Council Room.

Webb House was built in 1752 by Joseph Webb whose son Joseph, Jr., was Washington's host. It is a handsome white mansion as it stands now, but when Washington was there, it was painted red and had no front porch. Otherwise it is essentially the same as it was then, even to the original dark red flock wallpaper put on for Washington's visit. The Webb House is the headquarters of the National Society of the Colonial Dames of America in the State of Connecticut.

How to reach: 8 miles southwest of Hartford on Routes 5 alternate and 15.

Open: Weekdays, 10:00 A.M. to 5:00 P.M.; Sundays, 1:00 P.M. to 5:00 P.M.

Admission: 50¢. Special arrangements for groups of students.

Administration: National Society of the Colonial Dames of America in the State of Connecticut.

Washington's bedchamber. Note original flock wallpaper.

The Council Room.

The Glebe House

BIRTHPLACE OF AMERICAN EPISCOPACY

WOODBURY, CONN.

IT WAS in this house that Samuel Seabury was elected, in 1783, the first Bishop of the Anglican Church to serve in America. Architects estimate that the oldest portion of the building dates from 1690. It was enlarged and completed 1740-50 and was first used as a rectory in 1771. It is now restored to its eighteenth-century appearance with appropriate authentic furnishings. Of special interest to visitors is the escape hatch in the west room, through which Rector John Rutgers Marshall escaped from Non-Conformists who persecuted him for participating in Episcopal services.

How to reach: On U. S. Route 6.
Open: Weekdays, 10:00 A.M. to 5:00 P.M.; Sundays, 1:00 P.M. to 5:00 P.M.
Admission: Free. Guide service available.
Administration: Seabury Society for the Preservation of the Glebe House.

The Bishop's Chair in the Seabury Room.

The Tapping Reeve House

and

THE FIRST LAW SCHOOL IN AMERICA

LITCHFIELD, CONN.

TAPPING REEVE, a Princeton graduate, was the founder of the first law school in America. In 1773, when Reeve built his house to serve as home and law office, there were no law schools and prospective lawyers studied in the offices of members of the Bar. Reeve attracted a number of young men and by 1782 was delivering lectures on law to his students; he had also organized moot courts among them to teach them court practice. In 1784 Reeve erected a little building next to his home to house his law library and to serve as his lecture and moot court room. This became the center of his law school. In 1931 a group of lawyers including Chief Justice William Howard Taft acquired the Reeve buildings and restored them to their former condition. Several special groups—the Princeton Trustees, the Yale Corporation and the Harvard Alumni—also participated in this effort.

The first Law School in America.

How to reach: On Route 63, 1 mile south of Route 25.
Open: June 1 to November 1, daily except Sundays, 2:00 P.M. to 5:00 P.M.
Admission: 30¢.
Administration: Litchfield Historical Society.

Bowne House

A Shrine to Religious Freedom

FLUSHING, L. I., N. Y.

IN 1651, John Bowne of Derbyshire, England, came to Flushing and purchased a farm from the friendly Mattinecock (or Seawan-hacky) Indians. He paid for it eight strings of seawam or white wampum worth about thirty-two guilders in Dutch money or about fourteen of our money. That land, with the improvements on it, is now worth more than a million times fourteen now.

The most important improvement on that land is the home, still standing, that Bowne built in 1661. Bowne and his wife had become converted to the Quaker faith and he invited the Quakers to worship in his home in defiance of Governor Stuyvesant's ban on those whom he called "an abominable sect." Bowne was arrested and fined but he stood up for his religious rights, refused to pay the fine, was put in solitary confinement and then sent to Holland for disposal of his case. At his trial he made such an eloquent plea for "liberty of conscience" that he won his point. He was set free and the Dutch West India Company declared for freedom of religion in the New Netherlands province.

The Bowne case for freedom of religion ranks equally with the more famous case of John Peter Zenger for freedom of the press.

It was in the kitchen that the Quakers first held their meetings until Bowne's arrest. After his victory the Quakers continued to worship there until 1694 when the *Friends Meeting House,* still standing, was completed. George Fox in 1672 and William Penn in 1683 were guests at the Bowne House. The home was occupied by John Bowne's direct descendants until 1946 when the Bowne House Historical Society acquired it and began restoration.

The *Friends Meeting House,* at 137-16 Northern Boulevard, is open to the public for meeting for worship every Sunday at 11:00 A.M., otherwise by appointment.

———

How to reach: At the corner of Bowne Street and Fox Lane, just off Northern Boulevard.
Open: Tuesdays, Saturdays, Sundays, 3:00 P.M. to 5:00 P.M.
Admission: Free.
Administration: Bowne House Historical Society.

The kitchen. The fireplace was made large enough to roast an ox, and the fire, at least when John Bowne was there, was never allowed to go out.

Sagamore Hill

Home of Theodore Roosevelt

OYSTER BAY, L. I.

HIGH on a rolling hill overlooking beautiful Oyster Bay, and in the far distance on a clear morning the blue waters of Long Island Sound, stands a large, rambling old-fashioned house built by a dynamic man who for almost eight years ran our country. Theodore Roosevelt, the Rough Rider, the Indian fighter, the explorer, was a man of great courage, apparently unending stamina and wonderful charm, direct and decisive in everything he did and said. He was one of the most devoted when it came to his family, for he believed that the family, "which if broken means the dissolution of civilization," was the basis for lifelong happiness.

I knew Theodore Roosevelt well and he was my ideal during the years of my youth and early manhood. In my teens I spent many long summer evenings on the steps of the piazza of Sagamore Hill, at the feet of "my hero." Thus it was in 1917 when the United States entered the first World War and Theodore Roosevelt was no longer president that, fired by his patriotism and splendid courage, I ran away from my parents' home nearby and enlisted in the U. S. Army as a buck private. My parents did everything to get me out, but I went into the trenches of France and Flan-

ders with regular army troops. I never regretted it.

After I returned from the trenches on hospital leave (I had been gassed), I went back to Sagamore Hill one late summer evening while a party was in progress. The former president was sitting out on the piazza fanning himself with a huge brown palm-leaf. We discussed the conduct of the war, as of that moment, and he made me feel truly important, talking to a private in the U. S. Army as if he were one of its generals. The Trophy Room was a favorite of T.R.'s. Whenever a newcomer came, he pointed out his trophies and told how he had secured them. I remember his saying, "We men must stick together on our stories, or the women will run the earth."

Sagamore Hill was built in 1884 by T.R. It was the Summer White House when he was President of the United States, 1901-1909. Restored in Victorian style, the house looks as it did in the period 1890-1901. Furnishings are the family heirlooms, hunting trophies and gifts from famous people.

How to reach: On Route 106. Follow Sagamore Hill signs.
Open: Daily except Tuesdays, 10:00 A.M. to 5:00 P.M.
Admission: 75¢. Children under 12, free when accompanied by an adult. Special rates for groups of 20 or more.
Administration: Theodore Roosevelt Assoc.

The parlor.

The Trophy Room.

Fraunces Tavern

NEW YORK CITY

GEORGE WASHINGTON didn't sleep here, but he made it famous by patronizing it on several occasions, the most memorable of which was his touching farewell to his officers on December 4, 1783, when he retired to his plantation.

Not only is Fraunces Tavern the oldest restaurant in New York, it is the oldest building. It is still an excellent restaurant. My father took me there first when I was a child. His favorite dish was the superb oyster stew, half and half. I probably ate ice cream. My father told me that my great-great-grandfather, Commodore Cornelius Vanderbilt, used to take his meals and hold his business conferences here.

Since 1763, what started as the Queen's Head Tavern and later became known as Fraunces Tavern has been a restaurant. Samuel Fraunces, the founder, was of French extraction and came from the West Indies to New York where he had been an innkeeper since 1755. The excellent food, service and wine, especially the Madeira for which it was famous, attracted most of the leading citizens of the city, among them the most famous of all, General George Washington.

How to reach: 54 Pearl Street.
Open: Monday through Friday 10:00 A.M. to 4:00 P.M; Saturdays, to 3:00 P.M. Closed Sundays and holidays except Washington's Birthday. (Restaurant open usual hours.)
Admission: Free.
Administration: Sons of the Revolution in the State of New York.

Cooper Union

NEW YORK CITY

THE COOPER UNION for the Advancement of Science and Art has a rare dual distinction—it is historic both as a building and as an institution. Its Foundation Building is the forerunner of skyscraper construction and the Union itself is a celebrated monument to democratic education.

The founder was Peter Cooper who designed the building himself to house his educational institute. The cornerstone was laid in 1853 and the building was completed in 1858 at a cost of $650,000. It was one of the first buildings in which horizontal rolled iron beams were used and is now the oldest building in the United States supported by such means. Though elevators were not available in 1858, an elevator shaft was built in the structure because Cooper realized that elevators would have to be built some day.

When the doors of Cooper Union were opened in 1859, the American tradition of free education was just being formed. This institution designed by Cooper "to aid the efforts of youth to acquire that kind of useful knowledge which will enable them to find and fill valuable places . . . to the great possible advantage of themselves and the community" was an important factor in the development of the tradition.

Everyone knows of Lincoln's speech at Cooper Union in 1860 but few realize that twelve other Presidents of the United States made addresses in the Great Hall of Cooper Union.

Open: Generally, weekdays, 9:00 A.M. to 5:00 P.M.; Saturdays, 10:00 A.M. to 5:00 P.M.
Admission: Free. Guide service available.
Administration: The Cooper Union for the Advancement of Science and Art.

Roger Morris-Jumel Mansion

HISTORIC SHOWPLACE
NEW YORK CITY

I HAVE always been fascinated by the story of Eliza Bowen Jumel, the Providence girl of questionable origin who rose from poverty to become one of the richest women of her time, who overcame social ostracism to become a fabulous leader of society. The mansion she made famous had a remarkably checkered career.

In colonial days it was a gentleman's estate where the landed gentry assembled at brilliant social gatherings. Then it had a military period when within its handsome walls famous American and British generals planned their campaigns. Then it was a bustling hostelry until it became a farmer's home, deteriorating gradually and going into disrepair and decay. But Jumel bought it and it became a fabulous social center until Madame Jumel's death. Then the house passed through several ownerships and was about to be demolished when a group of women petitioned the city to buy the house and grounds and preserve it. The city did purchase the property and the custodianship was given to the Washington Headquarters Association founded by the Daughters of the American Revolution.

It was Roger Morris, who had married wealthy Mary Philipse, who built the house in 1765. The Morris family spent summers there until the Revolutionary War began. In 1776 American troops took it over and Washington made it his headquarters. When Washington abandoned it after five weeks the British moved in and General Sir Henry Clinton and his officers occupied it for the seven years that the British held New York. After the war the house was sold and resold many times. Eventually renamed Calumet Hall, it was a tavern on the stagecoach route to Albany. When President Washington visited it to see his old headquarters, it was the home of an unknown farmer.

The drawing room.

But in 1810 Stephen Jumel bought it for his wife who remodeled and refurnished it and made it one of the most beautiful homes in the country. It was in the style of that period—early nineteenth century—when the Federal influence was strong. Many notables and possibly royalty also were entertained. In 1833, a year after Jumel's death, Madame Jumel, now fifty-eight, married seventy-eight-year-old Aaron Burr but that marriage did not last long and ended in divorce. She died at ninety-three in 1865.

How to reach: Edgecombe Avenue at West 160th Street.
Open: Daily except Mondays, 11:00 A.M. to 5:00 P.M.
Admission: Free.
Administration: Washington Headquarters Assoc. of the Daughters of the American Revolution.

Office. Washington planned Harlem Heights campaign here.

The Frick Collection

A Private House Museum

NEW YORK CITY

Living hall.

THE Henry Clay Frick house is historic, in my opinion, not because it was for a time the home of a steelman who played an important part in the industrial history of our country, but rather because it is a shining example of the "American Palace," the home built by a fabulously rich man without regard for cost and yet with taste and judgment, under the supervision and according to the designs of experts. There was a golden decade or two of such construction in the early part of the century, but I do not think such private homes will ever be built again.

The Frick house was built 1913-14 according to plans of Carrère and Hastings, architects of the New York Public Library. It was the home of Mr. Frick until his death in 1919 and of Mrs. Frick until her death in 1931. Then, according to the Frick will, it became a museum, but the atmosphere of a private house was retained. All the great works of art, including a great collection of paintings, are displayed, not as in a large museum but as in a home—a regal, ducal or doge-like home, it is true, but a private house nevertheless.

How to reach: At 1 East 70th Street.
Open: Weekdays, except Mondays, 10:00 A.M. to 5:00 P.M.; Sundays and holidays, 1:00 P.M. to 5:00 P.M. Closed on May 30, July 4, December 25, and month of August.
Admission: Free. Children under 10 not admitted; children under 16 must be accompanied by adults.
Administration: The Frick Collection, Inc.

The Fragonard Room of the Frick House.

Van Cortlandt Mansion

WASHINGTON SLEPT HERE
NEW YORK CITY

THE VERY last stop on the Broadway branch of New York's subway is Van Cortlandt Park. There you can see and go through the house where during the Revolution on numerous occasions George Washington slept. It is said that it was from this house that he and his men started their triumphal march into New York City at the end of the war in 1783.

The handsome stone house was built in 1748 by Frederick Van Cortlandt and was restored and furnished by the National Society of Colonial Dames in the State of New York.

———————

How to reach: Broadway and 242nd Street.
Open: Daily.
Admission: 25¢ on Sundays, Mondays, Tuesdays, Wednesdays. Other days, free. School children accompanied by teachers, free.
Administration: National Society of Colonial Dames in the State of New York.

[41]

Philipse Castle

Residence of the First Lord of the Manor

NORTH TARRYTOWN, N. Y.

IN 1683 Frederick Philipse, who had been Peter
Stuyvesant's "carpenter" and associate, came to the
manor he had acquired in the wilderness—some
twenty-five thousand acres along the Hudson not many
miles from New York—and built a pioneer settlement
and trading post. The magnificent castle-like home, in
the true Dutch tradition, that he built that year still
stands—restored with the help of John D. Rockefeller,
Jr., and local philanthropists—as it was in its great
days.

Frederick Philipse was the wealthiest man of his day
and his area. Having acquired some twenty miles of
Hudson River frontage northward from Spuyten Duyvil and far eastward and having built a very profitable
toll bridge across the Spuyten Duyvil, he established
his vast holdings as the Manor of Philipsburg, which
remained in his family until confiscated as Tory property in 1779.

Philipse married twice and both his wives came from
prominent families, the Van Cortlandts and the Har-
denburghs. And it was natural that this fine and
luxurious house should be regarded as the social center
of the time. As succeeding generations took possession,
the castle and its Dutch tradition were replaced in
importance by the Philipse Manor House in Yonkers
where the more accepted English social life held sway.
But, later, when Gerard G. Beekman, husband of Cornelia Van Cortlandt, acquired the property, it was once

again "the great house" for a time. An addition was
built in 1785.

The restoration of Philipse Castle is rather novel.
There are twenty-four different rooms ranging in
period from 1683 to 1800, covering all aspects of the
Dutch tradition. Outside the castle are other restored
elements of manor life: the old barn, the slave cottage,
the smokehouse, the old mill, the church, the Dutch
garden, etc.

How to reach: Via Route 9.
Open: Daily, except Easter, Thanksgiving, Christmas, New Year's
  Day, 10:00 A.M to 5:00 P.M.
Admission: $1.00; children with adults, 60¢.
Administration: Sleepy Hollow Restorations, Inc.

*Lord of the Manor's
office. Note sand on
floor.*

The Widow Beekman's parlor (1785 section) in Philipse Castle.

Philipse Manor

RESIDENCE OF THE THIRD LORD OF THE MANOR
YONKERS, N. Y.

IT WAS the namesake and grandson of the original Frederick Philipse who made this manor a great social center from the 1740's to the Revolution. The first lord built the original stone section of the building about 1682; the third lord, Colonel Frederick Philipse, built the brick wing about 1745. George Washington came here to court Mary Philipse, Colonel Frederick's sister. But Washington was too much occupied as a colonial officer and "Polly" was won by the English captain Roger Morris and went to live in the Morris Mansion, now known as the Roger Morris-Jumel Mansion.

Colonel Frederick was a Loyalist, and after the Revolution his property was confiscated, broken up and sold. The Manor House at one time was used as the city hall.

How to reach: On Route 9.
Open: Weekdays, 9:00 A.M. to 5:00 P.M.; Sundays, 1:00 P.M. to 5:00 P.M.
Admission: Free.
Administration: State Education Department, State of New York.

Doorway, south entrance of Philipse Manor.

Sunnyside

Sleepy Hollow Land

IRVINGTON-ON-THE-HUDSON, N. Y.

The crow-stepped "snuggery" showing wisteria vine planted by Irving and the famous ivy from the home of Sir Walter Scott.

"I HAVE built me a little cottage on the banks of the Hudson in a lonely spot endeared to me by the recollection of my boyhood," Washington Irving wrote to Charles Dickens on May 20, 1841. He had acquired the property in 1835, when after years of travel abroad, he wanted to settle down in America. He named the place, which dated back to the 1780's, "The Roost," kept adding and rebuilding it in the quaint Dutch style until it was for him an "elegant little snuggery" which he loved. About 1841 he renamed the house Sunnyside and it was his home until he died in 1859. He wrote his *Life of George Washington* at Sunnyside, and of course the countryside nearby—the Sleepy Hollow country—was the scene of his best-known writings.

Sunnyside was restored, as was Philipse Castle, with the aid of John D. Rockefeller, Jr., and others, and appears now as it did in Irving's day. The furnishings include many of Irving's own possessions.

How to reach: Via U. S. Route 9.
Open: Daily, except Easter, Thanksgiving, Christmas, New Year's Day, 10:00 A.M. to 5:00 P.M.
Admission: $1.00; children with adults, 60¢.
Administration: Sleepy Hollow Restorations, Inc.

Alcove in Irving's study.

Bedroom showing Irving's original furniture.

Vanderbilt Mansion

HYDE PARK, N. Y.

THIS is "perfect American millionaire," a magnificent example of the kind of great estate built by American millionaires in the great expansion period following the Civil War. It was the home of my great-uncle Frederick W., grandson of the Commodore. Except for the fact that it is on American soil and that it represents a phase of our cultural history, there is very little that is American about it. The mansion itself, completed in 1898, was designed as an Italian Renaissance royal palace by McKim, Mead and White. The furnishings are mostly Italian and French. The grounds and gardens are beautiful. The estate was originally called Hyde Park, from which the town, which lies just south of it, took its name. The property was presented to the National Park Service in 1940.

How to reach: U. S. Route 9.
Open: Daily except Mondays, 9:00 A.M. to 5:00 P.M.
Admission: Nominal. Children and education groups, free.
Administration: National Park Service.

The drawing room. The chairs are French, the table is Italian, the piano is an American one that was sent to Paris to be decorated. On the wall is one of four Brussels tapestries that tell the story of the fall of Troy. Note Medici arms on the other tapestry.

Hyde Park

Home of Franklin Delano Roosevelt

HYDE PARK, N. Y.

HYDE PARK is one of the most beautiful estates in America. It lies on the banks of the Hudson, a gracious, comfortable house, surrounded by acres of trees and green lawns and gardens. The only president ever to be elected to four terms was born and buried here—in magnificent simplicity in a white marble tomb of marble from the same Vermont quarry from which the Jefferson Memorial in Washington, D. C., was made.

Franklin Delano Roosevelt was an old, old friend of mine. He used to say that he had known me longer than I knew him, since he had been a guest at my christening. I have been a frequent guest at Hyde Park, as a young man when F.D.R. was Governor of New York and later when he was President. His favorite room was his bedroom where he would sit propped up in bed, wearing a faded old sweater, writing, dictating, attending to the business of his country. Once during his so-called attempt to pack the Supreme Court, it happened that a well-known Wall Street broker was at his luncheon table. This gentleman had been damning Roosevelt from one end of the country to the other and he told the President why he hated him. Instead of flying into a rage, F.D.R. burst into one of his most contagious laughs and said, "Well, Hal, you are in good company. Lots of people hate me, too." The man was so astounded he nearly choked, and during the next election campaign his checks to the Roosevelt cause were among the largest received.

Isaac Roosevelt, whose portrait by Gilbert Stuart today hangs at the east end of the living room, was Franklin's great-great-grandfather. He was active in politics. His son James, whose portrait hangs at the west end of the living room, was a successful merchant. James' son Isaac, whose portrait hangs in the dining room, was a doctor who settled in the township of Hyde Park. His son James was a lawyer and businessman who, after the death of his first wife, married Sara Delano in 1880. Both her father and grandfather had been active in the China trade, which accounts for many of the Chinese objects in the house.

The house was originally built in 1826. James Roosevelt bought it in 1867 and Franklin Delano was born there January 30, 1882. The house underwent many changes. The old central portion, for instance, its clapboards removed, is covered with stucco. A porch, with balustrade and colonnaded portico, was added. By 1915 it was as it is now, and at the request of the late President, will remain so. Hyde Park is a home and a livable one, full of small knick-knacks and treasures many of which are "collections" made by members of the family.

How to reach: U. S. Route 9.
Open: Daily except Mondays, 10:00 A.M. to 5:00 P.M.
Admission: 25¢. Children under 12 and educational groups, free.
Administration: National Park Service.

Room in which Franklin D. Roosevelt was born.

President Franklin D. Roosevelt's study and Summer White House office.

Hasbrouck House

BIRTHPLACE OF THE
"ORDER OF THE PURPLE HEART"
NEWBURGH, N. Y.

GENERAL GEORGE WASHINGTON made his headquarters here from April 1, 1782, until August 19, 1783, when the Revolutionary War ended. From here General Washington replied to the proposal that he form a new government with himself at the head with the title of "King." Here on August 7, 1782, he proposed the military award known as the "Order of the Purple Heart."

The house was started in 1750 and two additions, also of fieldstone, had been made by 1770. The largest room, known as "the room of seven doors and one window," was used by Washington as a reception and living room.

On the grounds is a regional museum. The Hamilton-Burr dueling pistols are here, as is part of the chain and boom which spanned the Narrows of the Hudson River at West Point, barring passage upstream to the British fleet.

How to reach: On Routes 9W and 52.
Open: Weekdays, 9:00 A.M. to 5:00 P.M.; Sundays, 1:00 P.M. to 5:00 P.M.
Admission: Free.
Administration: State Education Department, State of New York.

Senate House

WHERE THE FIRST STATE SENATE MET
KINGSTON, N. Y.

THE New York Provincial Congress convened first in 1776 in New York City, but when capture of that city by the British seemed imminent, the Congress moved to White Plains, then to Fishkill and again to Kingston where the first State Constitution was adopted. The first Senate elected under it met at the house of Wessel Ten Broeck—built in 1676. When the British burned Kingston, the Ten Broeck house was not entirely destroyed and was soon rebuilt and used as a private residence by the Ten Broeck family until 1888. The State then acquired it as a historic house and restored it with furnishings of the period, including certain objects believed to have been saved from the British destruction.

How to reach: On Route 9W and 209.
Open: Weekdays, 9:00 A.M. to 5:00 P.M.; Sundays, 1:00 P.M. to 5:00 P.M.
Admission: Free.
Administration: State Education Department, State of New York.

Street of the Huguenots

The Earliest Group of Original Houses on One Street

NEW PALTZ, N. Y.

Memorial House.

THE SETTLEMENT of New Paltz was founded in 1678 by twelve Patentees, all French Huguenots. Five of the stone houses built by the early settlers —all on the same street, Huguenot Street—are still standing. The Huguenot Historical Society of New Paltz claims that these constitute the earliest group of houses in their original state on one street in this country. I do not know of any other group of houses that can dispute this claim.

The five houses are: *The Abraham Hasbrouck House* (1712); the *Louis Bevier* or *Bevier-Elting House* (1694); the *Daniel DuBois House,* or the *Old Fort* (1705); *Hugo Freer House* (1709); *Jean Hasbrouck House* (1712) which is also known as the *Memorial House* and is maintained as a historic house museum. The rooms are furnished in the period of the eighteenth century, and one of them, the Hasbrouck-Innis-Young Room, is furnished with items that belonged to the first Huguenot settlers. This house is open regularly to the public. All the other old stone houses are open to visitors all day on Stone House Day each year, generally in the first week of August.

The Old Fort.

How to reach: On Route 299.
Open: Memorial House is open daily except Mondays, 9:00 A.M. to 5:00 P.M.; Sundays, 10:00 A.M. to 4:00 P.M.
Admission: Free (donations).
Administration: Huguenot Historical Society of New Paltz.

Abraham Hasbrouck House.

Chimney of the Memorial House.

Fort Crailo

THE VAN RENSSELAER MANOR HOUSE

RENSSELAER, N. Y.

THE Van Rensselaer Manor lands at one time comprised some 700,000 acres, extending from the mouth of the Mohawk River to below Albany on both banks of the Hudson to a width of almost fifty miles. The original Manor House was erected about 1650 approximately at the center of the property, on the east bank of the Hudson opposite Albany. The present structure, Fort Crailo, is believed to have been built about 1704 on the foundations of the earlier building.

A wealth of anecdote clings to Fort Crailo which was given to the State of New York in 1924 at which time restoration and refurnishing in the Van Rensselaer tradition was begun.

How to reach: On Route 9.
Open: Weekdays, 9:00 A.M. to 5:00 P.M.; Sundays, 1:00 P.M. to 5:00 P.M.
Admission: Free.
Administration: State Education Department, State of New York.

The parlor, Fort Crailo.

Schuyler Mansion

ALBANY, N. Y.

ACROSS the Hudson from Fort Crailo is the impressive house built in 1762 by General Philip Schuyler who married "Sweet Kitty" Van Rensselaer, daughter of John Van Rensselaer of Fort Crailo. The Schuylers' daughter Elizabeth married Alexander Hamilton in 1780. The wedding, the most brilliant of the mansion's many such affairs, took place in what has since become known as the Hamilton Room.

How to reach: On Route 9.
Open: Weekdays, 9:00 A.M. to 4:30 P.M.; Sundays, 1:00 P.M. to 4:30 P.M.
Admission: Free
Administration: State Education Department, State of New York.

Mark Twain's Study

A LITERARY SHRINE

ELMIRA, N. Y.

IN THIS octagonal replica of a Mississippi pilot-house Mark Twain wrote most of *Tom Sawyer* and did much work on *Huckleberry Finn, A Connecticut Yankee in King Arthur's Court, The Prince and the Pauper,* etc. His sister-in-law, Mrs. Theodore Crane, built it for him in 1874 on her "Quarry Farm," located on East Hill overlooking the Chemung Valley. Twain was delighted with it and loved to work there.

In 1952, in order to insure its proper preservation, the study was moved to the Elmira College campus. Completely restored, it is open to the public.

How to reach: On Route 17.
Open: Summer, weekdays; 10:00 A.M. to 12:00 M.; winter, during college hours, 2:00 P.M. to 4:00 P.M.
Admission: Free.
Administration: Elmira College.

Herkimer Home

"OLD HONIKOL'S HOUSE"

LITTLE FALLS, N. Y.

ONE OF the most popular men in Mohawk Valley history was "Old Honikol," General Nicholas Herkimer, hero of the Battle of Oriskany in 1777 against the British, Canadians, Hessians, Tories and Indians under the command of Sir John Johnson, Barry St. Leger and the Indian chief, Joseph Brant.

The Herkimer House was built in 1764. Somewhat modernized in 1845, it is now partially restored. It contains much that was the property of the general.

How to reach: On Route 5S.
Open: Weekdays, 9:00 A.M. to 5:00 P.M.; Sundays, 1:00 P.M. to 5:00 P.M.
Admission: Free.
Administration: State Education Department, State of New York.

Cooperstown
The *Leatherstocking* Country

COOPERSTOWN, N. Y.

SAY "Cooperstown" to any American (or almost any European) and he'll identify it at once as the home of James Fenimore Cooper, the scene of the Leatherstocking books and the site of the Baseball Hall of Fame. James Fenimore Cooper was not born here but was brought when he was a year old to the little settlement that his father, Judge William Cooper, founded in New York State's lovely Cherry Valley. The judge gave the village its name and his son James made it famous throughout the world.

Now at Cooperstown there is the *Farmers' Museum* and a typical *Village Crossroads* restoration of the time Cooper wrote about (early nineteenth century) in his *Leatherstocking Tales* and other books. Here you can see a schoolhouse of 1810 (moved from Filer's Corners in the Butternuts Valley), a country store of 1820 (moved from Toddsville), a blacksmith shop of 1827 (moved from New Berlin), a printing office of 1829 (moved from Middlefield), a doctor's office of 1829 (moved from Westford), a druggist's shop of 1832 (moved from Hartwick), a lawyer's office of the 1800-1840 period, a tavern built about 1800 (moved from Ashland), a farmhouse built about 1797 (moved from

Main building of the Farmers' Museum.

Hinman Hollow, Hartwick), a log barn (moved from South New Berlin). Household activities of the early nineteenth century are carried on daily. The farm has a pair of working oxen, livestock and poultry, crops are raised and harvested. Nearby is *Fenimore House,* a

museum of American history and folk art. All these buildings are operated by the New York State Historical Association.

Also in Cooperstown is the *National Baseball Hall of Fame and Museum,* which is not exactly a historic house as I have used the term in this book but which of course cannot be ignored when we are talking of this village where the game of baseball is said to have been born. Besides the exhibits of plaques and baseball memorabilia within the Hall itself, there is *Doubleday Field,* constructed on the cow pasture where Abner Doubleday is supposed to have originated and named the game. Apparently there is some question as to whether or not this is so, but I think this is not the place to attempt to resolve the issue. It doesn't matter. The Baseball Hall of Fame is an excellent museum, thrilling to all baseball fans, and Cooperstown is a fine re-creation of elements of our past, authentically and superbly presented.

―――――

How to reach: On Routes 80 and 28.
Open: May through September, daily, 9:00 A.M. to 6:00 P.M.; other months, 9:00 A.M. to 5:00 P.M.
Admission: Farmers' Museum, $1.00; children, 15¢. Fenimore House, Baseball Museum, 75¢; children, 15¢. Reduced rates in combination.
Administration: New York State Historical Assoc., National Baseball Hall of Fame and Museum.

Doubleday Field.

(Left) *The Village Crossroads.* From right to left, *blacksmith shop, printing office, doctor's office, lawyer's office.*

National Baseball Hall of Fame and Museum.

Main entrance of French "Castle."

Old Fort Niagara

YOUNGSTOWN, N. Y.

THREE flags have waved over the ramparts of old Fort Niagara—the French *fleur-de-lis*, the Union Jack (twice) and the Stars and Stripes. Fourteen miles from Niagara Falls, it is the oldest masonry west of the Mohawk Valley in the north. Five of its stone buildings were constructed before the Revolution.

The present French fortress-castle, which was built in 1726 as a trading chateau to deceive the Indians, is the third fortification on the site. Its dormers sheltered gun platforms for cannon. The others were Fort Conti, built by La Salle in 1679 and the log Fort Denonville. The "Castle" appears today substantially as it was in the days of exploration and the French and Indian Wars. The drawbridge, complete with chains, windlasses and stone counterbalance weights, leads to the Gate of Five Nations. The main door, nearly six inches thick, is backed with double bars to withstand battering ram attack.

Within, names of some of the early prisoners and dates in the 1740's are scratched in the plaster of the jail cell. A solitary confinement cell is windowless. An interior well, sealed by the British in 1759, was un-

French powder magazine (center) and barbette guns.

The "Castle," north end.

covered during the restoration, as was a sealed holy water font in the Jesuit chapel, one of the first Christian churches on the frontier. The Castle also includes a barter room, military kitchen, guard rooms, with sleeping bunks and musket racks, officers' quarters, a gun deck—sometimes used for a drill room—and council chamber.

Fort Niagara fell to the British in 1759 after an eighteen-day siege. Sir William Johnson, first British commandant, was appointed superintendent of Indian affairs for the Northern Colonies. It is said he controlled half of North America from the council chamber.

During the Revolution, British guerrilla forces made forays from Fort Niagara into central New York. Redoubts, actually small forts with twelve-pounder cannon, were built in 1770-71 for protection of the flanks of the Castle. During the War of 1812, Fort Niagara, an American stronghold after the Jay Treaty, exchanged bombardments with Fort George on the Canadian side of the Niagara River. British troops captured it and held it until the end of the conflict. The final strengthening of the ancient fort was carried out at the time of the Civil War in preparation for an attack which never came. The brick walls of these casemate arches, mounting batteries of cannon, are seven feet thick and heavily reinforced with earth.

The work of restoration was begun by the Old Fort Niagara Association, Inc., in 1927 and completed in 1934.

Also of interest are the former French storehouse, now the Historical Institute, with scale models, maps and paintings; the French powder magazine, housing relics of colonial warfare; the postern gate, built in 1839, through which supplies were brought into the fort from the landing place below; the hot-shot furnace and battery (recalling Fanny Doyle's heroism in loading and firing red-hot shot in the War of 1812); and the old French bakehouse, with two bake-ovens still intact.

Beyond the Castle, at the edge of the bluff, is a stone platform commemorating the Rush-Bagot Treaty following the War of 1812, under which Britain and the United States agreed to cease their warlike activities on the Lakes and to limit their inland navies to small vessels carrying no more than one cannon, thus providing for an unfortified frontier between Canada and this country.

How to reach: On Route 18-F from Niagara Falls.
Open: Daily, except Thanksgiving, Christmas and New Year's Day, 9:00 A.M. to 4:45 P.M.; during July and August, 9:00 A.M. to 9:00 P.M.
Admission: 50¢; children and members of the armed forces, organized school groups, free. Adult groups of 25 or more, 30¢. Guide service available in summer.
Administered by: Old Fort Niagara Assoc.

English council chamber.

Jesuit chapel in the "Castle."

The George Eastman Birthplace

A PHOTOGRAPHIC SHRINE
ROCHESTER, N. Y.

ONCE when I was visiting Thomas Edison down at Fort Myers in Florida, George Eastman was there and we talked for quite a while. After Eastman left, Edison said, "George Eastman has contributed more to education in the world *we* live in than anyone else I can think of." "More than the inventor of the electric light?" I asked. "Yes," he said. There was no point in disputing the matter then, and none now. But the man, justly called the Father of Modern Photography, who did so much to make the camera and photography everyday things to almost everyone, who helped the pictorial view to take its place beside the written word, has a permanent high place in American social and cultural history.

On July 12, 1954, the one-hundredth anniversary of his birth in Waterville, N. Y., his birthplace, a rare example of a story-and-a-half Greek Revival house, was moved to Rochester, re-erected and restored to the period of the Eastman occupancy.

The house, in some ways typical of Oneida County houses of that time, was built in the 1830's and is notable for a number of unusual features.

How to reach: On Route 96.
Open: Weekdays except Mondays, 10:00 A.M. to 5:00 P.M.; Sundays, 1:00 P.M. to 6:00 P.M.
Admission: 25¢.
Administration: The George Eastman House, Inc.

Exterior view of the Eastman Birthplace and a view of the parlor. In the 1850's, when the Eastmans occupied this house, the parlor was the "Important Event" room, reserved for special occasions and seldom used or even entered in ordinary everyday living.

Nassau Hall

ACADEMIC AND HISTORIC SHRINE

PRINCETON, N. J.

NASSAU HALL, the famed "Old Nassau" of Princeton University, was the first, and for fifty years after it was completed in 1756, the only building of Princeton College. It *was* the College—housing classrooms, chapel, dormitory and dining rooms. But during the Revolution it achieved special importance. It served as a barracks and as a hospital. The first legislature of the State of New Jersey convened in it in 1776 and the Continental Congress conducted its June-November sessions there in 1783. The first minister of a foreign nation (van Berckel of the Netherlands) was officially received there.

In recent years Nassau Hall has been devoted solely to administrative offices, faculty meetings and other gatherings. It contains many interesting portraits, including a Charles Willson Peale painting of George Washington at the Battle of Princeton, showing Nassau Hall in the background.

How to reach: Just off U. S. 1.
Open: During college hours.
Admission: Free.
Administration: Princeton University.

The William Trent House

TRENTON, N. J.

WILLIAM TRENT, from whom the city of Trenton derives its name, built this brick mansion in 1719. He was a colonel, very active in colonial affairs, and at his death in 1724 was Chief Justice of New Jersey, regarded as the region's most outstanding citizen. The Trent House is notable for its first-rank collection of William and Mary and also Queen Anne period furniture. In the restoration, begun in 1934 and completed in 1936, the antiquarians had the guidance of a minutely detailed "True & Perfect Inventory of the Goods and Chattels, etc. of William Trent," made in 1726 and indubitably authenticated.

How to reach: On U. S. Route 1. 539 South Warren Street.
Open: Weekdays, 10:00 A.M. to 4:00 P.M.; Sundays, 1:00 P.M. to 4:00 P.M.
Admission: 25¢; children, 10¢.
Administration: Trent House Commission.

Drawing room of the Trent House, showing original corner fireplace.

Morristown

A Military Capital of the American Revolution

MORRISTOWN, N. J.

MORRISTOWN, thirty miles from New York and advantageously located for military purposes, was the scene of almost continuous American military action from 1776 to 1782. It was the site of Washington's military headquarters and the main encampment of the Continental Army during the winters of 1777 and 1779-80. In January, 1777, Washington established his winter quarters in the area near Morristown that came to be called, for some unknown reason, Fort Nonsense. Here he divided his forces, detailing one detachment "to Strengthen the Works . . . and erect such others as are necessary for the better defending it," while the main body was engaged in gathering the military material, wagons and supplies for the coming spring campaign. It was in nearby Jockey Hollow that the 10,000 men of the main Continental Army spent the hard winter of 1779-80 while Washington reorganized and re-inspirited them almost within sight of the British army in New York. It was here that Lafayette came, in May of 1780, to announce the second French expedition to help the Americans.

To preserve the area and restore the significant elements, the Morristown National Historical Park of almost 1,000 acres was established by Congress, July 4, 1933. Among the features are:

Officer's hut (reconstructed).

The Ford Mansion.

The *Ford Mansion*. This was the house used by Washington in 1779-80 as his headquarters. The mansion, built just before the war by Colonel Jacob Ford, was typical of the best American houses of the time. Now partially restored and furnished with authentic pieces of the period, it shows the general appearance of the mansion when Washington occupied it.

The *Wick House,* built about 1750, was used as quarters in 1779-80 by Major General Arthur St. Clair. It has been restored and furnished authentically to re-establish its colonial appearance and atmosphere.

The *Historical Museum* is a new structure built to house and display historical material. Exhibits illustrate the story of the Continental Army and include original objects of all kinds—prints, costumes, furnishings, etc.

Close to the National Historical Park is the *Schuyler-Hamilton House,* built before 1765. It was here that Alexander Hamilton courted Betsy Schuyler, who lived in the house as the guest of her aunt during the winter of 1779-80 when Washington and his aides were in residence nearby at the Ford Mansion. It contains many examples of colonial furniture and craftsmanship and there is a notable old-fashioned garden. Administered by the Morristown chapter of the Daughters of the American Revolution, it is open Tuesday to Friday from 10:00 A.M. to 12:00 P.M. and from 2:00 P.M. to 5:00 P.M. There is no admission charge.

The Wick House.

How to reach: On New Jersey Route 24 or 32, U. S. Route 202.

Open: Tuesday through Sunday, 10:00 A.M. to 5:00 P.M. (except *Wick House,* which is open Tuesday through Saturday from 1:00 P.M. to 5:00 P.M.

Admission: 25¢ for *Ford Mansion* and *Historical Museum.* Children under 12 with adults, free. Free guide service for groups may be arranged in advance.

Administration: National Historical Park, National Park Service.

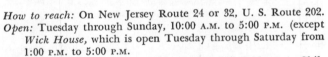

Kitchen of the Wick House.

Independence Hall

Shrine of Liberty

PHILADELPHIA, PA.

I HAVE visited Independence Hall on dozens of occasions for as many reasons. The first occasion was educational, when I was shown the place where "the United States was created on July 4, 1776," along with other students at Pine Lodge Academy where I attended boarding school. Later, from my office window at the *Saturday Evening Post*, I had an excellent view of this historic building and it was only then that I began to appreciate its history and its significance. It would "still be merely the old State House," as Carl Van Doren once said, "if independence had not been achieved and if the Constitution had not been ratified and put into effect. . . . On account of the Declaration of Independence it is a shrine honored wherever the rights of man are honored."

After my stint on Horace Lorimer's magazine, I was a legislative correspondent. My beat was Washington, D. C., and that meant I was on every presidential campaign train with every president after Wilson and every candidate for the presidency beginning with John W. Davis. With each of these I visited Independence Hall, though I admit many a time I wrote my story from memory while sitting in the presidential train.

Independence Hall is now a part of the Independence National Historical Park, which includes *Car-*

Independence Hall.

penter's Hall, Christ Church and other historic sites in Philadelphia. Not only is Independence Hall worth a long visit, but so are other preservations: the *Second Bank of the United States,* a fine example of Greek Revival architecture; *St. Mary's Church,* the principal Catholic church in Philadelphia during the colonial and Revolutionary periods; the late eighteenth-century *Dilworth-Todd-Moylan House;* the *Bishop White House,* where the Right Reverend William White, father of the American Protestant Episcopal Church, lived until his death in 1836; the *Philadelphia Merchants' Exchange,* built between 1832-34, which housed the Philadelphia Stock Exchange; the *First Bank of the United States,* built in 1795, probably the oldest bank building in the United States; *Carpenters' Hall,* built in 1770 as the guild hall of the Carpenters' Company of Philadelphia, organized in 1724.

Benjamin Franklin lived the last twenty-five years of his life in a house in Franklin Court, which was torn down in 1810. Two famous old churches in Philadelphia are *Gloria Dei (Old Swedes' Church),* built in 1700, the oldest church building in the city, and *Christ Church,* where Washington worshiped. In our eager-

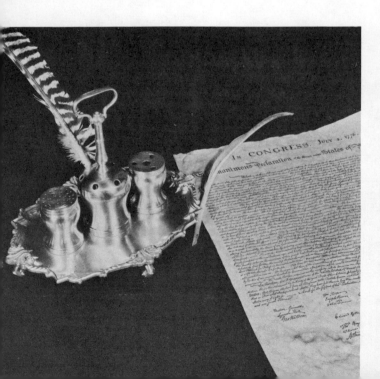

The silver inkstand used during the signing of the Declaration of Independence.

ness to see Independence Hall and the Liberty Bell, we are sometimes inclined to forget that these other buildings are among the oldest in the United States, still standing on their original sites and of paramount importance to Americans interested in our living past.

Philadelphia, "City of Brotherly Love," was settled in 1681 by Captain William Markham and a small band of colonists sent out by William Penn. Penn arrived the next year, laid out streets and named the city. By 1685, 7,200 people had settled in the city and in the pre-Revolutionary period it led the colonies in education, art, science, industry and commerce. The first Continental Congress met here at Carpenter's Hall in 1774; the Declaration of Independence was adopted here, as was the Constitution years later, and the city became the seat of the federal government. Here the first mint was established. The Continental Army, under George Washington, spent the bitter winter of 1777-78 at Valley Forge, twenty-one miles west of Philadelphia, now Valley Forge State Park.

***

How to reach: On Independence Square, Chestnut to Walnut Streets, Fifth to Sixth Streets.
Open: Daily, 9:00 A.M. to 5:00 P.M.
Admission: Free. Guide service for groups may be arranged.
Administration: National Park Service.

Carpenters' Hall (built in 1770), where the first Continental Congress met in 1774.

The Betsy Ross House

BIRTHPLACE OF THE FLAG

PHILADELPHIA, PA.

NOT ENOUGH credit for her art and skill has been given to Betsy Ross who made in this house the first "Stars and Stripes." She made that first official flag at the request of a committee consisting of George Washington, Robert Morris and George Ross (Betsy's husband's uncle). Mrs. Ross was the Schiaparelli of her day. She had learned her trade through long study and apprenticeship. Her skill as a seamstress and as an artist in needlework was well known and she was regarded as one of the best in her field.

***

How to reach: 239 Arch Street.
Open: Daily, 10:00 A.M. to 4:30 P.M.
Admission: Free.
Administration: City of Philadelphia.

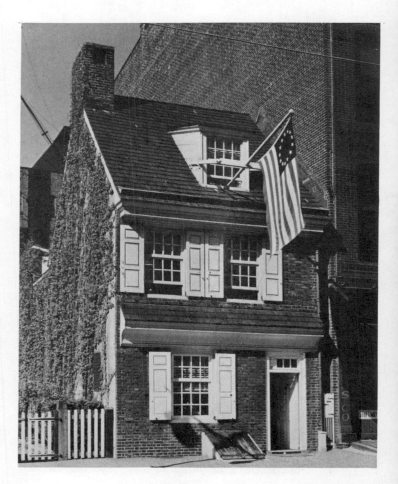

Christ Church

THE NATION'S CHURCH

PHILADELPHIA, PA.

FOUNDED in 1695, Christ Church has been called the "Nation's Church" because of its intimate association with men and events which brought forth this nation. It was the first Church of England parish in the colony. Two of its original members were pirates. By 1754 the church, with its 200-foot tower and steeple, was one of the largest buildings on the continent. Its bells, cast by the same company which cast the Liberty Bell, rang in unison with it on the announcement of the signing of the Declaration of Independence. The communion silver was presented to Christ Church by Queen Anne in 1709. The chandelier over the center aisle is probably the oldest in the country still in its original place.

Pews occupied by famous persons are marked: #58 is the Washington pew; #60, that of the Penn family; #70, the Franklin family; #52, the Robert Morris family; #12, Betsy Ross; #65, Francis Hopkinson; #55, Cadwalader family. In 1790, since Philadelphia was the capital, a pew, #58, was assigned to the Chief Executive. Washington used it during both his terms as President. After President Adams' term, the rector had the privilege of using it, with the reservation that it should always be available for the President of the United States. Lafayette occupied it during his second visit to this country and President Eisenhower occupied it, when he was General, at a victory service.

The cathedra, or bishop's chair, is probably the oldest one in America. The white-and-gold "wineglass" pulpit was made in 1770. The side windows were made in London. Christ Church's burial ground probably has a larger number of colonial and Revolutionary leaders interred in it than any other non-military cemetery in the country. The library, which was established through the efforts of the Reverend Thomas Bray in 1696, contains more than 1,000 volumes and rare folios, largely theological works. The older volumes, some printed in the 1500's, are preserved in the vaults of the Muniment Room.

How to reach: Second Street above Market Street.
Open: Daily, 9:00 A.M. to 5:00 P.M.
Admission: Free. Guide service available.
Administration: Part of Independence National Historical Park, Christ Church is administered by the Corporation of Christ Church in association with the National Park Service.

Elfreth's Alley

"EVER THE SAME AS YESTERDAY"

PHILADELPHIA, PA.

ELFRETH'S ALLEY is the only complete little street remaining in Philadelphia where the thirty-three houses have been lived in continuously for 200 years. William Penn planned wide-spaced streets for his fair country town, but his agents granted rights of way through the blocks. These developed into alleys and courts. Elfreth's Alley was originally surrounded by great forests of oak, maple, laurel and cedar, streams and ponds. Philadelphia then extended about four blocks back from the Delaware. On High Street, now Market, stood a duck pond. Town Hall, at Second and High Streets, was the center; Broad and Market Streets were woodland left to deer and wild turkeys. Jeremiah Elfreth came to Philadelphia about 1690 from England, having acquired land near the Blue Anchor Inn at Dock Creek. His nephew married the eldest daughter of a wealthy merchant who lived in the Alley. Gradually the street came to be known as Elfreth's Alley, then Cherry Street, then changed back to Elfreth's again.

It was originally paved with cobblestones; some may still be found in Bladen's Court and in the alley beside House No. 134. Seven houses bear fire-mark insignia placed by early insurance companies. Early directories show the kind of people who lived in the Alley: a cedar-cooper, a shipmaster, a wagoner, a pewterer, a Windsor chairmaker, a paperhanger, a whitesmith, a lodging-house keeper, a rabbi, a Friend, a French refugee. Elfreth's Alley, mentioned by Kipling in two of his stories, has a changeless look:

> The cats sleep on and the children play,
> The pigeons strut in the narrow way,
> Ever the same as yesterday,
> Ever the same—tomorrow.

The houses are mostly of the eighteenth century; one is probably late seventeenth. The Elfreth's Alley Association owns two houses in Bladen's Court and leases two houses. The rest are privately owned and many are being restored.

How to reach: Between Front and Second Streets, just north of Arch Street.
Open: Weekends when guide service is available.
Admission: Free.
Administration: Elfreth's Alley Assoc., Inc.

Fairmount Park
The Park of Mansions
PHILADELPHIA, PA.

FAIRMOUNT is one of the great American parks, probably the most famous in the country. Its 3,500 beautiful acres straddle the Schuylkill River for miles, starting not far from the center of the city.

At the entrance to the Park is the Philadelphia Museum of Art, one of the finest in the world. But Fairmount's really unique distinction is its wealth of beautiful mansions, its many historic houses, some of which are open to the public under the administration of the Museum.

Near 30th and Girard Avenue are:

LETITIA STREET HOUSE

This house, one of the earliest brick houses in the city, was built circa 1703-15 on land granted by William Penn to his daughter Letitia. It was removed from Letitia Street to its present site in 1883 and was restored in 1932. It is furnished in the Queen Anne style.

Open: Daily except holidays, 10:00 A.M. to 5:00 P.M.
Admission: 25¢; children, 10¢.

Letitia Street House.

First floor front.

CEDAR GROVE

Built in Frankfort about 1721, this unusual house descended in the Morris family to the late Lydia Thompson Morris, who removed it to its present site in 1927. The original furnishings, of William and Mary, Chippendale and Hepplewhite periods, were replaced in it.

————

Open: Daily except holidays, 10:00 A.M. to 5:00 P.M.
Admission: 25¢; children, 10¢.

Cedar Grove.

Parlor.

Dining room.

Bedroom, second floor rear.

MOUNT PLEASANT

Built by John Macpherson in 1762, this was regarded as one of the finest and richest houses in the colonies. John Adams called it "the handsomest seat in Pennsylvania." Benedict Arnold bought it for his bride, Peggy Shippen, but they never lived in it. It was restored in 1925. Furnishings are in the Chippendale style.

Open: Daily except holidays, 10:00 A.M. to 5:00 P.M.
Admission: 25¢; children, 10¢. Guide service available.

Besides the famous old houses in Fairmount Park administered by the Philadelphia Museum of Art are a number of others, under separate administration, in Philadelphia's "Colonial Chain."

Mount Pleasant.

Hall and stairway, first floor.

Parlor.

Dining room.

The "Colonial Chain"

SWEETBRIER

Notable for its delicate Adam ornament, Sweetbrier was built in 1797 and restored by the Junior League of Philadelphia in 1927. It is used as a clubhouse by the Modern Club, but is open to the public from 10:00 A.M. to 5:00 P.M. except Sundays. Admission fee is 25¢, in groups of 20 or more, 15¢. It is near Girard Avenue, between the Letitia Street House and Cedar Grove. It is administered by the Fairmount Park Commission.

WOODFORD

Notable for its fine carved chimney pieces, pedimented doorway and Palladian window, its lower story was built in 1734 and the rest of the present structure was completed in 1756. It is near Strawberry Mansion, at 33rd Street and Ridge Avenue, and is open to the public daily except Mondays from 1:00 P.M. to 5:00 P.M. Admission is free.

BELMONT

Notable for its early Georgian ornamental plaster work, this was a favorite resort of Washington and Lafayette. It dates back before 1742, but there were several later additions. Restored in 1926, it is now open as a restaurant with special hours for lunch and dinner. It is on the Belmont plateau near Belmont and Midvale Avenues.

Sweetbrier.

Woodford.

Belmont Mansion.

Famous Strawberry Mansion was built, or rather rebuilt, in 1798, by Judge William Lewis on the ruins of the house called Somerton which was burned by the British in 1777. It was restored in 1930. Judge Lewis, distinguished Quaker, drew up, together with Benjamin Franklin and Dr. Rush, the first law against slaves passed by any government in the world. It was adopted by the Pennsylvania Assembly in 1780.

The first strawberries successfully grown from Chilean roots were grown here—hence the name of the mansion. That was in Judge Joseph Hemphill's day. He had succeeded Judge Lewis as owner. It was here also that Hemphill Clinic became famous and here were bred the first coach dogs in the country—Dalmatians from England.

How to reach: Near 33rd Street and the Ridge.
Open: Daily, 11:00 A.M. to 5:00 P.M. except during August.
Admission: 25¢; children, 10¢. Special rate for groups.
Administration: Committee of 1926 under the Park Commission.

Strawberry Mansion.

Library.

Officers' hut.

Valley Forge

Symbol of the American Spirit

VALLEY FORGE, PA.

AFTER the defeats at Brandywine and Germantown and when the British were in complete control of Philadelphia, Washington moved what was left of his Continental Army to winter quarters at Valley Forge. The first night at the encampment, December 19, 1777, was bitterly cold. Washington and his officers huddled around open fires, as the soldiers did, and Washington refused more comfortable quarters until his men were better sheltered. That first night was only a sample of the terrible winter to come.

The cold became more intense, the provisions scarcer, and the situation seemed utterly desperate. Washington pleaded with the Continental Congress.

He wrote of his men: "Without arrogance or the smallest deviation from truth it may be said that no history now extant can furnish an instance of an army's suffering such uncommon hardships as ours has done, and bearing them with the same patience and fortitude. To see men without clothes to cover their nakedness, without blankets to lie on, without shoes,

Soldiers' huts. Muhlenberg's brigade.

Washington's headquarters.

for want of which their marches might be traced by the blood from their feet, and almost as often without provisions as with them . . . is proof of patience and obedience which in my opinion can scarce be paralleled."

It is to this "incomparable patience and fidelity of the soldiery" to Washington and to the ideal of liberty that Valley Forge is a monument.

The area took its name from an iron mill or forge built not later than 1751, along Valley Creek. The entire area, known as Mt. Joy Manor or Letitia Penn Manor, was a tract of 7,800 acres granted by William Penn in 1707 to his daughter Letitia. The present park and restoration comprise 2,033 acres. As far back as 1828, efforts were made to preserve the encampment ground as an historic site, but it was not until 1893 that the Commonwealth of Pennsylvania took over the property "for the purpose of perpetuating and preserving the site, to restore it as nearly as possible to its original condition as a military camp."

WASHINGTON'S HEADQUARTERS

On Christmas Eve, 1777, after nearly a week in a marquee tent, Washington moved into the house owned by Isaac Potts, a young Quaker minister who was a tenant of the widow Mrs. Deborah Hewes. A day before the army evacuated, General Washington gave Mrs. Hewes a check for 100 pounds, Pennsylvania currency, as rent for her house which he occupied for six months, the longest stay for the General at any headquarters. Here he planned future campaigns, addressed appeals to the Continental Congress and listened to the complaints of his suffering soldiers.

Martha Washington came to Valley Forge on February 21, 1778, and the next day celebrated her husband's birthday. Later in the month Lady Stirling and the wife of General Knox visited the camp. The women spent their time knitting socks for the soldiers. Mrs. Washington occupied the second floor front room, which is preserved today as her bedchamber. She left when the army was evacuated, June 19, 1778, to return to Mt. Vernon by coach.

In addition to the Headquarters, the old Fatland Fort Road over which the British first marched when they entered and left Valley Forge is maintained. The site of the bridge across the Schuylkill River, over which the Continental Army marched from Valley Forge to victories in New Jersey and the reoccupation of Philadelphia, is marked. Original houses occupied by four generals as quarters are preserved within the present park limits, as well as thirteen original farmhouses used by generals on privately owned land adjacent to the park. In the center of the park stands the original schoolhouse built in 1705, used as an emergency hospital during camp days and then continued in service as a school until about 1840.

Other features of the park are various cannon, huts of artillerymen and the stables. Besides statues, monuments and markers, there is the *Valley Forge Park Museum*, which houses about 500 relics, most of which were found on the encampment grounds.

How to reach: On Route 23.
Open: Daily, 9:00 A.M. to 5:00 P.M.
Admission: Free. Guide service available on request.
Administration: Valley Forge Park Commission (Commonwealth of Pennsylvania).

The Thompson-Neely House

"Where Washington Crossed the Delaware"

WASHINGTON CROSSING, PA.

AMERICA'S very own Christmas story is the famous Christmas Night (1776) crossing of the Delaware from the point in Bucks County now called Washington's Crossing. This area is preserved as a living memorial as Washington Crossing Park, a state park established by the Commonwealth of Pennsylvania. It contains monuments, old Ferry Inn, a memorial observation tower and other houses. But it was at the Thompson-Neely house where Washington held most of his conferences and where most of the planning was done. The final council of war just before the crossing was held in this house. Among those who were quartered here for many days before the crossing were Captain James Moore, who died there on Christmas Day, Captain William Washington, Lord Stirling and Lieutenant James Monroe, later fifth president of the United States.

It is an excellent example of early Pennsylvania architecture, built in three sections, the oldest in 1701, by John Pidcock, the first white settler in this part of the colony. Restoration was completed in 1950 with the original part of the house furnished with appropriate pre-Revolutionary furniture and the later section with post-Revolutionary pieces.

How to reach: On Route 32.
Open: April 15 to November 1, weekends, 1:00 P.M. to 5:00 P.M.
Admission: Free.
Administration: Washington Crossing Park Commission.

The John Morton Homestead

Commemorating the Swedish Contribution to Pennsylvania

NEAR PROSPECT PARK, PA.

IN 1638 a group of pioneer settlers from Sweden landed off present-day Wilmington, Del. They had come in two ships owned by the New Sweden Company, organized by Swedish and Dutch capitalists, and the commander of the expedition was the same Peter Minuit who had purchased Manhattan Island from the Indians. They established the colony of New Sweden, the first permanent white settlement in Pennsylvania, bought land and extended their holdings along the Delaware. Their property went as far north as the League Island Navy Yard. Eventually the Dutch, under Peter Stuyvesant, gained control of the little colony, but then lost it to the English in 1664. Nevertheless this Swedish prologue to Pennsylvania history is of considerable interest, even though it was William Penn and the Quakers who were to determine the main development of the region. To commemorate the Swedish contribution to Pennsylvania's development, the Commonwealth of Pennsylvania established as historic shrines the Governor Printz Park and the John Morton Homestead in Prospect Park,

Delaware County, which had been part of New Sweden. This log house, dating back to 1654, was the birthplace of John Morton, a famous descendant of the New Sweden colonists. He was influential and effective in colonial and Revolutionary affairs. He was a delegate from Pennsylvania to the various Congresses, 1774-77, and was a signer of the Declaration of Independence.

How to reach: Via U. S. Route 13.
Open: Daily, 10:00 A.M. to 5:00 P.M.
Admission: Free.
Administration: Pennsylvania Historical and Museum Comm.

[71]

Pennsbury

The Manor House of William Penn

NEAR MORRISVILLE, PA.

I HAVE visited William Penn's Bucks County home many times, and every time, but especially in the spring when the buds are beginning to open, I was impressed, as I was at Monticello and Mt. Vernon, with the peace and tranquility of the surroundings. The order of the minds of the great men of our early days was reflected in their mode of living. Certainly the calm spirit of the restored Pennsbury Manor reflects the character and dignity of this humane gentleman, who left a legacy of tolerance to his fellowmen. He counseled his family: "Of cities and towns of concourse beware; the world is apt to stick close to those who have lived and got wealth there; a country life and estate I like best for my children."

William Penn, Quaker gentleman, founder of Pennsylvania and one of the great men of colonial America, arranged in 1683 for the building of the original Manor House at Pennsbury, twenty-four miles northeast of Philadelphia. Restoration of the building was started in the 1930's and was completed in 1939. The task of furnishing it with authentic seventeenth-century furniture was completed in 1946. Besides the Manor House the estate consists of a bake-and-brew house, a smoke house, ice house and stone barn, formal, herb and vegetable gardens.

How to reach: U. S. Route 1 to Fallsington, Tullytown or to Morrisville. Markers show route.
Open: Daily, 10:00 A.M. to 4:30 P.M.
Admission: 50¢; children under 12 and service men in uniform, free. Guide service available.
Administration: Pennsylvania Historical and Museum Commission.

On the ground floor of the Manor House are the Great Hall, the Best Room, the Governor's Reception Room and the Withdrawing Room, with its closet, or secret place, for study, work and religious meditation. On the second floor are four bedrooms and a nursery, and there are several bedrooms and a large storeroom on the third floor.

(Top right) A view from the second floor of the bake-and-brew house, showing the smoke house, office, ice house and the entrance. (Left, center) A close-up view of the Manor House. Note unusual brick and picket fence. (Right, center) Reception room. (Below) Main dining room.

Hopewell Village

NEAR BIRDSBORO, PA.

RESCUED from its quiet mantle of abandonment, this early iron-making "plantation" flourished in the Schuylkill Valley woodlands for more than a century, then closed down completely in 1883 when hot-blast furnaces outmoded the manufacture of iron by the use of charcoal. It now provides an authentic picture of the humble beginnings of our great iron and steel industry.

The Hopewell furnace, erected about 1770, was the hub of the small settlement of furnacemen, moulders, colliers, wheelwrights, blacksmiths, wood-choppers and teamsters. The ironmaster occupied the "Big House" and provided small ones for his tenant-workers, some of whom were indentured servants. All were dependent on community gardens, orchards, shops, stable and "boarding-house" where meals were served.

A typical primitive eighteenth-century furnace, Hopewell turned out about 700 tons of "pig iron" a year. About two and one-half tons of iron ore, along with limestone, and 180 bushels of charcoal from cordwood were required to make a ton of iron. The ingots were later refined by forges into malleable iron for hardware, nails, etc. Pots, kettles, decorative stove plates all cast directly from the furnace are on display at the site, as well as tools and machinery. The contributions of iron and food made to the patriots' cause during the Revolution by the son of the founder of the Hopewell furnace resulted in his financial ruin. But demand for castings continued and the village prospered. During the last decade of operation its entire iron output went into railroad-car wheels.

The 848-acre area, which has been a unit in the National Park System since 1938, includes several restored buildings, water raceways and the waterwheel which powered the machinery.

How to reach: The Village is situated 5 miles southeast of Birdsboro, Pa., on U. S. Route 422.
Open: May to October, weekdays, 8:00 A.M. to 4:45 P.M.; Saturdays, Sundays and holidays, 9:00 A.M. to 6:00 P.M.
Admission: Free.
Administration: National Park Service.

The Daniel Boone Homestead

NEAR BAUMSTOWN, PA.

DANIEL BOONE, symbol of the pioneer spirit, was born here on November 2, 1734, in a log cabin (not the stone house shown here, which was erected around it about 1750). He spent his boyhood years in Pennsylvania, and the Pennsylvania Historical Commission has established his homestead as a memorial to Boone and as a shrine and inspiration for youth.

How to reach: One mile north from State Route 422, three miles north of Birdsboro.
Open: Daily, 10:00 A.M. to 4:30 P.M.
Admission: 25¢; children, free.
Administration: Pennsylvania Historical and Museum Commission.

[74]

The Drake Oil Well

THE WORLD'S FIRST SUCCESSFUL OIL WELL

TITUSVILLE, PA.

ON AUGUST 28, 1859, Colonel Edwin L. Drake brought in the first successful oil well ever drilled, thereby making history. He demonstrated in a practical way how petroleum could be produced in abundance, and his methods guided future drillers, stimulated and helped to create a major new industry. A faithful replica of the original well has been reproduced at Drake Well Memorial Park. At the site there is also a museum containing a large library devoted to the oil industry, documents, tools and the famous Mather collection of several thousand photographs of the early days of the oil industry.

How to reach: State Highways 8, 27, 89.
Open: Daily, 9:30 A.M. to 12:00 M., 1:00 P.M. to 5:00 P.M.
Admission: Free. Guide service available.
Administration: Pennsylvania Historical and Museum Commission.

ONE OF the fascinating phenomena of American life in the eighteenth and nineteenth centuries was the religious community. There were, I suppose, dozens of them, all over the East and the Middle West, that prospered for a time and then faded out. I could devote a whole book to pictures and descriptions of them, but in relation to their impact on our history, I think they have to be regarded, in the main, more as curiosities than anything else.

I have described a few in some detail elsewhere in this book, and I cannot resist including Ephrata. That was one of the earliest—unusual in many ways, yet also typical in some respects. It was started in the 1730's by one of the Pennsylvania Dutch, Conrad Beissel, and consisted of three semi-independent orders of the Seventh Day Baptists—a Brotherhood, a Sisterhood and a congregation of married couples, or "householders," all pledged to live an austere life of

Ephrata Cloister

AN UNUSUAL RELIGIOUS EXPERIMENT

EPHRATA, PA.

self-denial and humility. Ephrata grew and prospered, contributing much in the arts of music, manuscript illumination and printing, but the Cloister began to decline after the Revolutionary War during which many of its buildings had been offered as hospitals for the wounded after the Battle of Brandywine. In 1941 the Commonwealth of Pennsylvania acquired the property, set about restoring it and established it as a historic shrine. Seen below, left to right, are the parsonage, almonry and Saron, or Sisterhouse.

How to reach: Via U. S. Routes 222 and 322.
Open: Daily, 10:00 A.M. to 4:30 P.M.
Admission: Free.
Administration: Pennsylvania Historical and Museum Commission.

Winterthur
Home of 100 Period Rooms
WINTERTHUR, DEL.

THE MOST "historic" home I have ever encountered is that of Henry Francis du Pont. Here and there throughout the country, as in Greenfield and Shelburne, there are villages of assembled houses brought together as a kind of living museum. At Winterthur we have an assemblage of *parts of houses,* and in the case of a number of rooms, are the best examples of their particular type. One instance of this: In the Pennsylvania section of this book I wanted to show something of the Pennsylvania Dutch, but I never saw anything which better illustrated the Pennsylvania Dutch quality than the Fractur Room of Winterthur, shown here.

Winterthur was the family home of Henry Francis du Pont. It was built in 1839 by James Antoine Bidermann, who named it for his ancestral home in Winterthur, Switzerland. Bidermann had married the great-aunt of Henry Francis du Pont in 1814, and the house has remained in the family since it was built. In 1927 Mr. du Pont began to install in his home, in their original form, parts of houses collected from New Hampshire to North Carolina, with the purpose of showing how Americans really lived, as well as America's rich tradition of craftsmanship in architecture and household arts. In 1951 this home was opened to the public as the Henry Francis du Pont Winterthur Museum.

In about 100 period rooms, the Museum covers the domestic scene from 1640 to 1840. In the words of Joseph Downs, its former curator: "In rooms as they originally stood, here are 200 years of domestic architecture, furniture, ceramics, metalwork, textiles, paintings and prints chosen with the most meticulous regard for their quality and fitness of location. . . . Winterthur represents the largest and richest assemblage of American decorative arts, especially furniture, ever brought together."

———

How to reach: 6 miles northwest of Wilmington on Route 52.

Open: Daily except Sundays and Mondays. By appointment only. For six weeks in the spring the most important rooms and the azalea gardens are open to the public without advance reservation. For details of tours, write the Museum.

Admission: Half-day, $1.25; full day, $2.50. Special charges during spring tours. Luncheon available on full day tour. Guides accompany each group of four visitors.

Administration: The Henry Francis du Pont Winterthur Museum.

The Fractur Room is named for the examples of illuminated writing, or "fractur," which line its walls. The woodwork, from a farmhouse built in 1783 near Kutztown, Pa., carries the original mottled blue paint.

The Hart Room, the earliest in the Museum, is from a house built by Thomas Hart in Ipswich, Mass., about 1640. The late seventeenth-century gate-leg table is from Pennsylvania and the spice chest under the window is marked TH 1679, for Thomas Hart, son of the builder.

The Flock Room. The woodwork is from Morattico Hall, Richmond, Va., 1714 to 1725. The great joined table, in the Jacobean tradition, was made in New England 1670-1690.

The Chestertown Room is from the Brown House in Chestertown, Md., built about 1762. The tables, case pieces and clock are attributed to the Townsend-Goddard family of Newport. Above the mantel is a portrait on wood of the Washington family, done in 1789 by Edward Savage.

Phyfe Room. The woodwork is from the Moses Rogers House, New York. The furniture bill, signed by Duncan Phyfe, is dated 1807. The eighteenth-century Khotan weave carpet was made in Chinese Turkestan and the early nineteenth-century curtains are French.

The Du Pont Dining Room takes its name from the set of Sheraton-style chairs, du Pont family heirlooms. The three-part Hepplewhite table from Baltimore, remarkable for its size, has inlaid eagles in ovals above its square tapered legs. The eight-leg New York Hepplewhite sideboard dates from 1795-1800. On it is a set of silver tankards made by Paul Revere.

Holy Trinity (Old Swedes') Church

ONE OF AMERICA'S OLDEST STILL IN USE

WILMINGTON, DEL.

IN 1638, the year the Swedes established their first colony on American soil, Old Swedes' Church was founded. The present church was erected in 1698 and that original building is still in use for regular religious services. Originally Swedish Lutheran, it was transferred to the Protestant Episcopal Church in 1791, and the present services are according to the liturgy of the Episcopal Church.

The bricks of its floor were made in William Penn's Philadelphia brickyard in 1698. The pulpit is the original one, the oldest in the United States, except for importations. The balcony installed in 1773 remains intact. A small museum room houses a number of historical items.

How to reach: 802 East 7th Street, corner of Church Street, which is U. S. Route 13.
Open: Daily, 11:00 A.M. to 4:00 P.M. Sunday service, 11:00 A.M.
Admission: Free.
Administration: Holy Trinity Old Swedes' Church Foundation, Inc.

Great Falls Tavern

ON THE CHESAPEAKE
AND OHIO CANAL

GREAT FALLS, MD.

AS EARLY as 1754 George Washington fostered a system of river and canal navigation along the Potomac Valley to facilitate communication between east and west. Largely through Washington's efforts, the Potomac Company was organized in 1785. Active in its work, he served as its first president, resigning when he became President of the United States. The Potomac canals were substantially completed in 1802 when small raftlike boats brought furs, lumber, flour and farm produce to Georgetown. This system of canals, now called the Chesapeake and Ohio Canal, is one of the least altered of old American canals.

The most important element of the canal system was the skirting canal at the impassable Great Falls of the Potomac. Here, on the Virginia banks of the river, the company had built a 1,200-yard-long, 25-foot-wide and 6-foot-deep canal to get around an elevation of 76 feet. The fine tavern, built 1828-31, at this crucial junction was naturally very popular, and today the Great Falls area is most popular with visitors, many of whom are interested in the Chesapeake and Ohio Canal Museum in the main room of the tavern. But there is much to see all along the canal, and a trip along the towpath, especially in the spring, is bound to be charming and rewarding.

Great Falls Tavern.

How to reach: The Canal extends from Washington, D. C., to Cumberland, Md. Great Falls may be reached by Routes 28 and 112.
Open: Daily, 10:00 A.M. to 5:00 P.M.
Admission: Free.
Administration: National Park Service.

Lock House 13, a few miles from Great Falls, near MacArthur Boulevard and Persimmon Tree Road.

Hager's Fancy
THE HOUSE ON SPRINGS
HAGERSTOWN, MD.

BUILT circa 1740 by Jonathan Hager, founder of Hagerstown, this house was built over two free-flowing springs and has two spring rooms. It has remained remarkably intact and unaltered for more than two centuries. Because of a remarkable "find" of artifacts and fragments discovered in the underporch area which was enclosed by a stone foundation, it was possible to restore the house with remarkable accuracy.

Where the spring flows out from the foundation.

The northeast spring room.

How to reach: Immediately west of Route 11 and south of Route 40 on Key Street.
Open: By appointment with Mrs. Frank Mish, Jr., Falling Waters, West Va.
Admission: Free.
Administration: Washington County Historical Society.

Hammond-Harwood House
ANNAPOLIS, MD.

THIS is one of the few colonial houses which can be definitely attributed to a known architect—in this case, William Buckland, who built it in 1774 for Matthias Hammond. An excellent example of Georgian architecture, it is notable for its unconventional interior plan: no two rooms are of identical size, and there is no repetition of design in cornices and wainscoting.

How to reach: Maryland Avenue and King George Street.
Open: Summer, weekdays, 10:00 A.M. to 5:00 P.M.; Sundays, 2:00 P.M. to 5:00 P.M. Winter, weekdays, 10:00 A.M. to 4:00 P.M.; Sundays, 2:00 P.M. to 4:00 P.M.
Admission: 50¢.
Administration: Hammond-Harwood House Association.

The dining room.

The Poe House
Short Story Shrine
BALTIMORE, MD.

EDGAR ALLAN POE lived and worked here 1832-35 during the turning-point years of his writing career. When he came from West Point to live with his aunt in this house, he had already published three volumes of verse which brought him no money and little fame. But here he turned to prose fiction and made himself master of the type of short story that may be regarded as his own invention.

How to reach: 203 N. Amity Street.
Open: Wednesdays and Saturdays, 2:00 P.M. to 5:00 P.M., and by appointment.
Admission: 25¢; children, 10¢.
Administration: The Edgar Allan Poe Society of Baltimore, Inc., in association with the City of Baltimore.

Peale Museum
A "First" in Museums
BALTIMORE, MD.

THIS is the first building ever erected expressly as a museum in America and possibly in the world. Designed by Robert Cary Long, Sr., it was opened August, 1814, as "Peale's Baltimore Museum and Gallery of Fine Arts" by Rembrandt Peale, the famous painter-son of the painter Charles Willson Peale. The elder Peale had started, in Philadelphia in 1786, the first significant museum in this country.

The Peale Museum is now the Municipal Museum of the City of Baltimore; it displays a number of Rembrandt Peale portraits and has many other exhibits chiefly connected with Baltimore history.

How to reach: 225 N. Holliday Street.
Open: Memorial Day through Labor Day, except Sundays, 10:30 A.M. to 4:30 P.M. Labor Day to Memorial Day, Tuesday through Saturday, 10:30 A.M. to 4:30 P.M.; Sundays, 1:30 P.M. to 5:30 P.M.
Admission: Free.
Administration: Board of Trustees, Municipal Museum of the City of Baltimore.

Hampton

One of the Great Georgian Houses of America

TOWSON,
BALTIMORE COUNTY, MD.

THIS famous mansion, an outstanding showplace of Maryland and a National Historic Site, was built 1783-90 and was restored in 1948. It was the home of the Ridgely family for over 150 years.

It is one of the largest of the early houses of Maryland, designed for large-scale entertaining, as indicated by the dimensions of the drawing room and the great hall of which Henry Thompson noted in his diary that fifty-one persons sat down to dinner and "everyone had plenty of room."

How to reach: Just off Dulaney Valley Road.
Open: Weekdays except Mondays, 11:30 A.M. to 5:00 P.M.; Sundays, 1:00 P.M. to 5:00 P.M.
Admission: 50¢. Guide service is available.
Administration: National Park Service under custodial agreement with the Society for the Preservation of Maryland Antiquities.

The drawing room.

Pierce Mill
Industrial Survivor of the Early Nineteenth Century
ROCK CREEK PARK, WASHINGTON, D. C.

IT WAS through Charles Schwab's interest in the Pierce Mill that it was finally taken over and restored by the government. Schwab used to say that a better sampling of public opinion could be had from people who visited millsites than from all the expensive newspaper polls put together. Calvin Coolidge had affection for it for another reason. He would ride out to Pierce Mill on a spring morning and sit watching the rushing water tumbling over the dam. He told me once that it reminded him of Vermont and his youth.

Rock Creek used to be quite a milling center. More than 125 years ago there were at least eight mills operating along the beautiful stream that gives Washington's famous park its name, but now only one of them, the Pierce Mill, built about 1820, still operates, not on a commercial basis but rather as an educational and historic exhibit. You can see the process by which its waterwheels produce cornmeal and flour for government cafeterias and you may also purchase the water-ground cornmeal or flour at the mill.

How to reach: Tilden Street, near intersection of Park Road and Beach Drive in Rock Creek Park.

Open: Daily except Mondays, 9:00 A.M. to 5:00 P.M.; Sundays, 1:00 P.M. to 5:00 P.M.

Admission: Free. Miller explains operation of mill.

Administration: National Capital Parks System, operated by Government Services, Inc.

Joaquin Miller Cabin
ROCK CREEK PARK, WASHINGTON, D. C.

IF, ON A visit to Rock Creek Park, you wondered about that little cabin on Beach Drive north of Military Road, now you know the answer. It is the little cabin which Joaquin Miller, "Poet of the Sierras," constructed as a sort of hideaway, or workroom, in the woods. It was built on Meridian Hill of small logs from trees that grew nearby. Here he wrote a number of the poems that made him famous. In 1912 the cabin was moved to Rock Creek Park. At the present time the cabin, under National Park Service administration, is not open to the public.

The White House, south side.

The White House
The Executive Mansion
WASHINGTON, D. C.

I HAVE been going to the White House for nearly fifty years. The first occasion was an Easter egg hunt in the spring of 1906. My sister and I scampered over the lawn with thousands of other children, and as a result I came down with the mumps! So for many years I did not look forward to returning, but I did return to participate in the inaugural of William Howard Taft. I had been chosen with twelve other military school youngsters to ride in the parade. I remember how the outgoing president, Theodore Roosevelt, met us in the White House basement and took us through the many first-floor rooms, telling us about various paintings and the prominent guests who had sat in various chairs and what they had said. "Teddy" called me the "Junior Rough Rider" and we became fast friends. He gave me a greater appreciation of my native land than any other president except F.D.R.

Woodrow Wilson, who often asked me to serve as a sort of sounding-board, always used to call me "Master Neil" when I went to the White House with Colonel E. M. House from Texas. (The Houses often asked my mother, who loved to give parties, to entertain various notables from Europe with whom President Wilson was trying to strike a bargain. I can remember sitting in the Lincoln study, the President at the desk and Colonel House and I occupying large brown leather armchairs.) But after mid-April in 1917 both Theodore Roosevelt and Woodrow Wilson called me "Private Vanderbilt." Wilson asked me to write him from camp and from overseas and report what I saw, letting him know of any inequalities at once. I remember how proud I was that hot and humid mid-August day he sent for me—a private in the back-ranks. There were Marines at the White House gates and Secret Service men all over the grounds.

Warren Harding, Calvin Coolidge and Herbert Hoover saw me in the Lincoln study and in the Appointment Office. During Harding's and Coolidge's administrations I was at the White House mostly as a newsman covering various events. I remember one time calling on President Coolidge when he was in bed with a cold. I had been hopping back and forth across the ocean and had heard about the troubles of the captain of the S. S. *Leviathan*, which had been converted into the world's largest passenger liner: "If we come to the narrows of the Solent (at the Isle of Wight below Southampton) ahead of any of the great British liners whose captains have naval ratings of full captains, we are forced to heave to and wait until the British vessel passes in or out on the tide. If it's low we must cruise about for twelve hours or so, thus losing valuable time and cargo." When I reported the American captain's dilemma to Coolidge, he replied, "What can I do about it?" "Create the rank of Commodore, Mr. President," I said. "Lincoln did it for Commodore Vanderbilt. It gave him precedence over the merchantmen of his day." Mr. Coolidge whistled and said, "I'll do just that," and he did.

My fondest memories of the White House, however, go back to F.D.R. Though offered diplomatic and political positions, I chose to remain a private citizen, with access to the front or back door whenever I thought I had something to say that he ought to know. In the early years I was constantly bringing writers and correspondents to tea, which was served every afternoon between five and six-thirty in the upstairs hall. Sometimes this de-fanged the most critical ones.

The White House, for many years called the President's House or the President's Palace, was the first public building to be constructed in the new capital laid out by L'Enfant. Washington selected the site and approved James Hoban's plans, but John Adams was the first chief executive to occupy the classical-style mansion in 1800. Some of the interior was still unfinished and Mrs. Adams used the East Room to dry the family wash. Jefferson held open house every morning for all arrivals and the Madisons entertained

South portico, showing the "Truman Balcony," and (below) a view of the north side of The White House.

Entrance hall and lobby.

often and lavishly. The White House was burned by British forces in 1814, but the damaged sandstone walls were rebuilt in time for President Monroe's occupancy in 1817. Hoban supervised its reconstruction and the addition of the north and south porticoes, in 1824 and 1829.

From 1830 to 1902 no important structural changes were made, although there were many improvements —running water in 1834, gas lighting in 1848, hot water heating in 1853, central heating during Grant's administration, an elevator in 1882 and electric wiring in the 1890's. But during the administration of Theodore Roosevelt, the White House was strengthened and the main floor redone, enlarging the State Dining Room by the removal of the main stairway. During Wilson's administration guest rooms were made in the attic and in 1927 the roof and third story were remodeled.

In recent years the White House has acquired a swimming pool, an electric kitchen, a maintenance and storage basement, an air raid shelter off the new East Wing, a motion picture theater, a solarium and a gymnasium. In 1946 a balcony behind the columns

of the south portico provided a private porch for the President's family.

From 1948 to 1952 a major renovation program of the entire Executive Mansion was undertaken after ceilings began to sag perilously. Both the north and south porticos were given new steps and floors, the old walls buoyed with concrete foundations, and old wooden beams and interior brick walls supported by a steel framework. Every effort was made to retain or restore the original atmosphere and also to provide a more liveable home for the President and his family. The White House now has 132 rooms, twenty baths and five elevators.

Designed to preserve an air of restrained elegance rather than formal display, it retains the simplicity of its original appearance for the many visitors who come to admire the landscaped grounds and handsome rooms rich in historic associations. Furnishings of historic interest have been retained and much of the old furniture has been refinished and recovered to harmonize with the color scheme of various rooms. In general the decor is predominantly eighteenth-century Georgian.

The entrance lobby and the main corridor are divided by six classic columns of Vermont marble. On the marble-faced opening of the stairway are seals of the thirteen original states. The large white and gold East Room, now used for state receptions and balls, has been the scene of several Presidential family weddings and funeral services (for William Henry Harrison, Zachary Taylor, Abraham Lincoln, Warren G. Harding and Franklin D. Roosevelt). On the east wall hangs the Gilbert Stuart portrait of Washington which Dolly Madison ordered moved just before the British burned the White House in 1814. The large crystal chandeliers and enameled wood paneling date from 1902.

The second largest room, the State Dining Room, can comfortably seat 100 guests at a long oval table with Chippendale chairs. The oak paneling, installed in 1902, has been painted pale green to set off the gold damask draperies and to provide a background for the Healy portrait of Lincoln. The "over mantel" was a gift from the late King George VI of England. The private dining room has a vaulted ceiling, enameled wainscoting and a portrait of President Tyler.

The Green Room, used for informal receptions, has a deep green Savonnerie rug with the official seal in its center. The Italian marble mantel, originally in the State Dining Room, was imported at the time the White House was rebuilt after the War of 1812. During Monroe's administrations the Hannibal clock and vases on the mantel were purchased. There are portraits of Thomas Jefferson, John Quincy Adams, Martin Van Buren and James K. Polk.

The Red Room, where the First Lady receives guests, is identical in size and shape with the Green Room and has a duplicate marble mantel. On it are two eighteenth-century candelabra and a musical clock presented by the President of France. Rutherford B. Hayes took his oath of office as President here in 1877. On the walls are portraits of McKinley, Cleveland, Coolidge and Wilson.

The oval Blue Room, in which the President receives guests at state dinners and receptions, has been considered the most beautiful room in the White House. Here Grover Cleveland and Frances Folsom were married in 1886. On the gold and white mantelpiece are a French clock and gilt candlesticks purchased by President Monroe. Walls, draperies and upholstery are of a bright blue silk damask with a gold motif and the furniture and woodwork are white.

The second and third floors are reserved for the family and guests of the President. The austere Lincoln bedroom, in which his long specially made bed

The East Room.

stands, was restored in the Victorian period with a green and yellow color scheme.

On the ground floor the library, china room and cloak rooms are paneled in pine from the old beams of the White House, some of which show old nail holes. The china collection is one of the most interesting and valuable in the United States. Many presidents ordered complete dinner services. Presidents Wilson, Roosevelt and Truman preferred Lenox china; Washington and Jefferson, Lowestoft; Madison, Jackson, Monroe and others favored French porcelains; others, Wedgwood and Minton. Across the hall is the original kitchen in which the old sandstone fire-

places have been restored. It is now used for conferences and television and radio broadcasting.

Of special interest among the trees on the grounds are the magnolias planted by Andrew Jackson. In front of the north portico English boxwood has been planted, as old as the venerable White House.

How to reach: 1600 Pennsylvania Avenue.
Open: Tuesday through Saturday, 10:00 A.M. to 12:00 M. (except December 25-29 and other holidays).
Admission: Free.
Administration: National Park Service.

The Blue Room.

Colonial Williamsburg

"That the Future May Learn from the Past"

WILLIAMSBURG, VA.

"TO RE-CREATE accurately the environment of the men and women of eighteenth-century Williamsburg and to bring about such an understanding of their lives and times that present and future generations may more vividly appreciate the contribution of these early Americans to the ideals and culture of our country" is the purpose of the restoration of Colonial Williamsburg. And the millions of visitors who have come to see Williamsburg since its opening in 1932 are a living testament to the interest and validity of that purpose.

People come from all over the world—plain people, kings and queens, teen-agers, the President of the United States, the Crown Prince of Japan—and take away a new sense of the living past of our country. I have been many times to Williamsburg and stayed there once in my house-trailer for four days because I was so deeply impressed by the beauty and simplicity of the place. The buildings made me wonder about some of the original inhabitants—Thomas Jefferson, George Washington, George Mason, Patrick Henry, George Wythe, Peyton Reynolds, among others. And it seemed logical that greatness should grow in this place.

As I stood in the hall of the House of Burgesses I realized that while the British Governor of the Colonies was directing affairs for the Crown, our Revolu-

The Governor's Palace, rear gates, and (below) Duke of Gloucester Street, described by Franklin D. Roosevelt as "the most historic avenue in all America." Among structures visible are (at far left) Chowning's Tavern, The Brick House.

The hall of the House of Burgesses.

The Court House of 1770. When originally built, the portico was cantilevered to await the arrival of columns. But in the 1770's conditions were difficult and unsettled and the columns were never delivered.

tion was being planned in the houses around the capitol.

As I wandered around the narrow streets and passed the lovely old homes, it occurred to me that perhaps John D. Rockefeller, Jr., began giving money for this famous reconstruction because he felt as I did, that here was a touchstone of the essential American idea.

It is my impression, too, that this is one of the few places, with the possible exception of Natchez, Miss., where the inhabitants wear the original costumes of their forebears all year round. Though it is certainly colorful, the costumes don't look very comfortable. Williamsburg is a particularly wonderful sight at night when the windows of the public buildings and the houses are lit by candles made in the village. And the Great Hall in the Williamsburg Inn before dinner when champagne is served in large goblets at small candle-lit tables is a sight of grace and charm.

The site of Williamsburg was first occupied in 1633 by Middle Plantation, a stockaded settlement erected against Indian attack by hard-pressed colonists from nearby Jamestown. In 1698, when the Statehouse at Jamestown was leveled by fire, the legislators decided to move their capital to Middle Plantation, which they renamed Williamsburg in honor of the reigning English king, William III.

From 1699 until the war year of 1780, when the capital was moved to Richmond, Williamsburg was the political, social and cultural center of the entire colony. Until 1776 Williamsburg served not only as the seat of government for Britain's largest colony in America, but also as the political headquarters for Virginia patriots who were to have an important part in overthrowing the rule of the Crown. Here George Washington, Patrick Henry, George Wythe, Thomas Jefferson, George Mason and other patriots helped shape the foundations of our government. It was the scene of Patrick Henry's "Caesar-Brutus" speech and his defiant Resolutions protesting the Stamp Act; George Mason's Virginia Declaration of Rights; the May 15, 1776, Resolution for Independence, which led directly to the historic July 4th Declaration; the pioneering Virginia Constitution, which served as a model for most other states; and the introduction of Jefferson's famous Statute for Religious Freedom.

After 1780 Williamsburg stepped backstage in history, to resume its major role only when restoration work was begun in 1927. All funds for this project (some thirty-seven million dollars to date) have been the gift of John D. Rockefeller, Jr. The first exhibition building, the Raleigh Tavern, was opened to the public in 1932. By 1954, 82 original eighteenth-century buildings had been restored, more than 380 buildings had been reconstructed on their original foundations and 616 modern buildings had been removed from the historic area. In addition, 75 acres of gardens and greens had been restored or reconstructed.

The exhibition buildings of Colonial Williamsburg contain a distinguished collection of seventeenth- and eighteenth-century antiques, the furnishings of an English colonial capital. On view are many outstanding and rare examples of American and English furniture, as well as paintings, prints and maps. Noteworthy is the collection of English ceramics that contains some of the only known examples on public view in America. There are also an excellent variety of English silver and pewter, lighting fixtures, an excellent collection of textiles, including a wide range of costumes of the eighteenth century and rugs of the seventeenth and eighteenth centuries.

The eight main exhibition buildings of Colonial Williamsburg are:

The *Capitol,* originally completed in 1705 and twice burned, has been rebuilt on the foundations of the original structure and furnished in accordance with ancient records of the Virginia colony. It was one of the principal buildings of colonial America.

The *Raleigh Tavern,* near the Capitol, erected before 1742, was a center of social and political life before the Revolution. In the Apollo Room, it is believed, students of the College of William and Mary founded the Phi Beta Kappa Society in 1776.

The upper middle room of the Governor's Palace.

The supper room of the Governor's Palace.

The Capitol. From its cupola the British "Great Union" flag, no longer used, flies daily as it did two centuries ago.

The *Ludwell-Paradise House,* built about 1717 by Col. Philip Ludwell II, has been restored and now contains the Abby Aldrich Rockefeller collection of American folk art.

The *Brush-Everard House,* built 1717, is an example of an eighteenth-century home of a middle-income family. Typical period furnishings include numerous rare antiques and a complete library.

The *Governor's Palace,* used by governors from about 1720 to 1780, was destroyed by fire in 1781 when it was being used as a hospital for men wounded at Yorktown. It has been reconstructed on the original foundations and refurnished. The kitchen has a collection of old utensils and equipment.

The *Wythe House,* erected toward the close of the eighteenth century, was owned by George Wythe, classical scholar, teacher of Thomas Jefferson, first professor of law in an American college and a signer of the Declaration of Independence.

The *Public Gaol,* built about 1701, has been restored, including stocks and pillories for debtors, criminals and offenders.

Raleigh Tavern kitchen.

Raleigh Tavern dining room.

Main stairway, George Wythe House.

George Wythe House. The front is marked by an unusual difference in the size of the first- and second-story windows.

[95]

*Formal garden of the Governor's Palace. The simple topiary
pieces, hedges, pleached arbor, bulb and perennial plantings
were favorite garden ornaments of the period.*

The *Magazine* and *Guardhouse,* built 1716, was a storehouse of arms and ammunition for the colony during the eighteenth century. It has a display of military supplies.

In addition, Colonial Williamsburg operates eleven craft shops, where costumed craftsmen demonstrate eighteenth-century crafts. They are: the Ayscough Shop (cabinetmaker), the Raleigh Tavern Bakery, the Margaret Hunter Shop (milliner), the Deane Shop and Forge, the wigmaker, the bootmaker, the Governor's Palace scullery, the Wythe House weaving and spinning shop, the Pasteur-Galk Apothecary Shop, the Golden Ball (silversmith) and the printing office.

How to reach: U. S. Route 60, 50 miles east of Richmond. May be reached by boat, to Old Point Comfort, Va., overnight service from Washington, D. C., and Baltimore via the Old Bay Line. Frequent ferries from Kiptopeke. Both accommodate cars. Bus connections available.

Open: Daily. From April to September, 9:00 A.M. to 5:00 P.M.; October to March, 10:00 A.M. to 5:00 P.M.

Admission: Block ticket to eight buildings, $3.00; students and military personnel, $1.50. Block ticket to five buildings, $2.50; students and military personnel, $1.00. Children under 12, free if accompanied by adult. Tickets for individual buildings also available. Craft shops are open without charge.

Administration: Colonial Williamsburg, Inc.

Child's room in the Brush-Everard House.

Colonial printing office. An accurately reconstructed press of pre-Revolutionary days, requiring eleven different hand operations for each impression, is used for demonstrations and for souvenir printings.

Arlington House

Lee Mansion National Memorial

ARLINGTON, VA.

ARLINGTON HOUSE was originally the home of George Washington Parke Custis, foster son of George Washington. He began building it in 1802, the year his grandmother, Martha Washington, died. He named it Arlington in honor of the ancestral homestead of the Custis family on the eastern shore of Virginia. The house was to receive furniture and pictures, plate and china from Mount Vernon and the personal effects of George Washington. Mr. Custis is believed to have designed and supervised the original building; its remodeling was directed by the architect, George Hadfield, in 1820.

On June 30, 1831, Mary Ann Randolph Custis, only child of the Arlington Custis family, became the wife of Robert E. Lee, a young lieutenant in the U. S. Army. Most of Mrs. Lee's time was spent at her girlhood home, a good deal of it waiting for her husband to return from a tour of duty. Six of the seven Lee children were born here. When George Washington Parke Custis died in 1857, he left Arlington to his daughter. Lee was named executor, and Arlington was so badly run down that he obtained a long leave from the army and settled down to the life of a farmer. Three years later, however, he rejoined his regiment. On the news of the secession of Virginia, April 20, 1861, Lee resigned his commission in the U. S. Army and at the request of the Governor of Virginia left for Richmond. Mrs. Lee stayed at Arlington to dismantle the house and send the family possessions to a place of safety. But on May 24 the seizure of lands between Washington and Alexandria by Federal troops forced her to abandon what remained. Arlington, on the line of fortifications guarding Washington, became an armed camp, and after the first Battle of Bull Run, in July, 1861, was used as a field hospital.

How to reach: From Washington, D. C., via Constitution Avenue and 23rd Street across Arlington Memorial Bridge.
Open: October through March, daily, 9:30 A.M. to 4:30 P.M.; April through September, 9:30 A.M. to 6:00 P.M.
Admission: 25¢; children under 18, free. Guide service is available.
Administration: National Capital Parks, National Park Service.

View from parlor into family dining room. Robert E. Lee and Mary Custis were married under the center arch.

Mount Vernon

A Great American Shrine

MOUNT VERNON, VA.

MOUNT VERNON is an estate, not a town or a village. When George Washington owned it, it was made up of five farms as well as his home—the mansion, with lodges, greenhouses, servants' quarters, gardens, stables, smokehouse, wash- and coach-houses. To all these have been added a museum (1928) and Washington's tomb.

I visited Mount Vernon first when I was about twelve years old, on horseback, so I saw it from the same perspective as did its owner, the Father of Our Country. I still remember how moved I was at being where Washington had lived and walked and worked and slept. Many, many times later I visited it again, and I remember one time in particular with General John J. Pershing just after World War I when there was considerable talk about nominating him for the presidency. He told me then, as he did later at Walter Reed Hospital, that "George Washington was the only General who ever made good as President."

In 1726 Augustine Washington, father of George, bought the Hunting Creek Plantation and in 1735, when George was three years old, moved his family into it. In 1740 Augustine deeded it to George's half-brother, Lawrence. He married in 1743 and settled on the estate, renaming it in honor of Admiral Vernon under whom he had served in the Caribbean. In 1752 Lawrence died and two years later George Washington came into possession. From 1752 until 1759 Washington's military service as aide to General Braddock and commander of the Virginia militia allowed only infrequent visits. In 1759 he retired to private life and that year married Martha Dandridge Custis. But his retirement ended in 1775 when he was appointed Commander-in-Chief of the Continental Army. In the eight years of his presidency, he visited Mount Vernon fifteen times. On his retirement in March, 1797, he returned home and in the two and a half years which remained to him enjoyed a measure of the tranquility he had always wanted. He died December 14, 1799; Mrs. Washington died in May, 1802.

How to reach: On State Route 235.
Open: Daily, from 9:00 A.M.
Admission: Free.
Administration: The Mount Vernon Ladies Association of the Union.

George Washington's desk and chair.

WOODLAWN PLANTATION

Another part of the original Mount Vernon estate is Woodlawn Plantation, a few miles from the national shrine itself. The land—2,000 acres—was Washington's wedding gift to his adopted daughter, Nelly Custis, when she married his nephew Lawrence Lewis in 1799. They commissioned Dr. William Thornton, architect of the first capitol in Washington, to design the Woodlawn mansion, and the house was completed in 1805. It is now restored as an early nineteenth-century house, under the administration of the National Trust for Historic Preservation in the United States. The National Trust was established by Act of Congress in 1949 and Woodlawn was the first property accepted by it.

Open: March to October, daily 10:00 A.M. to 5:00 P.M.; November to February, daily except Mondays, 10:00 A.M. to 4:30 P.M. *Admission:* 50¢; children and service personnel in uniform, free. Groups of 20 or more, 25¢. Guide service is available.

Pohick Church (1772) at nearby Lorton, the parish church of Mount Vernon. George Washington was a vestryman from 1762-1784.

George Washington's Birthplace

A National Monument

WESTMORELAND COUNTY, VA.

GEORGE WASHINGTON was born in the Westmoreland County home of his parents at Popes Creek, sometimes called Wakefield. The national monument on the estate, a typical Virginia plantation house of the eighteenth century, is not a restoration. Extensive research uncovered insufficient reliable information to warrant an attempt at restoration, though the foundation on which the house was erected is believed to be the original. There were some artifacts including early bottle seals found in excavations at Wakefield but little to give a clue to the architecture of the house. The tilt-top table in the dining room is the only surviving piece known to have been in the original birthplace.

The progenitor of the Washington family, John Washington, arrived in Virginia in 1656. The *Seahorse of London,* on which he was second officer, ran aground in the Potomac River near the mouth of Mattox Creek. John remained in Virginia and soon married Ann Pope, daughter of Colonel Nathaniel Pope, a wealthy landowner living near Mattox Creek. It was their son, Augustine, who bought the land and built the home on Popes Creek which was first occupied some time in the years 1725-6. Augustine's first wife died in 1729 and he married his second wife, Mary Ball, in 1730. Their first son, George, was born at Popes Creek on February 11, 1732, according to the old-style calendar, or on February 22, 1732, according to the new-style calendar. George spent the first three years of his life here.

The Wakefield National Memorial Association and Mr. John D. Rockefeller, Jr., spent considerable time and money in acquiring land at Wakefield, and in 1931 turned the holdings over to the United States to restore the grounds and establish the place as a national shrine.

How to reach: Via State Route 3 to State Route 204. *Open:* Daily, except Christmas, 8:00 A.M. to 5:00 P.M. *Admission:* 25¢. Guide service is available. *Administration:* National Park Service.

Bottle seals found in excavations at Wakefield. The AW monogram may have been Augustine Washington's.

Gunston Hall

LORTON, VA.

HISTORIC Gunston Hall was built, according to the plans of the famous William Buckland by George Mason, 1755-58, one of the ardent leaders of his time. He wrote the Virginia Bill of Rights and helped to write the first Constitution of Virginia. He, with Patrick Henry, opposed the acceptance of the United States Constitution on the grounds that the essentials of his Virginia Bill of Rights should be included before acceptance. Though Mason and the anti-Constitutionalists lost, the United States Bill of Rights—the first ten amendments to the Constitution—is essentially that composed by Mason.

Gunston Hall, restored by the Colonial Dames of America to mid-eighteenth-century appearance, contains a number of original Mason pieces, including the Bill of Rights table.

How to reach: Four miles east of U. S. 1.
Open: Daily except Christmas.
Admission: 50¢.
Administration: Colonial Dames of America.

Stratford Hall

Birthplace of Robert E. Lee

WESTMORELAND COUNTY, VA.

A NUMBER of the famous Lees of Virginia, besides Robert E., were born and lived in this plantation home. The first Lee of Virginia was Richard, the "Emigrant," who landed in 1641. His grandson Thomas built Stratford on the "clefts" of the Potomac and the original buildings stand today essentially as they were built in 1725-30

A view of Stratford Hall showing the Great House, built in the form of an H and the two south annexes (there are four). The one on the left was Thomas Lee's office. The other is the kitchen.

The Great Hall.

Thomas was appointed to His Majesty's Council for life, was president of the council and acting governor of the colony. Two of his sons, Richard Henry and Francis Lightfoot, became signers of the Declaration of Independence. Later Stratford became the home of the famous Henry "Light Horse Harry" Lee. He married Ann Carter of Shirley and they became parents of Robert Edward, who was born January 19, 1807. In 1810 the family moved to Alexandria.

In 1929 the Robert E. Lee Memorial Foundation, Inc., purchased the Stratford Hall property and since then it has been maintained as a living colonial plantation and national shrine.

———

How to reach: Via State Route 3.
Open: Daily, except Christmas, 9:00 A.M. to 5:00 P.M.
Admission: 50¢; children, 25¢. In groups of 25 or more, 25¢ and 15¢.
Administration: The Robert E. Lee Memorial Foundation, Inc.

The nursery.

Historic Fredericksburg

Colonial - Revolutionary - Civil War Periods

FREDERICKSBURG, VA.

FREDERICKSBURG is the center of historic Virginia and its claim to being "America's Most Historic City" is well supported. Besides the places hallowed in American history that I describe below, there are many others—the *home of John Paul Jones;* the *Masonic Lodge* which initiated George Washington; the *Rising Sun Tavern; St. George's Church; Kenmore,* home of Colonel Fielding Lewis and Betty Washington Lewis; the *Confederate Cemetery;* the *Ferry Farm,* Washington's boyhood home. And in or near Fredericksburg are those famous battlefields: Fredericksburg, Chancellorsville, Spotsylvania, Wilderness, Salem Church, Manassas.

MARY BALL WASHINGTON HOUSE

George Washington bought this house in 1772 and moved his mother here to live the last years of her life "in the grandeur of simplicity." Thomas Jefferson, George Mason, John Marshall, the Lees and the Marquis de Lafayette came here to pay their respects to Washington's mother and it was here that the first president-elect of the United States came on March 12, 1789, to receive his mother's blessing before his inauguration. She died less than six months later.

This is the only house now standing in which Mary Washington lived. It was purchased in 1890 by the Association for the Preservation of Virginia Antiquities and in 1929 George A. Ball of Muncie, Indiana, provided funds for its restoration. The original mantels and paneling are of interest.

How to reach: On U. S. Routes 1 and 17 as well as State Route 3. 1200 Charles Street.
Open: Daily, 9:00 A.M. to 6:00 P.M. From December to February, daily, 9:00 A.M. to 5:00 P.M.
Admission: 50¢; children, 25¢. Groups of 20 or more, 25¢.
Administration: Association for the Preservation of Virginia Antiquities.

The bedroom.

James Monroe Law Office and Museum
A GREAT STATESMAN'S STUDY

View of the law office, showing the century-old mulberry tree.

JAMES MONROE started the practice of law here in 1786. It was his law office until 1791. In it may be seen the original furniture of the present White House, which President Monroe was the first to occupy when it was rebuilt after the original White House had been burned in the War of 1812. Monroe had bought the furnishings in France in 1794 when he was minister to that country. When he became President the furnishings were moved to the White House, and at the end of his two terms the Monroe family took their possessions with them to their new home. Now most of these are in the law office. The furnishings in the Monroe Room of the White House are replicas of these originals, copies commissioned by Mrs. Herbert Hoover in 1932.

How to reach: 908 Charles Street, Fredericksburg.
Open: Daily, 9:00 A.M. to 5:00 P.M .
Admission: 30¢. Guide service is available.
Administration: James Monroe Memorial Foundation.

James Monroe's Louis XVI desk, used by him in the White House. On it he signed the proclamation of December 2, 1823, which has come to be known as the Monroe Doctrine.

Stonewall Jackson Shrine

WHEN he was mortally wounded by the mistaken fire of his own men at the battle of Chancellorsville, Stonewall Jackson asked to be taken "across the river and into the trees." But it was in this house, now part of the Fredericksburg and Spotsylvania National Military Park at Fredericksburg, that Lee's most famous lieutenant died. Contained in the house are the bed on which Jackson died and other Civil War items.

How to reach: State Route 606. Guinea Station.
Open: Daily, except Wednesdays and Thursdays, 8:00 A.M. to 4:30 P.M.
Admission: Free. Guide service is available.
Administration: National Park Service.

Hugh Mercer Apothecary Shop

I LIKE to look at old shops and I find the colorfulness of apothecary shops especially fascinating. So I was delighted when I first saw this old drugstore where George Washington's friend and fellow officer, Dr. Hugh Mercer from Aberdeen, Scotland, sold drugs from 1763 until the Revolutionary War. I was told that the shop remains today much as it was in Dr. Mercer's time. When discovered and reopened, it was seen that apparently the deep shelves on which reposed the large bottles and jugs of the day had been kept boarded over. Scales, bowls, pestles and other equipment were intact. The shop is preserved as a shrine to pharmacists by the American Pharmaceutical Association.

How to reach: 1220 Caroline Street, Fredericksburg's main street.
Open: Weekdays, 9:00 A.M. to 5:00 P.M.; Sundays, 1:00 P.M. to 5:00 P.M.
Admission: 30¢; children, 15¢.
Administration: American Pharmaceutical Association.

The prescription department.

Richmond
Capital of the Confederacy
RICHMOND, VA.

SOMEHOW, whenever I think of Richmond, I recall an occasion when Woodrow Wilson visited the building known as the Confederate Museum, or the White House of the Confederacy because it was the house provided by the Confederate government for President Jefferson Davis and his family. President Wilson, recovering from an illness, was in a wheelchair. As he was wheeled into the Solid South Room, he bowed his head and prayed. Nobody heard his prayer, but there was a dramatic silence which had its impact on everyone there. It was somewhat like those two minutes of silence we came to establish after Armistice Day of World War I, to focus our thoughts on the brave men who died for their cause. (Because the White House of the Confederacy is a museum, it does not fall within the province of this book, and I mention it only in passing.)

Richmond has its share of historic places, notably the *Capitol,* designed by Thomas Jefferson; the *Lee House,* home of General Robert E. Lee's family during the Civil War, now headquarters of the Virginia Historical Society; the *Edgar Allan Poe Shrine;* the *John Marshall House,* designed and built about 1790 by the Chief Justice—and others besides the ones described here.

THE WICKHAM-VALENTINE HOUSE

This late Georgian house, believed to have been designed by the great Robert Mills, was built in 1812 by John Wickham. He was the eminent Richmond lawyer who successfully defended Aaron Burr in the famous treason trial. Wickham's friend and nephew, John Marshall, visited here as did also Henry Clay, John C. Calhoun, Daniel Webster, General Winfield Scott and William Makepeace Thackeray.

Successive owners made changes, and in the 1850's the house was completely redecorated in the French Second Empire and English Victorian styles. When the Valentine Museum acquired the property, it was decided to retain this decoration in the drawing room, but to restore the rest of the house to its 1812 appearance. Thus restored to its original appearance as a dwelling house, the home called the Wickham-Valentine House was opened to the public in 1930.

How to reach: Via U.S. Routes 1, 60 and 360. 1015 East Clay Street.
Open: Weekdays, 10:00 A.M. to 5:00 P.M.; Sundays, 2:30 P.M. to 5:30 P.M.
Admission: Free.
Administration: The Valentine Museum.

Wickham-Valentine House, garden front.

WILTON

This brick house, home of the Randolphs of Wilton, solidly built 1747-53, has remained practically intact, although suffering some damage during both the Revolutionary War and the War Between the States. Originally situated six miles below Richmond on the James River, it was removed to its present site 1933-35. The removal and re-erection was done carefully by experts, and the reconstruction was exact.

How to reach: South Wilton Road.
Open: Weekdays, 9:00 A.M. to 5:00 P.M.; Sundays, 3:00 P.M. to 5:00 P.M.
Admission: Free, except during Garden Week.
Administration: Colonial Dames of America in the State of Virginia.

The parlor. Note the paneling. Both first and second floors are completely paneled, including even the closets.

Monticello
Home of Thomas Jefferson
CHARLOTTESVILLE, VA.

MONTICELLO is one of the three great patriotic shrines of our country. The other two are Mount Vernon and Lincoln's birthplace. Mount Vernon and Monticello have some physical features in common: both were plantations with many buildings; both command magnificent views; both had unusual mansions.

Jefferson's genius as architect and inventor is immediately apparent as one steps through the east portico into the square hall. In room after room the evidences of his ingenuity and practicality are everywhere—the hall clock, the self-opening doors, his revolving desk, his camera obscura. But though this is impressive, it is only one side of the great man who did as much to shape American history, and perhaps human history, as any thinker or president. If his only monument was the Declaration of Independence, it would be enough to secure his greatness. But he wrote some of the most penetrating analyses of the meaning of democracy; he recognized the necessity for social and political changes—and these found their way into our Constitution as well as into the Statute of Virginia for Religious Freedom.

As I have walked through Monticello—and I have on many occasions—and strolled through the gardens, I have thought how this place, high on its mountaintop, remote and free, yet built to be lived in and enjoyed, was a perfect expression of architect and planner.

Monticello, built by Thomas Jefferson in 1769, was a unique plantation, in altitude 857 feet above sea level. He lived in it from 1770 until his death in 1826. It was privately owned from that time until 1923, when the Thomas Jefferson Memorial Association bought it. It was renovated in 1954.

Jefferson considered his home a one-story house (though it has rooms on the second and third stories which are not open to the public). He designed the house so that the necessary outbuildings—laundry, smokehouse, dairy, smithy, weaving house, stable and carriage houses, schoolhouse (when there was one) and kitchen—were made as inconspicuous as possible under the long terraces ending in two balanced outchambers. Beneath the south terrace are the kitchen, with its collection of contemporary cooking utensils, the cook's room, another servant's room, smoke room and dairy. The north terrace houses the stables, carriage house, ice house and laundry.

The mansion's main entrance is through the eastern portico in the ceiling of which is a wind vane operated by a weather vane on the roof. Over the hall door is a large clock which marks the days of the week by the descent of cannonball weights.

The drawing room, behind the hall, is separated from it by glass doors which open automatically by a system of chains wound around a drum beneath the floor. The piano, music rack and stand, a device for holding quartet music, are Jefferson's. His bedroom contains his famous revolving chair and revolving-top table. The library, occupying the entire south end of the house, contains the table at which he made drawings for his own house and the houses of many of his friends, as well as plans for the University of Virginia; an octagonal filing table; his camera obscura and a polygraph, an instrument used by Jefferson for duplicating letters.

How to reach: Routes 20 and 53 south from Charlottesville.
Open: Daily, 8:00 A.M. to 5:00 P.M.
Admission: 90¢; adults in groups of 15 or more, 50¢.
Administration: The Thomas Jefferson Memorial Association.

The boxwood garden approach to Ash Lawn.

The Napoleon parlor.

Ash Lawn
Home of James Monroe
CHARLOTTESVILLE, VA.

I NEVER realized, until I visited Charlottesville, that two of our greatest presidents, Thomas Jefferson and James Monroe, were close friends and neighbors. Only about two miles from Monticello is Ash Lawn, James Monroe's home, designed and built for him by Thomas Jefferson in 1796-99. When I refer to Monroe as one of our greatest presidents, I think not only of the eight years of his presidency but also of the fact that he was the author of the Monroe Doctrine, the negotiator of the Louisiana Purchase, four times Governor of Virginia, U. S. Senator, U. S. envoy to England, France and Spain and U. S. Secretary of State and War.

The historic boxwood garden has remained in a fine state of preservation, and when the original house was restored in 1930, a visit to Ash Lawn seemed like a visit to 1800.

———

How to reach: Via Routes 20 and 53 out of Charlottesville.
Open: Daily, 7:00 A.M. to 7:00 P.M.
Admission: 75¢.
Administration: Jay Winston Johns, owner.

In this fine old convex mirror, flanked by the silhouettes of President and Mrs. Monroe, can be seen the doorway and the boxwood garden of Ash Lawn.

Michie Tavern
Boyhood Home of Patrick Henry
CHARLOTTESVILLE, VA.

MAYOR John Henry, father of the great orator, built this house sometime in 1735 and it was young Patrick's home for the first ten years of his life. In 1746 the property was sold to the Michie Tavern who owned it until 1910. It was one of the most popular taverns of colonial days. Though not on its original site, from which it was removed to its present location near Monticello, the original tavern stands now, restored and furnished with possessions original to the house or to houses of the period.

How to reach: Route 53.
Open: Daily, 9:00 A.M. to 5:00 P.M.
Admission: 50¢.
Administration: Vestal Thomas Milton.

The Keeping Hall. This was used also as an informal living room.

Woodrow Wilson Birthplace
STAUNTON, VA.

THE enduring simplicity and dignity of Woodrow Wilson's family home in the Shenandoah Valley of Virginia make this a singularly peaceful shrine. In this columned manse, built in 1845 by the First Presbyterian Church for its ministers, the twenty-eighth President of the United States was born. His father was the second minister to occupy the square white house. The family Bible on the bedside table contains the record of Wilson's birth in 1856 and his crib stands in the white-washed nursery. The four-poster bed was used by Wilson when he was President of Princeton University. There are many family possessions, many donated by his widow—some of his mother's silver and china, a guitar and violin, a bookcase he bought for his room while he was a law student at the University of Virginia.

How to reach: On Alternate Route 11. 24 North Coalter Street.
Open: Daily, 9:00 A.M. to 5:00 P.M.
Admission: 50¢; children under 12, 25¢. Guide service is available.
Administration: Woodrow Wilson Birthplace Foundation, Inc.

The rear, or garden, entrance.

Colonial National Historical Park
Jamestown Site, Cape Henry Memorial and Yorktown
VIRGINIA

COLONIAL National Historical Park includes several areas: Cape Henry Memorial and Jamestown, which commemorate the first landing and settlement of the Virginia colonists in 1607 and the first century of the colonial area; and Yorktown, scene of Cornwallis' surrender to Washington in 1781.

The site of old "James Towne," though not rich in visible preservations—only an ivy-covered brick church tower, believed to date from 1639, remains—is memorable as the birthplace of many of the cherished American traditions of freedom. The English settlers of the London Company who founded this first permanent settlement as James Fort (the Roanoke Island colony on the Carolina coast had not endured) maintained trial by jury and their rights as free men. The first representative legislative assembly in the New World, the House of Burgesses, convened in a church here in 1619. The foundations of several seventeenth-century houses can still be seen, as well as those of two early State-Houses.

In 1624 the Virginia Company of London was dissolved and Virginia became a royal colony. The colonists chafed under the harsh administration of Governor Berkeley, resulting in the so-called Bacon's Rebellion of 1676. Jamestown never recovered from the burning of the town by the rebels and in 1699 Williamsburg became the state capital. By the time of the Revolution, Jamestown, its marshy isthmus washed away, was practically abandoned. The Association for the Preservation of Virginia Antiquities acquired title to Jamestown Island in 1893. It has been a National Historic Site since 1940. Excavations have been continued since 1934 and many objects found—dishes, keys, locks, jewelry, etc.—are on display in the Relic House.

How to reach: Jamestown Island is accessible from Williamsburg via State Highway 31 and from Richmond via State Highway 5. From the south, take State Highways 10 or 31 to the ferry across the James at Scotland.
Open: Daily.
Admission: 40¢; students under 18 in groups and children, free.
Administration: National Park Service and Association for the Preservation of Virginia Antiquities.

YORKTOWN

Yorktown became the scene of the climax of the American Revolution when the British, bottled up here by land and the sea blockade, requested a parley after three weeks of siege. Cornwallis surrendered on October 19, 1781. The British earthworks remain and several batteries and redoubts have been reconstructed.

The Moore House.

The official Articles of Capitulation were drafted and consequently signed by the commanding generals in the *Moore House* (restored and refurnished to create its 1781 appearance), about a mile outside the town. The Moore family lived in this frame house, which was built about 1725, throughout the siege.

Yorktown, a thriving port town during the peak of Virginia's tobacco trade, had many wealthy merchants with homes like Augustine Moore's. Many buildings date from the eighteenth century or earlier: the *Custom House, York Hall* (The Thomas Nelson House), the *Digges, Somerwell, Sessions and West Houses* along Main Street; the *Grace Episcopal Church,* originally built in 1697; the *Smith House* and *Pearl Hall.*

How to reach: Via Colonial Parkway and U. S. 17.
Open: The *Moore House* is open daily, April to October.
Admission: 25¢.
Administration: National Park Service.

Room in which Cornwallis surrendered.

Berkeley

CHARLES CITY, VA.

Berkeley, home of the Harrison family, was built in 1726 by Benjamin Harrison, leader in colonial affairs. His son, Colonel Benjamin, was a member of the Continental Congress, a signer of the Declaration of Independence, thrice Governor of Virginia. Colonel Harrison's younger son, William Henry, was "Old Tippecanoe," who, when elected President of the United States, returned to Berkeley to write his inaugural address in the room in which he had been born. Old Tippecanoe's grandson was Benjamin Harrison, also later elected President of the United States.

Berkeley was restored in 1938 and stands today in the elegant simplicity of its original design.

How to reach: State Route 5.
Open: Daily, 8:00 A.M. to 5:00 P.M.
Admission: $1.00.
Administration: Malcolm Jamieson, owner.

Appomattox Court House

APPOMATTOX, VA.

Appomattox, scene of Robert E. Lee's surrender of the Army of Northern Virginia to Grant on April 9, 1865, is a memorial to America's internal peace as a reunited nation. It was established in 1940 as a National Historical Park. The poplar tree on the far side of Appomattox Creek marks the spot where Lee returned to his men and wrote his farewell order, paroling the 28,000 Confederate troops in the area: "You will take with you the satisfaction that proceeds from the consciousness of duty faithfully performed."

At the time of the Civil War the village of Appomattox Court House consisted of the court house, law offices, blacksmith shops, stores, several residences, two of which have been renovated for Park Service staff use, the Clover Hill Tavern, a stage stop, now a Civil War museum, and the old county jail:

The *McLean House,* in the parlor of which the two generals signed the articles of surrender, was reconstructed, using as much of the original brick and wood as possible, in 1949 as the first step in the restoration of the village to its appearance in 1865. Period furnishings, including the original parlor sofa, have been assembled for this house built in 1848 and razed in 1893. Now restored and refurnished, the McLean House is open daily from May 1 to October 31, also April 9 and weekends until May 1.

How to reach: State Route 24.
Open: The village is open weekdays from 8:00 A.M. to 6:00 P.M.; Saturdays, Sundays and holidays, 9:00 A.M. to 5:00 P.M.
Admission: Free, except *McLean House,* 25¢. Guide service may be arranged for at the *Clover Hill Tavern.*
Administration: National Park Service.

The McLean House. In the room at the left of the main porch, Lee and Grant met on April 9, 1865.

The Chapel.

Lee Chapel and President's House

LEXINGTON, VA.

IN 1865 Robert E. Lee turned aside all other offers to accept the presidency of Washington College— and he died on its campus five years later. He is buried there in the Chapel which he designed. He also designed the President's House (1870). In the Chapel may be seen Lee's office and many personal effects of Lee and of George Washington.

How to reach: On U. S. Routes 60 and 11.

Open: Chapel: summer, weekdays, 9:00 A.M. to 5:00 P.M.; Sundays, 2:00 P.M. to 5:00 P.M. Winter, weekdays, 9:00 A.M. to 4:00 P.M.; Sundays, 2:00 P.M. to 4:00 P.M. *President's House:* not open to visitors.

Admission: Free.

Administration: Washington and Lee University.

(Left) *The President's House.* (Below) *Interior of the Chapel.*

The Washington Homes
of Jefferson County
CHARLES TOWN, WEST VA.

J EFFERSON County in West Virginia's eastern panhandle is Washington country and has been since 1748 when sixteen-year-old George Washington was sent to make surveys of Lord Fairfax's holdings— the northern neck of Virginia. Young Washington practically fell in love with the land and subsequently made many trips to it. At one time he controlled 35,000 acres in what is now West Virginia, and it was his enthusiasm that brought his three full brothers, and later their descendants, to build their homes here. There are still a number of old Washington family homes still standing in Jefferson County. First to be built was

HAREWOOD

This was erected in 1771 by Colonel Samuel Washington, who entertained many famous people here, besides his brother George. In the beautiful drawing room, in which Dolly and James Madison were married in 1794, may be seen one of the two handsome mantels sent by Lafayette to George Washington. The matching mantel is at Mount Vernon.

HAPPY RETREAT

Charles Washington, another of George's brothers, built this house in 1780. In 1786 he founded Charles Town, named for him. Happy Retreat is in an excellent state of preservation and is open to the public without charge, daily from 9:00 A.M. to 5:30 P.M.

CLAYMONT COURT

Claymont Court was built in 1820 by Bushrod Corbin Washington, grandson of George's third brother, John Augustine. The mansion was destroyed by fire in 1838 but was rebuilt almost immediately. In 1899

Harewood.

Claymont was purchased by Frank R. Stockton, who wrote his last books here. The home has since passed to other private ownership and may be visited by appointment only.

BLAKELEY

This home was also built in 1820 by Bushrod Corbin Washington's brother, John August Washington II. The home, now privately owned, has been restored.

Cedar Lawn (1825), *Beallair* (1830) and *Locust Hill* (1830) are other Washington homes in the area.

How to reach: On U. S. Route 340 and State Routes 9 and 51.
Open: Except as specified above, by appointment.
Admission: Free.
Administration: Private ownership.

Claymont Court.

Shepherd Hall

NOW KNOWN AS MONUMENT PLACE
WHEELING, WEST VA.

THIS fine stone house, built in 1798 by Colonel Moses Shepherd, is notable chiefly for its doorway and the woodwork of its mantels and paneling. For most of its existence Shepherd Hall was owned by two families, the Shepherds and the Lorings. Both families were prominent in the area, and such notables as Andrew Jackson, William Henry Harrison, Henry Clay, James K. Polk and Lafayette were entertained here.

Shepherd Hall, or Monument Place.

How to reach: On U. S. Route 40 at Elm Grove.
Open: Daily.
Admission: Free.
Administration: Osiris Temple.

Mansion House

WHEELING, WEST VA.

Dining room in the Mansion.

THIS handsome ante-bellum house, built about 1835 by Dr. Hanson Chapline, was the most magnificent of its time and area. Chapline's wife was the daughter of one of the first settlers, who bequeathed to her the 1,000 acres that are now Oglebay Park. A later owner, Earle W. Oglebay, bequeathed the property to the City of Wheeling.

Today the Mansion colorfully depicts, through period rooms, the tastes and furnishings of the frontier, the early nineteenth century and later eras. Also, the Mansion dramatizes the early culture of our country through exhibits of midwestern glass, eighteenth-century china, early pewter and a fine collection of early firearms.

How to reach: At Oglebay Park via Route 40 to Route 88.
Open: Weekdays, 10:00 A.M. to 12:00 P.M., 2:00 P.M. to 5:00 P.M.; Sundays and holidays, 2:00 P.M. to 7:00 P.M.
Admission: 50¢; children, free. Groups of 15 or more, half price.
Administration: Oglebay Institute with the cooperation of the Wheeling Park Commission.

Abraham Lincoln
National Historical Park
Where Lincoln Was Born
HODGENVILLE, KY.

The traditional birthplace cabin.

JUST about in the center of Kentucky, in a one-room log cabin on Sinking Spring Farm near Hodgen's Mill, Abraham Lincoln was born February 12, 1809. He was named for his grandfather who was killed by an Indian from ambush in 1786 when Kentucky was the wild west.

Grandfather Abraham's son Thomas, father of the Great Emancipator, bought the 300-acre farm known as Sinking Spring just three months before Abraham was born. The Lincolns lived there two and a half years, then moved to Knob Creek, ten miles away. Then, in 1816, they left Kentucky and moved to Pigeon Creek in Indiana.

Of the 116½ acres of Abraham Lincoln National Historical Park about 100 acres were in the original Sinking Spring farm. There is also a log cabin, traditionally the birthplace cabin, which is displayed within a new Memorial Building. No one can say definitely that this is the actual cabin in which Lincoln was born. But there does seem to be some evidence to support the belief that it is in fact the original.

How to reach: On U. S. Route 31E and State Route 61.
Open: Summer, daily, 8:00 A.M. to 5:00 P.M; winter, 8:00 A.M. to 4:30 P.M.
Admission: Free.
Administration: National Park Service.

The Lincoln Memorial which houses the cabin.

Ashland
Home of Henry Clay

LEXINGTON, KY.

O NE of the most popular shrines in Kentucky is Ashland, the home of Henry Clay from 1811 to his death in 1852. In 1805 James Clay, Henry's son, rebuilt the house because the walls had been weakened. Other minor changes have been made, but essentially what a visitor to Ashland, restored by the Henry Clay Memorial Foundation, sees now is what a visitor to Henry Clay himself might have seen.

How to reach: On U. S. Route 25.
Open: Weekdays, 9:30 A.M. to 4:30 P.M.; Sundays, 1:00 P.M. to 5:00 P.M.
Admission: 50¢; children, 25¢.
Administration: Henry Clay Memorial Foundation.

The drawing room. Note presidential campaign banner used in 1844.

The Library.

A bedroom at Ashland. The trunk and the hatbox were carried back and forth by Clay between Lexington and Washington. The silk quilt was made for him by "The Ladies of Philadelphia."

The dining room.

One of the icehouses at Ashland.

Harrodsburg

Cradle of Kentucky

HARRODSBURG, KY.

THIS is a town of so many firsts, it is difficult to decide where to start and which to mention. Here are a few which Harrodsburg claims: the first white settlement of Kentucky, 1774; the first white child born in Kentucky; the first white child buried in Kentucky; the first summer resort in Kentucky; the first court for Kentucky County; the first school taught in Kentucky; the first preacher; the first Presbyterian Church of Kentucky; the first representative for Kentucky in the Continental Congress; the first election in Kentucky, sending George Rogers Clark and John Gabriel Jones to the Virginia legislature; the first spinning wheel for the making of linsey; the first grist mill driven by water; the first woolen manufactory; the first race course; the first manufacture of pottery, fabrics, plows, etc.

For many years after 1774, when it was founded, Harrodsburg was the great refuge of the pioneer, the strong point for the stream of settlers moving through the Cumberland Gap and down the Wilderness Road and by flatboat down the Ohio River.

It was Daniel Boone who helped James Harrod lay out the town and here *Harrod's Fort* was built. Now you can see a replica of the Old Fort in Pioneer Memorial State Park which reproduces authentically not only the fort itself but also the stockade, blockhouses and cabins. In these buildings are preserved the furniture, utensils and household articles just as they were used by the early settlers. Thus you can see not only these things but also how life was for the settlers in those days.

In Pioneer Memorial State Park there are also the cabin in which Lincoln's parents were married (housed in a brick building called the *Lincoln Marriage Temple*), the *Pioneer Cemetery* and the *George Rogers Clark Memorial*. Just left of the park entrance is the *Mansion Museum,* with many appropriate displays, and in or near the town are a number of other historic places of interest.

How to reach: On U. S. Route 68 and State Route 35.
Open: Summer, daily, 8:00 A.M. to 6:00 P.M.; winter, 8:00 A.M. to 5:00 P.M.
Admission: 35¢; children, 10¢; groups, 25¢.
Administration: Commonwealth of Kentucky.

William Whitley House

NEAR STANFORD, KY.

THIS home, built 1787-1794 and restored in 1951 as a state shrine to perpetuate the memory of Colonel William Whitley, pioneer scout and Indian fighter, was the first brick house built west of the Alleghenies. It served not only as a home but also as a fort and stockade. The house has many unusual features, such as a dungeon, a hidden stairway, hand-carved doors on leather hinges, etc.

How to reach: Just off State Route 150.
Open: Daily, 8:00 A.M. to 6:00 P.M.
Admission: 35¢; children, 10¢; groups, 25¢. Guide service available.
Administration: Division of Parks, Commonwealth of Kentucky.

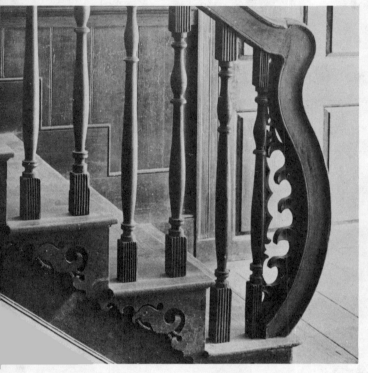

Stairway showing steps, of which there are 13, each carved with stylized eagle and olive branch. The newel post is thought to depict a harp, possibly Irish in origin, as was Whitley himself.

Duncan Tavern

PARIS, BOURBON COUNTY, KY.

THIS handsome stone building was erected by Major Joseph Duncan in 1788, while Kentucky was still part of Virginia. It had a billiard room, a ballroom, a bar, inside and outside kitchens. Restored by the Kentucky Society, D.A.R., the original building now stands as it did in the eighteenth century. The original woodwork of great beauty has been preserved and the furnishings are of the period. It is now the headquarters of the Kentucky Society.

How to reach: On Route 68.
Open: Daily, 9:00 A.M. to 12:00 P.M., 1:00 P.M. to 5:00 P.M.
Admission: 59¢.
Administration: Kentucky Society, D.A.R.

Federal Hill

"MY OLD KENTUCKY HOME"
BARDSTOWN, KY.

IN 1852 Stephen Collins Foster on his wedding trip visited his cousin John Rowan here. The Fosters spent the summer at Federal Hill, which became the inspiration for the famous song. The original rear wing of the house was built in 1795 by Judge John Rowan and additions were made in 1818. The home was restored in 1951 and it still contains some of the furnishings in use when Foster visited it.

How to reach: On Routes 68 and 150.
Open: Summer, daily, 8:00 A.M. to 6:00 P.M., winter, except Christmas Day, 8:00 A.M. to 5:00 P.M.
Admission: 60¢; children, 30¢; groups, 30¢.
Administration: Commonwealth of Kentucky.

The parlor. The portrait between the windows is that of Stephen Foster. The rosewood piano is more than 100 years old. Curtains, draperies, wallpaper and floor covering are reproductions of the 1852 period.

Wickland

HOME OF THREE GOVERNORS
BARDSTOWN, KY.

THIS mansion was built in 1813 by Charles Anderson Wickliffe, a native of Kentucky who grew up in a pioneer home near Springfield and became Governor of the state. His son Robert became Governor of Louisiana and his grandson, J.C.W. Beckham, was Governor of Kentucky from 1900-1907 and a U. S. Senator. The house is of brick made on the grounds, with fifteen-foot ceilings and eighteen-inch-thick walls, and the doorway is particularly beautiful. There are handsome period furniture, Aubusson rugs and fine stairways and mantels.

How to reach: On Route 62, east of Bardstown.
Open: Daily, 9:00 A.M. to 5:00 P.M.
Admission: 50¢; children, 15¢. Guide service is available.
Administration: Mrs. George Hagan, curator.

The operating room in which Dr. McDowell performed the first successful ovariotomy in 1809.

The front parlor, or Chippendale Room. The portrait over the mantel is of Dr. McDowell. His traveling case of drugs may be seen on the bottom shelf at the extreme left.

The Ephraim McDowell Memorial

A MEDICAL SHRINE

DANVILLE, KY.

ONE OF the important events in medical history occurred in this house—home of the man who has been called the father of abdominal surgery—on Christmas Day, 1809. Here Dr. Ephraim McDowell performed the first successful ovariotomy. He removed a twenty-pound ovarian tumor from his patient, forty-five-year-old Mrs. Jane Todd Crawford. During the operation, which was performed without anesthesia, Mrs. Crawford, who believed she would probably die under the knife, kept repeating the Psalms. In five days she was out of bed and in twenty-five days she went home, completely recovered. She lived another thirty-three years.

Dr. McDowell studied medicine under Dr. Alexander Humphries and at the University of Edinburgh, and took up practice in 1795. Though he never obtained a medical degree, other than an honorary M.D. from the University of Maryland in 1825, he was for many years the foremost surgeon west of the Alleghenies.

The frame structure of his handsome house was built in 1779; the brick additions of dining room, kitchen and office were built in 1802. It is restored with all furnishings of the period 1779-1830.

How to reach: One block off Route 150, three blocks from Route 35.
Open: Daily, 9:00 A.M. to 4:00 P.M.
Admission: 50¢; children, 15¢.
Administration: Kentucky State Medical Association.

The Rob Morris Memorial

LA GRANGE, KY.

ROB MORRIS founded the Order of the Eastern Star. Traveler, poet, composer and lecturer, he was called the Poet Laureate of Free Masonry and was one of its leading lights. The house in which he lived until his death in 1888 was built in 1830 and was restored in 1928.

How to reach: State Routes 146 and 53.
Open: Daily.
Admission: None.
Administration: The Order of the Eastern Star of Kentucky.

Study in Rob Morris home showing desk he used and original Eastern Star signet.

The Hermitage
Home of Andrew Jackson
NASHVILLE, TENN.

ANDREW JACKSON, hero of the Battle of New Orleans, first senator from Tennessee, Governor of Florida and seventh President of the United States, lived happily on this estate for many years with his wife Rachel. Jackson had bought the property, a group of log houses on a 425-acre tract, in 1804. He converted the principal log house, which had been a blockhouse in the days of Indian alarms, into a dwelling. The central portion of the present brick mansion was erected 1818-1819 and in 1831 wings were added. Fire destroyed much of the interior in 1834, but most of the furniture was saved. The mansion, as it stands today, was fully restored the next year.

The Hermitage is the only old national shrine completely furnished with original pieces. Though it was established as a memorial to a great hero, it is, I think, also a family shrine. General Jackson was devoted to his mother, who saved his life when he was stricken with smallpox during the Revolutionary War. Later she died of yellow fever while nursing some neighbors confined on a British hospital ship in Charleston harbor. Jackson never forgot her, and on his forty-eighth birthday in 1815 in New Orleans he said of her to some members of his military family: "I wish she could have lived to see this day. There never was a woman like her. She was gentle as a dove and as brave as a lioness. Her last words have been the law of my life."

Almost her last words were in a letter of advice she sent to her son when he was fourteen: "Andrew, if I should not see you again I wish you to remember and treasure up some things I have already said to you. In this world you will have to make your own way. To do that, you must have friends. You can make friends by being honest, and you can keep them by being steadfast. . . . In personal conduct be always polite but never obsequious. None will respect you more than you respect yourself. Avoid quarrels as long as you can without yielding to imposition. But sustain your manhood always. Never bring a suit in law for assault and battery or for defamation. The law affords no remedy for such outrages that can satisfy the feelings of a true man. . . ."

Andrew Jackson was equally fortunate in his wife, Rachel, who was a woman of strength and devoted to him. She wanted a tranquil life with her husband more than fame for him. And the Hermitage somehow stands as a symbol of the love of Andrew and Rachel as well as a shrine to the courage and far-sightedness of a great man.

How to reach: On U. S. Route 70N.
Open: October to March, daily, 8:30 A.M. to 4:00 P.M.; April to September, 8:30 A.M. to 6:00 P.M.
Admission: 50¢; children, 10¢.
Administration: Ladies' Hermitage Association.

The spacious entrance hall, showing the original wallpaper imported from France.

Ancestral Home of James K. Polk

COLUMBIA, TENN.

JAMES KNOX POLK, eleventh President of the United States, acquired more land for the country than any other President. He risked war with Great Britain to get Oregon and Washington. He did go to war to acquire California and most of our Southwest. He secured the annexation of Texas. He has been ranked as one of our "near great" Presidents along with Theodore Roosevelt, Grover Cleveland and John Adams, and his stature among historians is steadily increasing.

The Polk home, a modest structure of handmade brick, was built by Samuel Polk, the President's father, in 1816 and was deeded to the Polk Memorial Association and the State of Tennessee in 1929 for preservation as a shrine. The house contains some original Polk furniture.

How to reach: High Street and West 7th Street. State Routes 31 and 43, U. S. Highway 31.
Open: Weekdays, 9:00 A.M. to 12:00 P.M., 1:00 P.M. to 5:00 P.M.; Sundays, 1:00 P.M. to 5:00 P.M.
Admission: 50¢; children, 10¢.
Administration: Polk Memorial Association.

Belle Meade

Home of Thoroughbreds

NASHVILLE, TENN.

ONE OF the loveliest plantations in Tennessee, situated on the old Natchez Trace, Belle Meade was once the showplace of Nashville. But its national and international fame was due not to its loveliness but rather to the many distinguished thoroughbred race horses bred and owned there.

The official beginning of the Belle Meade stud is considered to have been 1835 when William Giles Harding, son of John Harding, who started the accumulation of the once 5,300-acre plantation, started breeding race horses. The thoroughbred nursery lasted until the last owner of the Harding-Jackson family died and the land was sold for division in 1904.

Belle Meade stands in a handsome park just outside the city limits of Nashville. The original building was erected by Giles Harding in 1810, but this burned down in 1853. After the fire William Strickland was retained to reconstruct the house, and it stands today, with the exception of a later addition of a porte-cochere, much as he finally left it.

The Belle Meade mansion.

The dining room.

The walls of the original structure appear to have remained substantially intact, as the main block of the house certainly dates from before Strickland's time. However, across the entire front he built a magnificent portico of eight Ionic piers of Tennessee limestone, each pier consisting of two immense blocks. The interior, though simple in plan and detail, is as impressive as the exterior. The trim is Greek of an extremely simplicity but of great boldness and scale.

How to reach: On U. S. Route 70S about 6 miles from Nashville or via State Route 100.
Open: Weekdays, 10:30 A.M. to 4:30 P.M.; Sundays, 1:30 P.M. to 4:30 P.M.
Admission: 50¢; teenagers, 25¢; children, free.
Administration: Association for the Preservation of Tennessee Antiquities.

(Below) *The drawing room.* (Right) *The parlor.*

The Governor William Blount Mansion

KNOXVILLE, TENN.

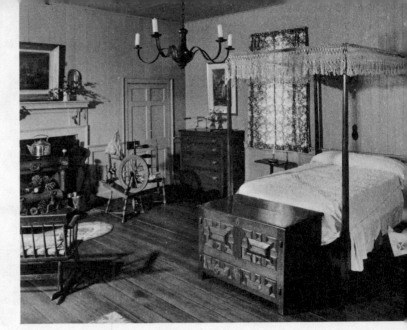

The Green Room. Scene of the important social functions of the day, this room was cleared for receptions and dancing. At other times it served as the family sitting room and has been restored accordingly.

THIS HAS been described by the well-known Tennessee historian John Trotwood Moore as the most important historic spot in Tennessee. It is closely identified with the origin of the State of Tennessee, which until 1790 had been North Carolina territory. Following the collapse of the attempt to establish this territory as the State of Franklin, North Carolina ceded the area to the United States. Congress accepted it and created the Territory of the United States south of the Ohio River.

William Blount, prominent in North Carolina as a merchant, manufacturer, Speaker of the North Carolina House of Commons and delegate to the Constitutional Convention, was appointed by Washington as Governor of the Territory. He selected White's Fort, the site of present-day Knoxville, as the seat of his territorial government, laid out the town and built his mansion, which was completed in 1792.

Blount established the Territorial Legislature, which had its first session in 1794, and one of its first acts was to establish Blount College, now the University of Tennessee. It was through Blount's efforts and suggestions that the Territory was admitted to the Union in 1796. Blount became one of its two United States Senators. Though expelled from the Senate because of alleged plotting for the seizure of the lower Mississippi area, he was exonerated by his fellow citizens. Impeachment proceedings were decided in his favor and subsequently he was made Speaker of the State Senate, a position which he held at the time of his death in 1800.

How to reach: Via U. S. Routes 11, 70, 441. 200 West Hill Avenue.
Open: June through October, weekdays, 9:30 A.M. to 5:00 P.M.; Sundays, 2:00 P.M. to 5:00 P.M. Other times by appointment.
Admission: Free.
Administration: Blount Mansion Assoc.

Andrew Johnson Birthplace

RALEIGH, N. C.

I ONCE visited here with Josephus Daniels, who was then a newspaper publisher in Raleigh. Mr. Daniels, who was a "teetotaler," told me with high pride that "so was Andrew Johnson," but the lady representing the local historical society disagreed and a lively debate ensued.

In this small house Andrew Johnson, seventeenth President of the United States, was born in 1808. Apprenticed at fourteen to a tailor, he became skilled in this trade in several Carolina towns before he and his family decided to go beyond the mountains to seek work in Tennessee.

The home has been preserved in its original form for almost a century and a half, though it has been moved twice. It was presented to the City of Raleigh about 1904 by the Wake County Committee of the Colonial Dames of America, when it was placed in Pullen Park. The house contains furniture in common use during the early nineteenth century—trundle bed, blanket chest, loom, kitchen items.

How to reach: U. S. Routes 1, 70, 64.
Open: Daily except Saturdays, 2:00 P.M. to 5:00 P.M.
Admission: 25¢; children, 10¢.
Administration: City of Raleigh.

Old Salem

WINSTON-SALEM, N. C.

OLD SALEM, which was founded as a planned community in 1766 by Moravian Brethren from Pennsylvania, is one of the best preserved eighteenth-century settlements in the country. Forty of the old buildings which centered about a public square are still standing. A program to restore the old village was initiated in 1950, under the non-profit organization called Old Salem, Inc.

Most notable is the *Home Moravian Church* and graveyard. This old church, with its weather vane and gilded ball atop the cupola, attracts about 50,000 visitors annually. The exterior, with its hooded doorways and eyebrow-arched windows, has remained unchanged since it was consecrated in 1800. Its German clock, made in 1790, still keeps time, and its bell was rung for the first time in 1772. Ten windows portray the life of Jesus.

God's Acre, the old tree-shaded graveyard with its "pillow" stonemarkers, is the closing scene of the Moravian Easter sunrise service, which has been held for over 100 years.

The Home Moravian Church (above); *parlor or family room of the John Vogler House* (center); *and* (below) *scale model (on display at Old Salem, Inc., Headquarters) of the village as it appeared about 1820.*

How to reach: Via U. S. Routes 311, 421, 52.
Open: Daily.
Admission: Free. Guide service is available.
Administration: The Moravian Church.

The *John Vogler House,* at South Main and West Streets, built in 1819 by John Vogler, silversmith and lockmaker, has been restored and his workshop has been re-established.

Other Old Salem points of interest include *The Fourth House,* oldest building in Salem; the *Lick-Boner Block House* (1787); *Cape Fear Bank,* built in 1847, was the first bank in Salem.

The *Wachovia Museum* houses one of the largest collections of local antiquities in the country.

Open: Weekdays, 10:00 A.M. to 4:00 P.M.; Sundays, 2:30 P.M. to 4:30 P.M.
Admission: 50¢; children, 15¢.
Administration: Old Salem, Inc.

Biltmore House
One of the Great Country Houses of America
NEAR ASHEVILLE, N. C.

OF THE Vanderbilt mansions now open to the public, Biltmore House is probably the least ornate and most tastefully arranged. My father's uncle, George, built it and lived in it until he died, when it passed to his daughter Cornelia.

Most of my memories of Biltmore are from childhood—not of art objects or of splendid rooms, but of sliding down the balustrade of the grand spiral staircase. Cornelia, my sister and I almost killed ourselves at the bottom, of course, but it didn't stop us from getting up for a game of hide-and-seek in the library.

My most recent memory of Biltmore was the occasion on which, as a buck private. I was assigned to drive General J. Leslie Kincaid and Colonel Taber Loree to Biltmore. At the gate, the gatekeeper refused us admission: "Cornelius Vanderbilt, Junior, is a general, not a buck private. If you don't get off this property at once, I'll call the sheriff."

How to reach: Via U. S. Routes 25, 70, 19, 74. South of Asheville.
Open: April 1 to September 30, daily, 9:00 A.M. to 6:00 P.M.
    October 1 to March 31, 9:30 A.M. to 5:00 P.M.
Admission: $2.40; children, $1.40.
Administration: Biltmore Estate.

A corner of the Tapestry Gallery.

The grand spiral staircase.

The Duke Homestead

DURHAM, N. C.

THIS little six-room house is a sort of tobacco industry shrine. It was built in 1851 by Washington Duke, and he and his wife, daughter and two sons, Benjamin Newton and James Buchanan, lived here for many years. James Buchanan Duke later became the founder of Duke University.

Washington Duke was in the Confederate service during the Civil War. When he returned to his homestead he found that the farm had been thoroughly raided by Union soldiers who had carried away just about everything movable. His entire capital consisted of two blind army mules and fifty cents in hard money. But he found a small quantity of leaf tobacco that had been overlooked by the raiders. He treated the tobacco, packed it in bags, loaded it into a covered wagon drawn by the mules and set out with his sons "Ben" and "Buck" over the state to sell and barter. That was the beginning of the great Duke tobacco empire, now the American Tobacco Company. Now restored, the homestead is the property of Duke University.

The third Duke tobacco factory. When the demand for bright leaf tobacco increased, crude machines were installed to "beat out" the leaf.

How to reach: On State Route 501.
Open: April 1 to October 1, Sundays, 2:30 P.M. to 5:30 P.M. and by appointment made by calling Duke University.
Admission: Free.
Administration: Duke University.

Oconaluftee Indian Village

CHEROKEE, N. C.

AT THE entrance to Great Smoky Mountains National Park is the 50,000-acre Qualla Reservation on which some 3,700 Cherokee Indians live and work. The Cherokee present at this Mountainside Theatre a drama, "Unto These Hills," which tells their story. There is in September an annual Cherokee Fair with displays of Indian arts, crafts and products. But perhaps most interesting is the Oconaluftee Indian village, a re-created community of two hundred years ago, presenting the old Cherokee way of life.

How to reach: Via U. S. Routes 19, 441 and State Route 107.
Open: May to October, weekdays, 9:30 A.M. to 4:30 P.M.; Sundays, 1:00 P.M. to 4:30 P.M.
Admission: $1.00; children, 25¢. Guide service is available.
Administration: Qualla Reservation.

Fort Hill

Home of John C. Calhoun

CLEMSON, S. C.

JOHN C. CALHOUN, the "states' rights" champion who served the South and the nation for over forty years—in Congress, as Secretary of War, Secretary of State and Vice-President—eagerly returned each spring to his family at Fort Hill where he enjoyed plantation life until Congress convened in the late fall. His old homestead now stands on the grounds of Clemson College, maintained as it was when he lived there.

The 1,100-acre estate came into Calhoun's possession in 1825. He enlarged the small two-story house, which had been built in 1803, adding three huge-columned piazzas, a separate kitchen, an office, a springhouse and quarters for house and field servants. He gave the plantation the title Fort Hill in honor of old Fort Rutledge, which was built on the place in 1776 as a protection against the Indians.

Most of the furnishings are original pieces. Mrs. Calhoun's spinet, made in England about 1800, stands in the parlor. A chair and a sofa belonged to George Washington. According to tradition the carved eagles on the back of the sofa were used by the mint as models for the eagles on the first American silver dollars. A red velvet chair was a gift from King Leopold I of Belgium. In the state dining room are a huge Duncan Phyfe mahogany banquet table and twelve horsehair-covered chairs. The sideboard, a gift to Calhoun from Henry Clay, was made from mahogany paneling taken from the officers' quarters of "Old Ironsides" (the *Constitution*).

On the spacious lawn are three trees of historic interest: a Canadian hemlock, gift to Calhoun by Daniel Webster; an arborvitae, presented to him by Henry Clay; and a varnish tree brought from Madagascar by Commodore Stephen Decatur.

***

How to reach: Routes 123 and 76.
Open: Winter, weekdays, 10:00 A.M. to 12:00 M. and 2:00 P.M. to 5:00 P.M.; summer, 10:00 A.M. to 12:00 M. and 2:00 P.M. to 5:30 P.M. Sundays, afternoons only.
Admission: Free.
Administration: Clemson College and the South Carolina Division of the United Daughters of the Confederacy.

A view of the parlor. The goldleaf cornices and tiebacks at the window are original. The painting is of Calhoun's daughter, Anna Maria, who was married in this room to Thomas Green Clemson. Note the hand-carved eagles on the sofa.

Another view of the parlor showing Mrs. Calhoun's spinet, the King Leopold chair and footstool.

Historic Charleston

Seat of Old Southern Culture

CHARLESTON, S. C.

CHARLESTON is a many-hued city, but the Charleston I like best is the old, old city just back from the Battery and extending no farther than the City Hall and some of the most outstanding churches. But there are other Charlestons, too; there is the Charleston of the waterfront and the Charleston of the Navy and the Charleston of industry, and others.

Some years ago when I was visiting here, my host took me on a tour of the older part of the town at dusk. We ambled along the ultra-narrow sidewalks, on cobblestoned streets, through grilled ironwork gateways, peering into the tidy backyards of a score of little brick or frame houses, as clean and spotless as could be. Here, my friend pointed out, is where DuBose Heyward wrote *Porgy* and there is Catfish Row. Across the street is where Caroline Pinckney Rutledge, sister of the well-known author of nature stories, lived, and over there is the historic Heyward House where George Washington was entertained in the spring of 1791. And, as in an aside, he added that of course Heyward was a signer of the Declaration of Independence.

The Sword Gate.

The Miles Brewton House.

St. Michael's.

Down from the corner, he said, is the studio of Elizabeth O'Neill Verner, an etcher of note; originally the little house had been lived in by Ladaveze, the famous confectioner. Nearby, he said, is Anna Heyward Taylor's studio; she was a member of Dr. Beebe's expedition to South America where she painted botanical studies. On the corner stood a very fine old house, now an antique shop, and just beyond it a building built by Peter Porcher in 1740 after the original building on the same site, once owned by Miles Brewton, had been destroyed by fire. Next door, in what was formerly an old coach house, is a very fine old inn, the Brewton Inn, overlooking its own lovely flagstoned gardens. The house beyond was where the Council of the Province used to hold its meetings, and a little farther down the street a house built in 1710, once owned by Richard Capers, a planter of Christ Church Parish. Next came the First Baptist Church, the first of its denomination to be organized in the South. By this time, my head was whirling and I could no longer read my notes.

Next day, when I visited the churches, the slave-market, the old capitol, the city hall, Fort Sumter and some of the museums, I thought, this is the only historical city in America today in which people still live as they used to live, where life continues as it was in the time of our forefathers. It isn't botched up with a lot of modernity, skyscrapers, dirty streets, subways and buses. It is still a closely knit old place with exquisite old houses, lovely furnishings, interesting people and a penchant for keeping history historical in the niche it should always be.

We have only a few cities left with a real flavor of their own—Boston, Washington, New Orleans, St. Augustine, San Antonio, San Francisco, San Diego. But we have only one Charleston, and it is to the people of Charleston, with their love of the gracious way in which our ancestors lived, that we owe a real debt of gratitude for keeping Old Charleston old.

Charleston, named for King Charles II, who granted the province to eight favorite noblemen, the Lords Proprietors, was founded by the English in 1670. It was the capital of Carolina until 1790. For many years it was the largest city in the South, one of the four largest in the country, rivaling Boston, New York and Philadelphia in commercial and cultural importance.

The way of life established by the Lords Proprietors was far different from that in the other colonies. There were lordly titles, great estates, much travel to the Old World, education abroad and close association with European culture. It was the metropolis and capital of a rich territory, made prosperous by money crops such as indigo and then rice. It was natural that Charleston should experience a golden age of grandeur, splendor and the flowering of the arts. Beautiful homes were built, magnificent gardens were laid out and well cared for. Charleston is world-famous for its plantation

The Dock Street Theatre.

gardens, started 100 or more years ago, notably Magnolia, Cypress and Middleton. And despite wars, sieges, bombardments and other disasters, Old Charleston stands today, a beautiful example of the South's living past.

———

How to reach: Via U. S. Routes 17, 176, 178.

The sword gate gives the *Sword Gate House* its name. The gates were made in 1838, installed in 1849. The house, built during the 1800's, is famous for its lovely ballroom and its fine furnishings. On Tradd and Legare Streets, it is open Monday through Saturday, 10:00 A.M. to 1:00 P.M., 2:30 P.M. to 5:00 P.M. Admission, $1.00. Privately owned.

The *Dock Street Theatre* is one of the earliest playhouses in America. It opened on February 12, 1736, and the first recorded American performance of a Shakespearean play was given here the following year. Originally the theatre entrance was on Dock Street (later renamed Queen Street). The present structure is a restoration and it is used by two local theatre groups who have made it one of the best-known theatres in the country. It is at Church and Queen Streets. Owned by the city of Charleston; leased to the Dock Street Theatre, Inc.

The *Miles Brewton House* was built 1765-69. This house was headquarters for Sir Henry Clinton and other British commanders during the Revolution and for the federal commander in 1865. It is an excellent example of the Charleston "double house." At 27 King Street, it is open to visitors from 9:00 A.M. to 5:00 P.M. Admission, $1.00. Privately owned.

The Manigault House.

The *Manigault House*, built in 1803, has special architectural interest because of its Adam style, includes elliptical porches and bays. Now the property of the Charleston Museum, it is open from 10:00 A.M. to 2:00 P.M. with an admission fee of $1.00. It is at 350 Meeting Street.

St. Michael's Episcopal Church is almost a duplicate of St. Martin's-in-the-Fields in London. Its cornerstone was laid in 1752. George Washington, Lafayette and Lee are among those who attended services here. At Broad and Meeting Streets, it is open to visitors daily from 9:00 A.M. to 5:00 P.M. without charge.

Magnolia Gardens (below), first planted in 1830, is world-famous for its century-old camellias and azaleas. At one time the Baedeker guides listed only three top attractions in the United States—Niagara Falls, the Grand Canyon and the Magnolia Gardens. Open January 1 to May 1. Charges range from $1.20 to $2.00. The Gardens are on State Route 61.

Beth Elohim.

Beth Elohim, founded in 1749, was the cradle of Reform Judaism in America, which began in 1824 when a group of members of Beth Elohim organized "The Reformed Society of Israelites." The present building was erected in 1840. It is open to visitors from 9:00 A.M. to 1:00 P.M. without charge. It is at 90 Hasell Street.

Middleton Gardens (above), the oldest formal gardens in America, were begun in 1741 by Henry Middleton, later President of the Continental Congress. They are among the most magnificent and remarkable gardens in the western world and are open the year round from 9:00 A.M. to 6:00 P.M. The admission fees range from $1.00 to$ 2.00. The Gardens are on State Route 61. Privately owned. Cypress Gardens (below), are part of Dean Hall, once a great rice plantation, built 1750. A reservoir for its rice fields was transformed into this strange and unusual spectacle. There are other cypress gardens in the country, but this is by far the oldest. The Gardens are open from January to May from 9:00 A.M. to 6:00 P.M. Admission fees range from $1.20 to $2.00. Privately owned.

Picturesque Savannah
Historic Waterfront City

SAVANNAH, GA.

SAVANNAH is one of the most beautiful old cities in the country and, apart from its many places of historical interest, the city itself may be regarded as part of the Living Past of America, not so much because of historical events that occurred here but rather because preserved in the city is the quality of its old way of life, the color of its great days as Cotton Capital.

I know it well, and since the days of my childhood I have always been fond of the old city. My uncle, the late Richard T. Wilson, had a plantation up the May River, across from Bluffton. Here he raised Egyptian cotton, which was weighed, sorted and inspected at the famous place called Factors' Row, on the waterfront of Savannah. I used to go there often.

My mother was from a Southern family, and it was no wonder that she wanted to spend the holidays with her family in the South. Every Christmas we used to journey here in Father's private railroad car. We would be met in Savannah by Uncle Dick, who would put us aboard an old stern-wheeled river boat which would puff upstream to the Wilson plantation. I remember that the boat went past a sort of lighthouse where a lady used to come out on a catwalk and wave to us and other passing vessels. The story was that she was looking for her lover. She had told him she would wait for him forever, but forever never came.

It seems to me that Savannah houses are truly magnificent, its parks wonderfully spacious, its old buildings beautifully kept up, its clubs genuinely excellent and its citizens as proud as they come.

In the early days at the turn of the century when we came here, everything seemed so slow-moving compared to the great cities of the North. It was almost unbelievable that here was a place where life still moved as it might still be moving if we had not harnessed the machine. The waterfront was crowded with sailing ships and steamers loading cotton for the great ports of the world. (The first steamship sailed from Savannah in 1816.) There was a sort of willowy mist over everything, perhaps coming from the swamp fires or maybe from the smokestacks of the steamers themselves. Through a thick morning fog the waterfront looked eerie; even the mule-drawn wagons seemed to steam either from the perspiration of the mules, or from the fog itself.

Wherever you went in Savannah there were trees— huge shady ones—and iron railings. There were flowers galore and short stubby palm trees and all kinds of green growing plants. Every other house had a red geranium and there were miles and miles of purple bougainvillea and orange honeysuckle. The main residential street was one of the most beautiful streets in America, ranking along with Peachtree Street in Atlanta and Bellevue Avenue in Newport.

How to reach: Savannah is on U. S. Routes 17, 21 and 80.

Factors' Walk. The lower level is what was specifically called Factors' Walk; the whole stretch is sometimes called Factors' Row. The bridge seen in this picture has since been destroyed.

FACTORS' WALK

The early mercantile life of the city is represented by the area of Factors' Row or Factors' Walk, the term applied to the second level of the waterfront section on Bay Street, where cotton factors walked from warehouse to warehouse, inspecting bales of cotton stored there. These storage rooms are beneath the street-level stories of the buildings which flank the city on the north, the backs of which drop five stories to the river level. The street-level stories of the buildings were used for sampling rooms for cotton.

The row extends several blocks along the waterfront, the buildings facing the city and separated from it by ramps which lead down to the river. The ramps are spanned by old iron bridges. The ramps wind from city level to the river and are paved with the stones once used as ballast in the ships which came into port. Cotton merchants used the iron balconies overlooking the river in the old days to view incoming and outgoing vessels and to see across the river to the slips, warehouses and docks.

The exact dates of construction of the buildings are not known, but the area was developed shortly after Savannah was founded in 1732 by General James Edward Oglethorpe. Beginning about 1840, upper levels were added to the lower ones which had been made of the stones used on the ramps. With the decline of cotton shipments from the port, the buildings passed into other hands and are now used for various purposes. It seems inevitable that this historic waterfront section will soon be lost.

There is no administration and no admission fee. Guide service, however, is available.

THE OWENS-THOMAS HOUSE AND THE REGENCY GARDEN

This Savannah house that exhibits the most charm in its ante-bellum structure has been described as the purest example of Regency architecture in America, and the American Institute of Architects considers it one of the outstandingly beautiful examples of old American architecture. Almost all the other distinguished architecture of historic association in Savannah—the Habersham House, the Hermitage, the Birk, the Scarborough House—have gone and it is fortunate that this handsome mansion, begun in 1816 and finished in 1819, has been preserved.

It was designed for Richard Richardson by William Jay, a young English architect, and the acclaim it received, together with other notable houses he designed, helped him attain distinction as one of the great architects who have worked in this country. George W. Owens acquired the property in 1830 and it remained in the family until the death of his granddaughter Margaret Owens Thomas in 1951. She bequeathed it

Pirates' House (1759), situated in the Trustees' Garden, was a traditional headquarters for Blackbeard and other pirates. It is folklore in Savannah that the prototype of Treasure Island's Captain Flint died on the second floor of Pirates' House, attended by Billy Bones, Long John Silver and Tom Morgan.

to the Telfair Academy of Arts and Sciences which started the work of restoration and opened the home, on Oglethorpe Square, to the public in 1954.

———

Open: Sundays, 3:00 P.M. to 6:00 P.M.; Mondays, 2:00 P.M. to 5:00 P.M.; other days, 10:00 A.M. to 5:00 P.M.
Admission: $1.00.
Administration: Telfair Academy of Arts and Sciences.

TRUSTEES' GARDEN VILLAGE

Trustees' Garden Village, recently restored, was the birthplace of the Royal Colony of Georgia and is a landmark in early American history. It was established in 1733, when General Oglethorpe laid out the plot within a month after the original colonists landed. Its purpose was to introduce, foster and develop in the colony the growing of plants and products that England needed: grapes for wine, mulberry trees for silkworms, peaches, spices, bamboo, coffee, oranges, herbs. And, most notably, upland cotton was first introduced into this country through this ten-acre tract.

The garden, landscaped to accentuate the beauty of the growing trees, became a favorite park. But as the city grew and as the essential objective of the garden was accomplished, it was neglected and it fell into disuse. But in 1947 the South Atlantic Gas Company acquired the property and arranged to restore it as a colorful residential area with a number of dwelling units and business locations. It is administered by the Trustees' Garden Village, Inc.

The Little White House

WARM SPRINGS, GA.

I KNOW and love this place for itself and for the memories I associate with it—memories of F.D.R., the greatest man I have ever known, when he was able to relax and enjoy a measure of anonymity. My first visit preceded F.D.R.'s by two years, and with each later visit I could understand better his deep love for it.

I remember the beginning and the end. When plans for the house were drawn, F.D.R.'s mother, Mrs. James Roosevelt, thought the rooms were too "dinky," but F.D.R. thought the whole place exactly right for getting close to nature and as removed as possible from the pressures of the world. He especially liked the sun-deck from which he could see only trees; at night he would sit on it in his wheelchair and gaze at the stars. Sometimes, as I sat with him, I thought I could hear him praying.

I was with F.D.R. at Warm Springs a day or two before his death. It was just after Yalta that he telephoned to ask if I could meet him at Warm Springs. I motored to Columbus, Georgia, and saw him the next morning on the sun-deck. He discussed the events at Yalta with me, his hopes and plans for it. It was then, too, that he told me of the United Nations Conference at San Francisco which was to begin in April. Finally he said, "I was talking the other day to a pretty lady who owns a string of newspapers. I suggested to her that it might be a good idea to have a fellow like you cover the Conference. You could not only write what you saw and heard, but you could telephone me from time to time what you felt."

The President's bedroom, where he died.

The next day I accepted the job and started off almost immediately for California. Two days out of New York, I picked up a news flash. F.D.R. was dead. I couldn't believe it—just as millions of Americans couldn't believe or accept it. And through the whole Conference I felt his presence.

The building, begun in 1931, was occupied April, 1932, and used by President Roosevelt until his death, April 12, 1945. It was willed by him to the Georgia Warm Springs Foundation, which deeded it to the State of Georgia for memorial purposes. Renovated by the state, it was opened to the public in October, 1948. The furnishings have been left in all the rooms just as they were. F.D.R.'s Ford, which used to stand outside the front door, is now on display in the garage.

How to reach: U. S. Route 27 alternate, State Highways 41 and 85W.
Open: Daily, 9:00 A.M. to 5:00 P.M.
Admission: 75¢; children, 25¢. Guide service is available.
Administration: Franklin D. Roosevelt Warm Springs Memorial Commission.

The dining room.

The ruins of Fort Frederica. Note the Frederica River, part of the intracoastal waterway, behind the fort.

Christ Church. Not the original building in which the Wesleys preached. The present building was erected in 1884.

Fort Frederica

SAINT SIMONS ISLAND, NEAR

SEA ISLAND, GA.

THE RUINS of the eighteenth-century English Fort Frederica, commanding the winding inland waterway, are a grim reminder of the Anglo-Spanish tug-of-war for southeastern America. Here, as early as 1566, Spain had established Franciscan missions, and from St. Simons Island, ships loaded with deerskins and sassafras introduced American products to Europe. Here pirates lurked in inlets, lying in wait for Spanish treasure galleons. These Golden Isles were in the heart of the old Spanish Main.

Soon after General James Oglethorpe established his colony at Savannah in 1733—a challenge to Spanish domain—he constructed several coastal forts, the major one, strategically located Fort Frederica on St. Simons Island, as a buffer against the Spanish in Florida. The defenses of the citadel and barracks were substantially improved and the town was enclosed by a ten-foot earth and timber wall and a moat, now overgrown with giant trees. The founders of Methodism, John and Charles Wesley, first preached under the moss-hung oaks where Christ Church now stands.

The War of Jenkins' Ear began in 1739 over a Spanish sea captain's insistence on the "right of search" of English trading vessels suspected of engaging in smuggling. The Battle of Bloody Marsh, fought on St. Simons Island in 1742, was the first decisive battle in the New World, undertaken by the governor of Florida as a reprisal for Oglethorpe's attack on St. Augustine in 1740. The Spanish withdrawal ended the last military attempt to dislodge the British from this area, which soon came to be regarded as neutral ground. Fort Frederica lost its importance and by 1754 was in ruins, the twenty cannon on its walls dismounted and useless.

How to reach: St. Simons Island, twelve miles from Brunswick, Ga., may be reached by the Brunswick-St. Simons Highway (toll bridge) or by the inland waterway.

Midway Church

MIDWAY, GA.

THE MIDWAY CHURCH and Society was founded here in 1754 by descendants of Puritans who migrated here from Dorchester, Mass. The present church was built in 1792 and remains essentially unchanged. From this congregation came two signers of the Declaration of Independence, Dr. Lyman Hall and Button Gwinnett, and among its preachers were Abiel Holmes, father of Oliver Wendell Holmes, and Jedidah Morse, father of Samuel F. B. Morse. Sherman's cavalry camped here during the Civil War, stabling their horses in the churchyard and using the melodeon as a meat block.

How to reach: Via U. S. Route 17.
Open: Daily. Key may be obtained from nearby filling station.
Admission: Free.
Administration: Midway Museum, Inc.

Ivy Green

BIRTHPLACE OF HELEN KELLER

TUSCUMBIA, ALA.

HERE on a beautiful ten-acre estate was born America's First Lady of Courage, one of the most remarkable women in our time. Helen Keller, though a normal child at birth, lost both her sight and hearing at two. She first learned the meaning of words when she was seven years old. Her teacher, Miss Anne Sullivan from Boston, took her to the garden pump, pumped the water over the child's hand and spelled the word "water" into the other. The story of how she overcame her major handicaps and traveled all over the world, bringing inspiration and hope to millions of handicapped persons, is a famous one.

Though I have met Miss Keller on many occasions and sat next to her at dinner on many others, twice at the White House, I am never conscious of her disability. Her thoughtful sincerity leaves you completely dumfounded when you realize the obstacles she has had to face since about 1880. I recall one dinner party at my parents' home in Newport at which a distinguished admiral beside whom she sat had not caught her name and did not seem to realize her condition. He became rather perturbed at the length of time it took her to reply to one of his more profound questions. Miss Keller's companion, who was sitting on her other side, finally broke into the conversation. "She says, Admiral, that she may be dumb but she isn't stupid." The distinguished naval gentleman was evidently ruffled by the reply, but later on, after learning who Miss Keller was, he went up to her with tears in his eyes and humbly asked her to forgive him.

The main house of Ivy Green plantation, built by Miss Keller's grandfather in 1820, has a large porch and square rooms with individual fireplaces. The name comes from the English ivy which grew in abundance all over the plantation's buildings and fences. The nearby office became an annex by the addition of a dressing room and porch; it served as a bridal suite for Miss Keller's parents. The slave quarters on the grounds include a bedroom and a kitchen with a large open fireplace.

How to reach: West of Routes 72 and 43. G300 North Common.
Open: Weekdays, 8:00 A.M. to 5:00 P.M.; Sundays, 1:00 P.M. to 5:00 P.M.
Admission: 50¢. Guide service available.
Administration: Helen Keller Property Board and the State of Alabama.

Rosemount Mansion

FORKLAND, ALA.

The Bride's Room. The small spindle-back chairs were called "gossip chairs" because the women could quickly get about the room with them.

"THE GRAND MANSION OF ALABAMA" was built in 1830 atop a star-shaped hill near Forkland, a beautiful example of Greek Revival architecture. The cupola surmounting the twenty-room mansion has been called by some architects the prize of all cupolas in the South. Built by Williamson Allen Glover, cotton planter and shipping master, the house remained in the family for 116 years.

How to reach: Via Routes 43 and 11.
Open: Daily, 8:00 A.M. to 6:00 P.M.
Admission: 50¢.
Administration: Mrs. E. F. de Vesci, owner.

Arlington Historical Shrine

BIRMINGHAM, ALA.

BUILT in 1842 by William S. Mudd, a young lawyer who later became a judge, this house was completed thirty years before Birmingham was founded. It is restored and preserved as a typical antebellum home. In 1865 the Union General James H. Wilson made his headquarters here. It contains period furniture—Empire, Victorian, Early American. Now owned by the City of Birmingham, it is operated by the Arlington Historical Association.

How to reach: U. S. Route 11. 331 Cotton Avenue, S. W.
Open: Daily, 9:00 A.M. to 5:00 P.M.
Admission: 50¢; children, 25¢.
Administration: The Arlington Historical Association.

Living room. It is furnished with authentic pieces of the period: antique Waterford chandelier; rosewood piano which belonged to a governor of Alabama; a Chippendale mirror (1779); a French porcelain mantel clock and candelabra and an early oil painting.

Arlington Historical Shrine.

Dining room.

Old St. Augustine

Oldest City in the Country

ST. AUGUSTINE, FLA.

THERE is no city in America quite so old-world Spanish and no city so old. Yet it is very much a living city at the same time that its origin and a good deal of its history are visible as one walks along its narrow streets and looks at its walls, its gates, its fortress, its moat with a medieval torture chamber, its old houses and oldest schoolhouse. Architecturally, it is a storehouse of interesting detail. Historically, it makes us aware of our ties with Europe and gives us a sense of the continuity of our living history.

It was an established town fifty-five years before the Pilgrims landed on Plymouth Rock and forty-two years before the English settled Jamestown. By the time of the American Revolution it was 210 years old. It was a possession of the Spanish, the British and again the Spanish before it became part of the United States. It has survived numerous battles and wars by the fighting men of our countries.

The harbor here was visited by the Spanish explorer, Juan Ponce de León, April 3 to 8, 1513. It was on its shore that he first landed in his search for the fabled Fountain of Youth. Here he took possession for the Spanish monarchy and named the land he had discovered "La Florida." This was the first formal possession taken for a European nation of any part of the North American Continent.

The city of St. Augustine was founded September 8, 1565, by Pedro Menéndez de Avilés, captain-general of the Spanish Armada of the Indies. The ancient Spanish part of the city is located on a narrow peninsula formed by Matanzas Bay and the San Sebastian River. It is bounded on the north by Castillo de San Marcos and the City Gates (the only land entrance during colonial times); on the east by the bay; on the south by St. Francis Street and on the west by Córdova Street—an area approximately one mile long and less than a half-mile wide.

The earliest form of architecture was a crude frame of tree branches thatched on walls and roof with fronds of the saw palmetto. Next came the wooden buildings with a red cedar frame, cypress siding and roof of cypress slabs. A form of Spanish *tapia* (Anglicized, "tabby") was of early introduction. Called *ostion* by the Spaniards, this consisted of a mixture of oyster shells, shell lime and sand pounded into a wooden form. With the discovery of large deposits of coquina, a rock composed of broken sea shells and sand, on Anastasia Island, east of the city, this material was used in the construction of the Castillo de San Marcos, begun in 1672, and other public works, as well

The "Oldest House."

as in private residences. A typical feature was the semicircular arch.

Many buildings of Spanish colonial architecture remain, and can be classified in three periods: First Spanish (1565-1763), First Spanish as modified or added to by the English (1763-1783) and Second Spanish (1783-1821). Most notable are:

GERONIMO ALVAREZ "OLDEST HOUSE"

Built in the First Spanish period, extensive additions were made during the English period. It was the residence of Geronimo Alvarez, first *Alcalde Mayor*

The oldest wooden schoolhouse.

The Spanish governor's mansion.

under the Spanish Constitution of 1812. It contains a miscellaneous collection of Spanish and United States colonial period furniture.

———

How to reach: Via U. S. Route 1. 14 St. Francis Street.
Open: Daily, 9:00 A.M. to 6:00 P.M.
Admission: 50¢. Guide service is available. Admission fee includes admission to museums and library in adjoining buildings.
Administration: St. Augustine Historical Society.

THE OLDEST WOODEN SCHOOLHOUSE

This was built in the First Spanish period (1565-1763), but the exact year is not known. During the Spanish-English period (1763-1783) a school was established here and it continued in use as a schoolhouse until 1864. The schoolroom is furnished with colonial period wooden benches, schoolmaster's desk, globes, slates, inkwells, etc. Mannequins dressed in costumes of 1864 represent the last class. The upper room is furnished as a bedroom, and a detached kitchen in the rear contains many implements of the colonial period. With the exception of repairs to the roof, few changes have been made in the original structure.

———

How to reach: 14 St. George Street.
Open: Daily, 8:00 A.M. to 5:00 P.M.
Admission: 50¢. Guide service is available.
Administration: St. Augustine Historical Society.

THE SPANISH GOVERNOR'S MANSION

Built in 1680 by the Spanish governor Don Pablo de Hita y Salazar, who built the walls of Castillo de San Marcos, it was occupied by him and his descendants until 1763. At 37 St. George Street, the structure has been restored to its original condition, but is not yet open to the public.

OLD SPANISH TREASURY

This structure was built in 1690 with a coquina first story and a wood second story, which was rebuilt by

Patio of the old Spanish Treasury.

*The Old Curiosity Shop. Built 1813-52 as a residence, it was pre-
served by the St. Augustine Historical Society and has been
leased as an antique shop.*

Dr. Seth Peck about 1812. Its strong room contains a collection of Spanish coins. One room is occupied as a salesroom of the Women's Exchange. The remainder of the building is furnished with authentic furniture of the Dr. Peck period.

Besides these buildings and the Castillo (described separately), there are many others. In addition, the Slave Market and the City Gates are well worth visiting.

How to reach: 143 St. George Street.
Open: Weekdays, 9:00 A.M. to 5:00 P.M.
Admission: 25¢. Guide service is available.
Administration: The Women's Exchange. The building is owned by the City of St. Augustine.

*The Prince Marat House, built about 1790, became famous as the
home of Prince Achille Murat, nephew of Napoleon and son of
the King of Naples.*

Castillo de San Marcos
THE OLDEST MASONRY FORT
IN THE COUNTRY

STANDING on the waterfront at the northern end of the old Spanish part of the city, Castillo de San Marcos is the finest example of Spanish colonial fortification in the United States. Built of coquina, with walls from nine to sixteen feet thick and surrounded by a water-filled moat forty feet wide, its only entrance was across a drawbridge protected by a ravelin.

Construction of the Castillo was initiated in 1672, but it was not until 1693 that the seventeenth-century part was completed. Besieged three times by the English, under James Moore, governor of Carolina in 1702, under Colonel Palmer in 1728 and under General James Oglethorpe in 1740, the Castillo was never taken.

During the Second Seminole Indian War two Indian leaders, Osceola and Coacooche, were imprisoned here, the latter making his escape in 1837. Except for a short Confederate occupation, during the Civil War, the Castillo remained a prison. Here, during the 1880's, Geronimo's band of Apaches was confined. Among them, Captain R. H. Pratt conducted his experiments which later led to his founding of Carlisle Indian School. The Spanish-American War period marked the last active military use of the fort, when about 150 court-martialed American soldiers were confined here. The Castillo is now a national monument.

How to reach: Via U. S. Route 1.
Open: Daily, 8:30 A.M. to 5:30 P.M.
Admission: Nominal; children and educational groups, free.
Administration: National Park Service.

The great house of Vizcaya seen from the top of the water stairway.

Vizcaya

Palace of a Merchant Prince

MIAMI, FLA.

IN EXTREME contrast to old St. Augustine is Vizcaya, which is unique in America. Of the many palaces built by the merchant princes of America, none has the taste or the grandeur of this one. It stands in a setting of wild orchids, roses and tropical trees, of acres of carved marble, coral and ornamental stonework. It was left by its builder, James Deering, a bachelor, to his nieces and nephews, two of whom have made it available to the public by transferring the property to Dade County, which administers the estate as the Dade County Art Museum.

I attended school in Florida when Vizcaya was being built, and together with Deering's nephew, who was a classmate, I used to bicycle to the estate and watch the construction. I recall that artisans and workmen

The Marie Antoinette Salon.

were imported from all over the country, and young Deering told me that his uncle had bought the roofs of dozens of Cuban houses because the color of their tiles was exactly what he wanted.

Vizcaya was the home of the late James Deering from Christmas Day, 1916, until his death in 1925. It is a sixteenth-century palace, Italian in style and spirit, designed and built under his supervision. It houses an art collection of extraordinary interest and value.

The gardens are Italian, formal in treatment and unduplicated in America. With the palazzo at one end and a small casino on a mound at the other, they are conceived as a vast room walled in with formally arranged gardens and forests, an arrangement of flower beds and plots, trimmed with borders and paths which are flanked by statues and fountains. At one end of the gardens is the sea wall.

James Deering, born in South Paris, Maine, was the son of the inventor of the harvesting machine and became a major stockholder and vice-president of the International Harvester Machine Company. After his retirement in 1919 he devoted himself to travel and artistic and philanthropic interests. For some twenty years before he began building Vizcaya, he started collecting the art which went into it and planning the design of the palace. To him as well as to his architects, F. Burrall Hoffman, Jr., and Paul Chalfin, go the credit for the perfection of the details of every part of the palace and the gardens.

How to reach: Via U. S. Routes 27 and 41. 3251 S. Miami Avenue.
Open: Daily except Christmas Day, 10:00 A.M. to 5:00 P.M.
Admission: $1.75; students, $1.00; children under 12, 50¢. Guide service available for school groups.
Administration: Dade County Art Museum.

The tea room. The legends on the wall panels, from the Iliad, *show the sack and destruction of Troy.*

The Putnam House

MARIETTA, OHIO

THE FIRST settlement in Ohio was established at Marietta in 1788, when General Rufus Putnam and a group of pioneer settlers erected the fortification called Campus Martius. A section of this fortification, which housed fifty to sixty families, was the Rufus Putnam House, in which General Putnam and his family lived from 1788 to 1824, when he died.

This house was purchased by the State of Ohio in 1918 and is now enclosed in a wing of the Campus Martius Museum. It is furnished as it might have been prior to 1830. The Ohio Company Land Office, originally built in 1788, is also part of the museum, having been acquired by the state and moved to the present site in 1953.

How to reach: One block west of Routes 77 and 21. Second and Washington Streets.
Open: March 1 to November 1, weekdays, 9:00 A.M. to 5:00 P.M. November 2 through February, weekdays, 9:00 A.M. to 5:00 P.M.; Sundays, 1:00 P.M. to 5:00 P.M.
Admission: Free.
Administration: Ohio State Historical Society.

U. S. Grant Birthplace

POINT PLEASANT, OHIO

ULYSSES SIMPSON GRANT, christened "Hiram Ulysses" but given the former name by the Congressman who appointed him to West Point, was born in 1822 in a small bedroom off the living room-kitchen of this small house. The birthplace of the tanner's son who was to become the leader of the Union armies and the eighteenth President of the United States was restored to its original site in 1936. Many personal effects of the Grant family are on display. The furniture is of the period around 1822.

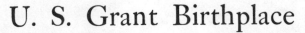

How to reach: On U. S. Route 52, Ohio River Drive.
Open: April 1 to October 31, daily except Mondays, 9:00 A.M. to 5:00 P.M. November 1 to March 1, daily except Mondays, 1:00 P.M. to 5:00 P.M.
Admission: Free. Guide service is available.
Administration: Ohio State Historical Society.

Thomas Edison Birthplace

MILAN, OHIO

THOMAS ALVA EDISON was born in this house February 11, 1847. It contains personal and family mementos, furniture of the period, including a rope bed, a "thousand-shell" design bedspread, spinning wheel and highchair. Models of some of Edison's inventions may be seen, the original phonograph and one of the original electric lights, the latter surrounded by a collection of its ancestors, including a rare "time lamp."

How to reach: At the intersection of Routes 250 and 113.
Open: Tuesday through Saturday, 9:00 A.M. to 5:00 P.M.; Sundays, 1:00 P.M. to 5:00 P.M. Closed during December.
Admission: 50¢; children, 25¢. Guide service is available.
Administration: Edison Birthplace Association, Inc.

Adena

CHILLICOTHE, OHIO

THIS was the home of one of Ohio's great statesmen, Thomas Worthington, one of the first two U. S. Senators from Ohio, later governor for three terms. It was built 1806-07 from plans drawn by the famous Benjamin Henry Latrobe. Originally the home was called Mount Prospect Hall, but later Worthington changed it to Adena, which, he noted in his diary, in the Hebrew language "was given to places remarkable for the delightfulness of their situations." This was apt, for the beautiful stone house, with its handsome gardens, is situated on a hill overlooking the lovely Scioto Valley. The large two-story central building is flanked by two smaller attached wings. Among the many guests at Adena who figured in the nation's history were President Monroe, DeWitt Clinton, Tecumseh, Blue Jacket and Henry Clay. Adena has been authentically restored to its magnificent early nineteenth-century appearance.

How to reach: On U. S. Routes 23, 35 and 50. At the end of Allen Avenue.
Open: Daily except Mondays.
Admission: 50¢; children, 25¢. Guide service is available.
Administration: The Ohio Historical Society.

The east façade of Adena as it appears through one of the arches in the pleached allée.

The drawing room. The portrait of 23-year-old Thomas Worthington, painted in 1796, hangs over the mantel. The side chairs, attributed to Henry Connelly of Philadelphia, are mates to a pair in the Winterthur Museum.

Zoar Village State Memorial

A TYPICALLY UNIQUE RELIGIOUS COMMUNITY

ZOAR, OHIO

A corner of a room in the Number One House.

ZOAR, a cooperative settlement established by a religious group, was one of the most unusual villages in the country and yet, in a way, typical of the surprisingly many outwardly similar communities that flourished in nineteenth-century America. It was established by a group of 300 Separatists from Wurttemburg in Germany who came to the United States in 1817 to find religious freedom. Philadelphia Quakers helped them and financed their purchase of a 5,500-acre tract of land in Tuscarawas County, Ohio. There they erected their first shelters, called their village Zoar and planted their first crop on the land only recently vacated by Indians.

They had a difficult time, and decided that since their plan of private holding and cultivation of land did not work, they would have to resort to a cooperative system. All property and wealth were pooled and held by the Society of Separatists of Zoar. Each member was at the command of the Society and received his sustenance from it. Since there was a larger number of women than men, the women were drafted to work in the fields and shops. Furthermore, to ensure the availability of this female labor force, the men agreed to practice celibacy until the Society's mortgage was paid off. The system, the celibacy, hard work and thrift combined to achieve prosperity and in 1834 the mortgage was paid off and the policy of celibacy was abandoned.

Zoar was a community with equal rights for men and women, a simple direct religion based on an abiding belief in the Bible and in the second coming of Christ on earth. Life there was pleasant, marked by close ties, group activities and social events. Arts and crafts flourished and music was not only a natural accompaniment for daily tasks but a favorite for recreation. There were concerts, choir singing, orchestras, waltzes and keen discussions about Wagner.

Zoar was really a town in an apple orchard, for apple trees were planted everywhere—the Zoarites' fondness for and skill at gardening matched their love of music. The Zoar Garden was laid out with geometrical precision, symbolic of the New Jerusalem described in The Revelation, and contained many varieties of exotic plants.

Until 1853 the Society was truly prosperous. By that time its membership was 500 and its assets were valued at more than $1,000,000. But after 1853 Zoar declined and in 1898 the community was dissolved.

The Ohio Historical Society maintains Zoar's *Number One House* as a museum of the Zoarites and has custody of the community garden.

How to reach: Ohio Route 212.
Open: April 1 to October 31.
Admission: Number One House, 25¢. Museum, free. Guide service is available.
Administration: Ohio Historical Society.

The Zoar garden.

Schoenbrunn Village

NEW PHILADELPHIA, OHIO

SCHOENBRUNN was the first town established by white men in what is now Ohio. It was built in 1772 by two Moravian missionaries, David Zeisberger and John Heckewelder, and over 200 Indians who had converted to Christianity. During the Revolution it was a buffer between the English at Fort Detroit and the Americans at Fort Pitt. But in 1777 the town was abandoned and almost lost to history, when in 1927 the Ohio Historical Society started restoration of the village and its thirteen log buildings, including eleven cabins, a trading post, church and schoolhouse.

How to reach: Via State Route 16 and U. S. Route 250.
Open: Daily.
Admission: Free. Guide service is available to large groups by prior arrangement.
Administration: Ohio Historical Society.

The Pioneer Home

DAYTON, OHIO

THE PIONEER HOME, built around 1815, was originally located several miles south of Dayton. In 1953 it was torn down, moved to Carillon Park and rebuilt, using the original stones and timbers. It is now used as an information center for the Park. The Deeds Carillon in Carillon Park is, I think, with the possible exception of the Bok Singing Tower in Florida, the most perfect example of a true carillon in the United States. Since it has no special historical significance, it is not treated in this book, but I do want to mention that, in connection with it, there is a living museum park containing unique historical exhibits, some of them outdoors and most relating to the history of transportation.

How to reach: Via U. S. Route 25. On South Patterson Boulevard.
Open: May 1 to October 31, Tuesday through Saturday, 10:00 A.M. to one hour after sundown; Sundays, 1:00 P.M to one hour after sundown.
Admission: Free.
Administration: Educational and Musical Arts, Inc.

Hawthorn Hill, Home of Orville Wright

DAYTON, OHIO

Hawthorn Hill.

LOCATED in the Oakwood suburb of Dayton, this home was completed in 1912 shortly after the death of Wilbur Wright, one of the two brothers who made the historic flight at Kitty Hawk. Following Orville Wright's death in 1948, it was acquired by the National Cash Register Company for use as a guest house. Only the library remains exactly as it appeared when Mr. Wright lived there.

Rubicon Homestead, the Patterson Memorial

DAYTON, OHIO

RUBICON HOMESTEAD, restored in 1939 and presented in 1953 to the City of Dayton as the Patterson Memorial Center, was built in 1816 by Colonel Robert Patterson, famed Indian fighter, founder of Lexington, Kentucky, and one of the original owners of the site of Cincinnati. John H. Patterson, grandson of Colonel Robert and founder of the National Cash Register Company, was born here. For more than fifty years it was the center of social and cultural life in the Miami Valley. At present there are no regularly scheduled visiting hours.

Patterson Memorial Center.

Sitting room of the Patterson Memorial Center.

Territorial Capitol

VINCENNES, IND.

FROM 1800 to 1813 this frame building, with its stoop porch and green shutters, was the seat of government of the vast Indiana Territory, created by Congress out of the Northwest Territory. It was also the capitol of the District of Louisiana in 1804-05. Except for the national capitol at Washington, no other building has been the governing place of so vast a territory.

A governor and three territorial judges sat at the odd-shaped walnut table in the legislative hall on the upper floor. Here laws were signed for the area which now includes Indiana, Illinois, Michigan, Wisconsin and that part of Minnesota which lies east of the Mississippi. In the governor's office, first occupied by William Henry Harrison, still stands the desk of General John Gibson, secretary of the Territory, equipped with quill pens and candles. In 1813 the Hoosier capital was moved to Corydon, Indiana, which was nearer the center of population.

Restored by the Fortnightly Club of Vincennes in 1933, the Territorial Capitol was moved to the present site in 1949 by the Indiana Department of Conservation and reopened the following year.

How to reach: On U. S. Routes 41 and 50. On North First Street.
Open: Daily, 9:00 A.M. to 5:00 P.M.
Admission: 10¢.
Administration: Indiana Department of Conservation.

Harrison ("Tippecanoe") Mansion

WILLIAM HENRY HARRISON—who was to become the ninth President of the United States in 1841—built this stately home, known as "Grouseland" and also "The White House of the West," in 1804 when he came to Vincennes as the young Governor of the newly formed Indiana Territory. Son of Benjamin Harrison of Berkeley Plantation in Virginia, the first governor of the unexplored Northwest Territory, William Henry had made a reputation in the West under General Anthony Wayne as an Indian fighter and negotiator of treaties. The Council Chamber of the Mansion was the scene of many meetings with Indian tribes and official functions.

The foundations are of stone and the bricks were made in the vicinity. A closet reveals secret access from the rear building, connected by a covered passage, which includes a kitchen, wine room and powder magazine. Near the house is a well to furnish water in case of siege. Originally the front of the house had six false windows, indicated by shutters, but four were cut through.

After the battle in 1811 that earned Harrison his famous nickname at Tippecanoe, he moved his family back to North Bend, Ohio, where he continued his political life. His eldest son lived in Grouseland for some years, after which it was used as a granary and a hotel. About 1909 the old house was saved from destruction by the D. A. R. chapter. A careful restoration was undertaken in 1949.

How to reach: At 3 West Scott Street "under the water tower."
Open: Weekdays, 9:30 A.M. to 5:00 P.M.; Sundays, 12:00 M. to 5:00 P.M.
Admission: Free.
Administration: Francis Vigo chapter, D. A. R.

Council Chamber of the Harrison Mansion.

Lincoln Pioneer Village

ROCKPORT, IND.

Judge John Pitcher law office.

The Lanier Home

MADISON, IND.

I'VE ALWAYS been fascinated by the spiral stairway in the old Lanier mansion, which was a palace in its day (built in 1844) and still is a handsome home. James F. D. Lanier was a pioneer financier. He helped Indiana through the difficult days of the Civil War with a loan, of the then enormous sum of $1,000,000, through his New York banking house. The mansion is now the J.F.D. Lanier State Memorial.

How to reach: On U. S. Route 421, State Routes 7, 56, 62. At 500 West First Street.
Open: Daily, 9:00 A.M. to 4:30 P.M.
Admission: 25¢; children, 10¢.
Administration: Indiana Department of Conservation.

ABRAHAM LINCOLN spent fourteen of his formative years in Spencer County, Ind. During the years 1935-37 the Spencer County Historical Society and the Rockport City Board, in association with the W.P.A. of the federal government, created this village of replicas as a memorial to Lincoln and his pioneer neighbors and friends. Besides the *Judge John Pitcher law office,* to which Lincoln walked twenty-two miles from his home to borrow a book, there are the *Jones Store,* where Lincoln was a clerk; the *Grigsby Home* (Sarah, Abe's sister, married Aaron Grigsby); the *Pioneer Schoolhouse;* the *Lincoln Homestead* and many other replicas.

How to reach: On State Route 66. In City Park.
Open: Daily, 7:00 A.M. to 5:00 P.M.
Admission: 50¢; children, 25¢.
Administration: Lincoln Pioneer Village.

James Whitcomb Riley Birthplace

GREENFIELD, IND.

THE HOOSIER poet was born in this eight-room frame house, built by his father in 1849, and spent his boyhood years here. Many of Riley's poems refer to parts of this house, for example, "the rafter room, cubby hole and press" from "Little Orphan Annie."

How to reach: On U. S. Route 40. 238 West Main Street.
Open: May 1 to November 1, weekdays, 9:00 A.M. to 4:00 P.M.; Sundays, 1:00 P.M. to 5:00 P.M.
Admission: 25¢; children, 10¢. Hostess guides available.
Administration: Riley Old Home Society.

A corner of the library.

The drawing room, where Riley entertained friends and famous visitors.

The Lockerbie Street Home of
James Whitcomb Riley

INDIANAPOLIS, IND.

THIS HOME, in which Riley lived for thirty-five years and wrote many of his best works, was purchased immediately after his death in 1916 and was retained exactly as it was. It is not a restoration, it is an essentially exact preservation. I show these views of an Indiana home of the late nineteenth and early twentieth centuries as documents of a way of life. This is how it actually was under the Victorian influence. James Whitcomb Riley was never married.

The hallway.

How to reach: Via U. S. Routes 36, 40 and 52. 528 Lockerbie Street.
Open: Daily except Mondays, 10:00 A.M. to 4:00 P.M.
Admission: 25¢; children accompanied by adults, free.
Administration: James Whitcomb Riley Memorial Association.

The bedroom, where the poet died.

The old fort.

Dormitory Number Two.

New Harmony
Scene of
Two Utopian Ventures
NEW HARMONY, IND.

NEW HARMONY, a cooperative community, was founded in 1814 by George Rapp and his associates, religious zealots searching for religious freedom. They built their church in 1816, in the form of a Maltese cross. They were originally from Wurttemberg, Germany, but had spent some time in Pennsylvania. They believed in the immediate millennium, lived as the early Christians and practiced celibacy. They had separate dormitories for men and women. Number Two was for men. The Rappites, intelligent, industrious and frugal, were prosperous. Their industries ranged from distilling whiskey to manufacturing textiles. To protect themselves in the rough country they built a fort.

In 1824 the Rappites, needing eastern markets, sold their town to Robert Owen, industrialist and philanthropist, who wanted it for his "Community of Equality," another Utopian experiment by which Universal Education would achieve Universal Happiness. Among the principles of the followers of Owen were community of property, acquisition of knowledge, courtesy in all encounters. Owen established a scientific laboratory which became the center of scientific and educational pursuits of the developing West. While the Owen community did not last long, it had considerable impact and influence on the culture of

its area. It was among the earliest in America, and possibly the first, to establish a kindergarten, trade school, geological survey and other advances.

Some of the buildings belong to the State of Indiana, which is considering reorganization and reactivation of its New Harmony Historical Commission to restore the village. Among the notable New Harmony houses are the *Workingmen's Institute*, a *Museum* and the *Old Fauntleroy Home*, once occupied by Robert Owen.

How to reach: On U. S. Route 460.
Open: Old Fauntleroy Home, June 1 to November 1, daily, 10:00
    A.M. to 4:30 P.M.
Admission: 25¢.
Administration: The Golden Rain Tree Association and the
    State of Indiana.

Original door of Rappite church.

Greenfield Village

The Henry Ford Museum

DEARBORN, MICH.

THE RESTORATIONS in Greenfield Village preserve the physical surroundings in which American customs and institutions developed. "When we are through," Henry Ford said, "we shall have reproduced American life as lived; and that, I think, is the best way of preserving at least a part of our history and tradition. . . ."

The *Henry Ford Museum*, with Greenfield Village, presents a graphic history of the growth of agriculture, manufacturing and transportation in this country. The name "Greenfield" was for a township near Dearborn where Mrs. Henry Ford spent her girlhood. The buildings, forty-four in all, are from many parts of the United States. There is an old mill which still grinds grain into flour, a blacksmith who still shoes horses and a stern-wheeler which paddles up the Suwanee River. Only horse-drawn carriages are allowed on the streets where the houses of Luther Burbank, Noah Webster and William Holmes McGuffey now are. Most of the shops, mills and handicrafts industries are on the Main Street. Across from the gristmill is the 58 Bagley Avenue Ford workshop, the birthplace of the first Ford car finished in 1896, complete with the first Ford car.

SHOPS AND MILLS

Village Print Shop and Bookbindery, example of small print shop in early America.

Loranger Gristmill, pioneer Michigan grist and sawmill, built about 1832. Flour ground by old buhrstone method.

Edsel Ford Building, with playthings and tools of Edsel Ford as a boy.

Armington & Sims Machine Shop.

Hanks Silk Mill, from Mansfield, Conn., built in 1810.

Plymouth Carding Mill, showing two hundred years of the history of weaving, from handloom to power loom, from hand-knitter to automatic loom.

Blacksmith Shop, complete with bellows, forge, anvil, hammers, ox-sling, in the shade of a chestnut tree.

Kingston Cooper Shop, built in Kingston, N. H., in 1785. Oldest American craft shop in Greenfield Village.

Currier Shoe Shop. William Currier, shoemaker of Newton, N. H., worked in this building in the 1890's.

Toll House Shoe Shop, built 1828 on the Merrimack River beside a covered bridge linking Rocks Village and West Newbury, Mass. The first toll collector made shoes as a sideline and the majority of his successors followed the practice.

Tintype Studio, built in Greenfield Village to represent tintype studios common in larger communities between 1880-90. Visitors may have tintypes made here.

Post Office and Apothecary Shop, built in Phoenixville, Conn., in 1803. The oldest registered post office in operation

Birthplace of the Ford— 58 Bagley Avenue. Replica of the little red shed in which Henry Ford began to build his first automobile, which was completed in 1896. It was made of bicycle wheels, plumbing pipe and other oddities. The shed originally stood behind the Ford home in Detroit.

Wright Homestead and Cycle Shop.

today. The apothecary shop is equipped with shelves of drugs, liquors, tonics, elixirs for medicinal purposes; case of drawers filled with herbs; jar for leeches.

Four clock and watchmaking shops: *Sir John Bennett Jewelry Shop,* exact reproduction of the building at 65 Cheapside Street, London. The oldest clock in the shop was made in 1630. The Gog and Magog clock above the doorway announces the time to the Village on the quarter-hour. *Grimm Jewelry Store,* first jewelry shop on Michigan Avenue, Detroit, opened in 1878 by Englebert Grimm. Young Henry Ford often stopped here to chat with the owner or to buy parts to repair watches. *Magill Jewelry Shop,* from 444 Baker Street, Detroit, where Henry Ford worked as a boy of sixteen in the back workroom, cleaning and repairing watches at a salary of fifty cents for four hours' work at night. *Swiss Watchmakers' Chalet,* typical of those in the Neuchatel district of the Jura Mountains in Switzerland.

Wright Brothers' Cycle Shop, originally in Dayton, Ohio, where the brothers built bicycles and produced the motor and parts of the first successful airplane. Much of the original machinery was found and put in its proper place in the shop with the assistance of Orville Wright. The wind tunnel was reconstructed.

AROUND THE GREEN

The public buildings are on the Green as they were in early American communities:

The *General Store,* a white frame building built in 1854, the principal store of Waterford, Mich., with original counters, spice and coffee grinders, cracker barrels, hoop skirts, slates, comic valentines, etc.

Clinton Inn, from Clinton, Mich., where it stood a century ago on the great Sauk Indian Trail.

Herb Garden, thirteenth-century herb garden beyond the Inn, an expression of the late Mrs. Henry Ford's interest in herb gardening.

The *Martha-Mary Chapel,* named for the mothers of the late Mr. and Mrs. Ford.

Scotch Settlement School, originally in a community near Dearborn, used today, furnished as it was eighty years ago.

Logan County Courthouse, from Postville, Ill., built 1840.

As a young man Abraham Lincoln occasionally practiced law in this building. The first floor, which was used as a courtroom, is furnished with several pieces of Lincoln furniture, an original corner cupboard made by young Abe and his father; Lincoln's wardrobe; a table from one of his law offices; chairs and other pieces from his Springfield home, as well as the chair in which he sat in the theatre the night he was assassinated.

Slave Huts, from the Hermitage Plantation near Savannah, Ga.

Town Hall, typical of many town meeting places of the nineteenth century.

HOMES OF THE VILLAGE

Most of the houses are furnished. Some are the birth-places of famous Americans, which have been moved to Greenfield Village; others were brought here as examples of American architecture at different periods.

George Washington Carver Memorial, cabin built in honor of the famous scientist.

Mattox House, originally a cottage at Richmond Hill, Ga., used in the days of slavery.

Suwanee. A typical paddle-wheel river boat on a miniature Suwanee River near the site of the Stephen Foster Memorial in Greenfield Village.

William Holmes McGuffey Birthplace, originally in Washington County, Pa., furnished with McGuffey furniture.

McGuffey School, constructed of logs from the farm where the birthplace of the pioneer educator originally stood.

Chapman House, home of John Brainer Chapman, one of Henry Ford's elementary school teachers, formerly located on a wooded trail close to the Rouge River and the old Ann Arbor stagecoach route.

Adams House, home of a Baptist minister at Saline, Mich., shortly after the Civil War, and birthplace of George Matthew Adams, newspaper columnist.

Steinmetz Camp, summer camp built in 1896 by Charles Steinmetz on Viele Creek near Schenectady, N. Y., where he wrote his textbooks on electricity.

Stephen Foster Memorial House, on the banks of the Suwanee River, built 1830, in Lawrenceville, Pa., thought to be Foster's birthplace. Furnished with heirlooms of Foster family.

Birthplace of Luther Burbank, originally in Lancaster, Mass.

Ann Arbor House, fine example of Greek Revival architecture.

Edison Homestead, originally in Vienna, Western Ontario, Can., home of Thomas Edison's father and grandfather.

Secretary House, from Exeter, N. H., the home of the first Secretary of State of New Hampshire.

Noah Webster House, home of the great American lexicographer, where Webster compiled his famous dictionary. This stood on the campus of Yale University from 1822 to 1937.

To trace the beginnings of the American home, cottages from the Cotswold in England have been brought to Greenfield Village to give some sense of

Cotswold or Rose Cottage.

our English forefathers' life in the first half of the seventeenth century. Most of the inhabitants of these cottages were sheep farmers; their houses were built largely of native sandstone and limestone:

Rose Cottage, with simple furniture of oak. Lighting from rush lamps and Betty lamps, leaded windows, kidney iron or spit, fireside settee from early 1600's.

The Barn, Dove Cote and *Cotswold Forge* are near the Rose Cottage.

Cape Cod Windmill, believed to be the oldest in America, resembles a Dutch windmill. It was built by the Pilgrims, who had spent some years in Holland before coming to the New World.

Logan County Courthouse.

Plympton House, the oldest of the American homes in Greenfield Village, was built in Sudbury, Mass., by Thomas Plympton, who was killed by Indians in 1676.

Susquehanna House, with its dormers and wide verandas, built in 1652 in southern Maryland at the mouth of the Patuxent River, where it stood for nearly three hundred years.

Other houses, not in the residential district of Greenfield Village, are:

Gardner House, typical home of Michigan pioneers, originally located near Dearborn.

Plymouth House, from Plymouth, Mich., representative of a modest midwestern home of the middle nineteenth century.

Wright Home, where Orville Wright was born in 1871 and where the Wright Brothers grew up, with some of the original furniture.

Henry Ford Birthplace, built on the dividing line between Dearborn and Springwells townships. Henry Ford was born in this house July 30, 1863. House, fence, barn and shed are arranged in their original positions.

MENLO PARK

The buildings at Menlo Park, N. J., where Thomas Edison made his brilliant discoveries, have been reconstructed or copied from the originals and have been placed in their original positions.

Little Glass House, first used as a photographic studio by Edison. This is the original building where the first successful lamp bulb was blown in 1879.

Machine Shop, the first central station for incandescent lighting in the world, houses the Edison dynamos, the original boiler for Menlo Park, the first electric light chandeliers and other relics.

Electric Railway, first of its kind in the United States, built by Edison in Menlo Park in 1880. The first run, with twenty passengers, was made that year. The original locomotive and reproductions of the two cars are on display.

Carpenter Shed and *Carbon Shed* adjoin the laboratory, the former, a distillation plant for manufacturing gas, the latter, a plant for making lampblack for use in the manu-

Cape Cod Windmill.

facture of telephone transmitters.

The *Laboratory,* which has been restored to its appearance in Edison's day, has many of the original instruments and apparatus, as well as models of many of his inventions, electric lighting system, first phonograph, microphone, telephone transmitter, etc.

Other Edison buildings include his laboratory from Fort Myers, Fla., his summer home; the Edison Homestead (mentioned above), the Smith's Creek Depot, the Edison Illuminating Company plant (where Henry Ford worked from 1891-1899 as an engineer for $40 a month) and Mrs. Sarah Jordan's boarding house, where several of Edison's workmen lived. Wires were run from the machine shop to the boarding house, which was the first house to be lighted by Edison's incandescent lamp.

Waterford General Store.

THE INDUSTRIAL SECTION

Behind the craft shops are the mills and shops typical of those in America after the industrial revolution:

Sandwich Glass Plant, with demonstrations of glass-blowing by hand.
Planing Mill, which provided doors, trim and woodwork for many Village buildings.
Sorghum Mill, reassembled from an old sugar mill in Louisiana.
Cotton Gin Mill, brought from Ways, Ga., and used before the Civil War.
Rice Mill, brought from Georgetown, S. C.
Circular Sawmill, used to cut lumber.
Cider Mill, which formerly operated every fall.

Others are the *Walking Beam Engine,* from Orange County, Va.; the *Spofford Sawmill,* built during the seventeenth century in Georgetown, Mass.; the *Mack Avenue Plant* from Detroit, a reproduction of the original building where the early Ford cars were assembled from 1903 to 1906; *Brick and Tile Works; Pottery Shop; Tripp Sawmill,* built in 1855 in Franklin Township, Mich.; and the *Macon Carriage Shop,* which stood after 1850 in Macon, Mich.

Also of special interest are:

The *Luther Burbank Office,* used by the famous horticulturist at his nursery in Santa Rosa, Calif., where Ford and Edison frequently visited him.
Deluge Fire House, the engine of which was built in 1845 for Rocks Village, Mass.
Owl Night Lunch Wagon, famous in Detroit around the turn of the century, and popular with late workers and newspapermen around the City Hall.
Ackley Covered Bridge, built in 1832 and brought from Wheeling Creek in Pennsylvania.
Steamer *Suwanee,* which is kept in operating condition and used by the children of the Greenfield Village schools, is anchored on the Suwanee River, on the banks of which stands the Stephen Foster Memorial House (described above).

How to reach: Near Detroit, Mich., via U. S. Route 112.
Open: Weekdays, 9:00 A.M. to 5:00 P.M.; weekends and holidays, 9:00 A.M. to 5:30 P.M. During July, 9:00 A.M. to 8:00 P.M.
Admission: Various fees, 85¢ to $1.50. Special rates for groups and students.
Administration: Henry Ford Museum and Greenfield Village.

Birthplace of Henry Ford—the Ford Homestead, a typical midwestern farm of the mid-1800's. This room, the Sunday Parlor, it furnished as it was in Ford's boyhood.

[161]

New Salem State Park
"The Lincoln Village"
NEAR PETERSBURG, ILL.

The Onstot Cooper Shop. An ash-hopper may be seen just to the left of the tree in the left foreground.

ON A HILL overlooking the Sangamon River valley stands the re-created village of New Salem. Here a tall young stranger from Kentucky, whose flatboat had been stranded on the town's grist-mill dam, first made the name of Abraham Lincoln immortal in the annals of the American nation. The six formative years he spent here, from 1831 to 1837, marked a turning point in his career; it was from New Salem that he was first elected to public office, as a representative in the Illinois legislature.

The rustic village, set among red-haws and wild crab trees, has been restored in authentic detail to its appearance in the early 1830's before its decline. A tavern, carding mill and wool house, blacksmith and shoemaker shops, a schoolhouse-church and thirteen simple log cabins, each with its ash-hopper for making lye soap, many of the houses furnished with articles used by the New Salem pioneers of Lincoln's time, give visitors to this beloved shrine a vivid impression of a thriving community. The collection includes wheat cradles, candle molds, flax shuttles, wool cards, wooden chests for dough and cornmeal, old pewter and earthenware. In the two doctors' offices are mortars and pestles, old medical texts and surgeons' instruments; in the cobbler's shop, awls and lasts; and on the store shelves, bolts of calico and jars of typical merchandise.

Here in the *Onstot Cooper Shop* (the only original building remaining) Lincoln studied lawbooks and literature by the light of a fire kindled by burning shavings. Here he clerked, sleeping in a back room or lean-to and boarding at a neighbor's, ventured—unsuccessfully—into storekeeping. Here he served as postmaster and deputy surveyor, drilled with fellow volunteers in the Black Hawk War. Here he met the tavernkeeper's daughter, Ann Rutledge, and the cousins of Herndon, who was to be his law partner in the Springfield days. The village the young legislator left in 1837 seems to live again as the visitor turns the bend in the footpath between the trees and strolls through the same rough streets.

The cornerstone of the first reconstructed building of the village, the *Lincoln-Berry Store,* was laid in November, 1932, by the State of Illinois, which had owned the area since 1918. The first step toward re-creating New Salem was taken by William Randolph Hearst, who had become interested in the preservation of the site while lecturing in nearby Petersburg. After acquiring it in 1906, he transferred it in trust to the Chatauqua Association. The Old Salem Lincoln League, which assembled many of the furnishings in the buildings, was formed in 1917 in Petersburg to carry on research and keep alive public interest in the vanished community.

How to reach: On State Routes 123 and 97.
Open: Daily, 8:00 A.M. to 5:00 P.M.
Admission: Free.
Administration: State of Illinois, Department of Conservation.

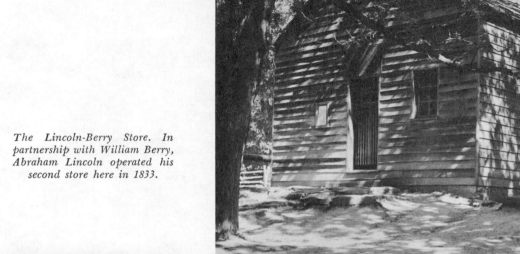

The Lincoln-Berry Store. In partnership with William Berry, Abraham Lincoln operated his second store here in 1833.

Interior view of Dr. Francis Regnier's office.

A view of the saw and grist mill showing the mill-dam where Lincoln was stranded.

The sitting room. The rocking chair at the far left was Mrs. Lincoln's, the small chair at the right was Tad's.

Abraham Lincoln's Home

The Lincoln Country

SPRINGFIELD, ILL.

SPRINGFIELD and the area round it is quite properly "Lincoln country." Abraham Lincoln lived in Springfield for many years. He practiced law here, was married here, and he was buried here, where his tomb at Oak Ridge Cemetery is now the Lincoln Tomb State Memorial.

Abraham Lincoln bought this home in 1844 from the Reverend Charles Dresser, the Episcopal rector who had married him and Mary Todd on November 4, 1842. Three of Lincoln's sons, including Thomas, "Tad," were born in this house. The Lincoln family occupied the home except for one year (1847-48) until February, 1861. It was in the north parlor that on May 19, 1860, Lincoln received the committee notifying him of his nomination for the presidency.

Lincoln and his heirs retained ownership until 1887 when Robert Todd Lincoln deeded the property to the State of Illinois. The property has been completely restored and the interior furnished to conform to pictures of the room shown in *Leslie's Weekly* in 1861.

How to reach: On U. S. Routes 66, 36 and 54.
Open: Daily, 9:00 A.M. to 5:00 P.M.
Admission: Free.
Administration: State of Illinois, Division of Parks and Memorials.

Two parlors. Photo taken from the back parlors, showing the first floor parlors on the north side of the house. It was here that Lincoln received the notification committee.

Ulysses S. Grant Home

GALENA, ILL.

THE PROUD citizens of Galena, Ill., presented a fine brick house, built in 1857, to ex-General Ulysses S. Grant at his triumphal homecoming celebration in 1865. Before the railroads came, this Mississippi River town, with its busy levee, was the metropolis of the lead and zinc mining industry of the area. I have often visited Grant's home on Bouthillier Street and have always been impressed by its famous occupant, who rose to great heights through his sincerity and courage. They say he never told a soldier to do anything he couldn't do himself.

Known as taciturn "Sam Grant" of Grant's Leather Store on Main Street (now restored to its appearance in 1860), he had left the town in 1861, an obscure drill-master of volunteers. After graduation from West Point at eighteen, he served fifteen years in the army. He failed as an auctioneer, as a bill-collector, even as a farmer in St. Louis. But he was to become the most successful general of the Civil War, Secretary of War

under Andrew Johnson and President of the United States for two terms. He was a familiar bearded figure, with an inevitable cigar, on the steep cobblestone streets of Galena when he returned here to live for two years after his trip around the world.

His son, Frederick Dent Grant, deeded the family home to the city in 1904 and Galena presented it to the State of Illinois in 1932. On display are the china and silver used in the White House, Grant's carriage, his favorite armchair, military trophies and world-tour souvenirs.

How to reach: On U. S. Highways 20 and 80.
Open: Daily, 9:00 A.M. to 5:00 P.M.
Admission: Free.
Administration: Illinois System of Parks and Memorials.
The *Grant Leather Store* on Main Street is open to visitors without charge daily from 1:00 P.M. to 5:00 P.M. from April 27 to November 1. It is administered by the Historic Shrines and Edifices Committee of the Galena Chamber of Commerce.

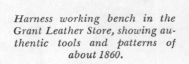

Harness working bench in the Grant Leather Store, showing authentic tools and patterns of about 1860.

Pendarvis
THE CORNISH RESTORATION
MINERAL POINT, WIS.

Pendarvis at left, Trelawny at right.

MINERAL POINT, in the heart of the old lead and zinc mining section, was Wisconsin's most important town in the 1830's. The need for help attracted men from all over, and while the lead and zinc rush was nothing like the later gold rush, the fever did reach Cornwall, England, where times were hard, and many Cornish miners migrated with their families to southwest Wisconsin to establish themselves as American miners. Here they established a sort of New Cornwall. They built their cottages and furnished them in Cornish style, retained their old traditions and gave their old way of life roots in the new country. A group of houses—called Polperro, Trelawny and Pendarvis—has been restored in the spirit of the original builders.

How to reach: Via Routes 23 and 39. Shake rag Street.
Open: Daily, May to November.
Admission: Free.
Administration: Pendarvis House.

(Below) *Polperro, third-floor bedroom.* (Right) *North side of Polperro, showing second-floor entrance from garden between Pendarvis and Polperro.*

Waelderhaus

KOHLER, WIS.

AN OLD-WORLD echo in sharp contrast to Pendarvis is this reproduction of the Austrian Alpine ancestral home of John Michael Kohler, erected as a memorial to him and presented to the Girl Scouts of Kohler by Marie Christine Kohler, the industrialist's daughter. Waelderhaus is a fabulous place, fascinating for its carvings, wrought-iron work, its unique architectural features and its quality of precision and orderliness. It was completed in 1931 and is situated on a wooded bluff near the Sheboygan River in the village of Kohler, which is itself a model village, carefully planned and ordered, being perhaps a reflection of the nature of its founder.

How to reach: Via U. S. Route 141, State Routes 23, 32, 42.
Open: Daily.
Admission: Free. Guide tours may be arranged.
Administration: Girl Scouts of Kohler Village.

The kitchen, showing the cooking area. An open fire may be built in the recess beneath the kettle.

[167]

Hallway on the second floor.

One of several Italian marble fireplaces in the Lincoln-Tallman House.

Lincoln-Tallman House

JANESVILLE, WIS.

ABRAHAM LINCOLN slept here, in 1859, and it is the only Wisconsin house in which he ever spent a night. Begun in 1855, it was completed in 1857 by William M. Tallman who had left his practice in New York to settle in Janesville. He was an abolitionist and this house was a station on the "Underground Railway." You can see the secret stairway for escaping slaves, their original benches, the signal window to summon them from the river.

Among other notable visitors to the Tallman home were his friends William H. Seward, Stephen Douglas and Cassius Clay. The home is an excellent restoration of the Civil War period and what I found most interesting was the wonderful firearms collection in the study.

———

How to reach: Via Routes 13 and 11. 440 North Jackson Street.
Open: May 15 to November 1, daily, 10:00 A.M. to 5:00 P.M.
Admission: 50¢; students, 25¢; children, 10¢. Guide service is available.
Administration: Rock County Historical Society.

Milton House

MILTON, WIS.

ANOTHER station on the "Underground" was Milton House, which is the oldest concrete building in the United States and one of the few hexagonal historic landmarks in the country. It was built in 1844 as an inn. Deeded in 1949 to the Milton Historical Society, it has been restored with the aid of state appropriations, private funds and donated labor.

———

How to reach: Just off State Routes 26 and 59.
Open: May to October, daily, 10:00 A.M. to 5:00 P.M.
Admission: 50¢; children, 10¢.
Administration: Milton Historical Society.

Kilbourntown House

MILWAUKEE, WIS.

BENJAMIN CHURCH, pioneer architect and contractor, built this Greek Revival house—remarkably like the George Eastman birthplace, now in Rochester—in 1844. It is one of the oldest in the area and has many unusual structural features. Work had already started on the demolition of the house on North Fourth Street, which had been condemned as unfit for habitation, when Frederic Heath, president of the Milwaukee Historical Society, and Alexander Guth arrived and persuaded the wrecking contractor to stop work. The Historical Society got permission to move the building to Estabrook Park. Then the work of restoration began, and through the help of the Colonial Dames of Wisconsin, it was furnished in keeping with its historical period.

How to reach: Via U. S. Routes 16, 18, 41. Enter parkway from Capitol Drive on Hampton Road.
Open: Memorial Day to Labor Day, Sundays, 2:00 P.M. to 5:00 P.M.
Admission: Free.
Administration: Milwaukee County Historical Society.

The Dewey Homestead

CASSVILLE, WIS.

STONEFIELD, the home of Wisconsin's first governor, now restored, is part of the Nelson Dewey State Park which contains also the first official state farm in the country. Built in 1860-70, the home and its outbuildings are in the Virginia plantation style, one of the few such farms in the midwest.

How to reach: On State Routes 133, 81.
Open: May to October, daily, 9:00 A.M. to 5:00 P.M.
Admission: 50¢; children, 10¢.
Administration: Wisconsin Conservation Department.

Grand Portage
National Historic Site

GRAND PORTAGE, MINN.

THE FIRST white settlement in Minnesota was at Grand Portage where the Northern Fur Company established a fort in 1778. Grand Portage is on Lake Superior just about at the point where the Pigeon River, the Canadian boundary line, empties into the Lake. Here supplies for the Northwest arriving from the Lake had to be transferred to canoes and sent westward via the connecting lakes or taken in other directions by voyageurs and traders. Here also trappers brought their furs for transport and sale to the East. For twenty-five years Grand Portage was the great trading center and meeting-place of the area. The village is almost entirely Indian, but the stockade and the main building, restored by the Minnesota Historical Society, is now a National Historic Site.

How to reach: Via U. S. Route 61.
Open: Summer, Tuesday-Saturday, 10:00 A.M. to 5:00 P.M. Sundays, 2:00 P.M. to 5:00 P.M.
Admission: Free.
Administration: National Park Service.

Fort Snelling

MINNEAPOLIS, MINN.

FORT SNELLING, one of the first United States military forts in the West and the northernmost for many years, was established in 1819 where the Minnesota River empties into the Mississippi, just south of Minneapolis. The fort is now a Veterans' Administration center, but its famous *Round Tower* has been preserved and contains a museum of Indian and military exhibits. It is open to visitors, by appointment.

Bedroom of Hoover birthplace.

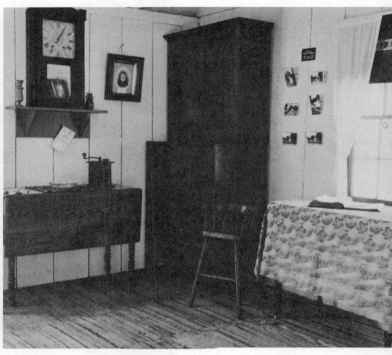

Kitchen-living room.

Herbert Hoover Birthplace

WEST BRANCH, IOWA

IN THIS small two-room cottage Herbert Clark Hoover—later to become the thirty-first President of the United States, and the first born west of the Mississippi—was born August 10, 1874. He was the second son of Jesse and Huldah Minthorn Hoover, both Quakers. While Jesse worked at his blacksmithing trade in an adjoining shop, Huldah, in addition to caring for her family, acted from time to time as minister of the West Branch Society of Friends. Hoover lived here until he was eleven when his uncle took him to Newburg, Oregon, to be educated there in the Quaker tradition.

There must have been thousands of little cottages just about like this all over the midwest in the latter part of the nineteenth century. Apart from its historic importance as the birthplace of a President, it has additional interest as a typical home, as typical for its time and place as the pioneer's log cabin was in its day.

How to reach: On State Route 1.
Open: Daily.
Admission: Free.
Administration: Herbert Hoover Birthplace Society, Inc.

Herbert Hoover Birthplace.

The Bolduc House, built before 1785.

Ste. Genevieve

Missouri's Oldest City

STE. GENEVIEVE, MO.

THE FIRST permanent settlement in Missouri was at Ste. Genevieve, founded by the French in 1735. Many of its old buildings still stand, some dating back to 1785, and one of them, the *Bolduc House,* even predates that year. 1784 was the year of the Great Flood when the overflow of the Mississippi was greater than ever known before—or since. The valley was one vast sea and the old town on the west bank of the river had to be abandoned. The town of Ste. Genevieve was re-established in Le Grand Champ, a large common field three miles away. The frame of the Bolduc House was salvaged, however, and moved to the new location. It can be seen today, still in a remarkable state of preservation. Among other old houses generally open to visitors are the first brick house west of the Mississippi, the *Valle House* (1785), the *Guibourd Home* (1784), the *Green Tree Tavern* (1790), the *Bantz House* (1800). A French-Indian trading post, built about 1790, is open from April to November from 11:00 A.M. to 5:00 P.M.

How to reach: Via U. S. Route 61.
Open: Various hours.
Admission: 10¢ generally.
Administration: Privately owned homes, advisory commission, Missouri Division of Resources and Development.

The oldest brick house in Ste. Genevieve, built 1785, which is claimed to be the first west of the Mississippi.

Mark Twain's Boyhood Home

HANNIBAL, MO.

The boyhood home of Samuel Clemens, later famous as Mark Twain.

THE YARNS and lore surrounding the man who knew so well how to captivate the hearts of young—and old—America still abound in this Mississippi River town. The flavor of Tom Sawyer's escapades with Huck Finn seems to linger about the whole locale and the simple white frame house with green shutters built by Samuel Clemens' father in 1844. Even the proverbial "white-washed fence" provides a reminiscent chuckle. Next door is a museum containing memorabilia of Mark Twain. It was in front of the old print shop on Main Street, where he worked as a printer's devil, that he found the page from *The Life of Joan of Arc* that started him on his career as a writer. Across the street from the Clemens home is the *Becky Thatcher House*, the home of pig-tailed Laura Hawkins. Her parlor and bedroom have been restored —even to a pair of long white stockings laid on the chair beside her bed.

Each room of the Mark Twain boyhood home at 208 Hill Street has been furnished with pieces in use during the 1850's. In the dining room is his own lap writing desk. Here is Mark Twain's own room from which, like Tom Sawyer, he used to steal down the drain-spout to join a companion on a midnight adventure—perhaps to the same cave, along the Mississippi, the Mark Twain Cave, two miles away, which is such a magnet for visitors today.

In my boyhood I knew Sam Clemens well, and I still remember listening, wide-eyed, to the exciting cat-stories he used to tell me. In a measure, I think Mark Twain and his adventures influenced me more than any other writer. As the years went by I went out camping and exploring and later roaming all over the world in my house-trailer, with camera and typewriter at hand. I like the inscription on his statue atop a bluff in Hannibal's Riverview Park: "His religion was humanity, and a whole world mourned for him when he died."

How to reach: U. S. Routes 36 and 61.
Open: Daily, June 1 to September 21, 7:30 A.M. to 6:00 P.M., remainder of year, 8:00 A.M. to 5:00 P.M.
Admission: Free.
Administration: Mark Twain Municipal Board.

Mark Twain's bedroom.

St. Louis

Gateway to the West

ST. LOUIS, MO.

ST. LOUIS, at the confluence of the Missouri and Mississippi Rivers, long known as the Gateway to the West, was founded in 1756 by French traders. Until it became a part of United States territory through Jefferson's Louisiana Purchase, it served as a center of French and Spanish interests.

The old waterfront area on the west bank of the Mississippi from which the city grew is being developed as the Jefferson National Expansion Memorial. Here Lewis and Clark returned from their expedition, fur traders brought beaver-loads, steamboats crowded the wharves. For many years the area served as a supply depot and market place for the frontier, when the waves of new settlers—via covered wagon and flatboat—transformed the Mississippi Valley from wilderness to a rich inland empire, then pushed even farther west—to Oregon, California and Santa Fé. Three historic buildings have been preserved and the land surrounding them cleared, pending further landscaping.

THE OLD ROCK HOUSE —
THE LISA WAREHOUSE

The oldest building is the Manuel Lisa Warehouse, built in 1818 by a Spanish fur trader. The John Jacob Astor Company used it for storage, and during the California Trail days many a tarpaulin and wagon-cover was sewed by a sail-maker in its loft. The rear wall is one large chunk of the original limestone bluff, while the side walls and front are made of rubble blasted from the bluff. It was restored in 1941.

How to reach: Via U. S. Routes 40, 50, 66, 67. Southwest corner of Chestnut Street and the Levee.
Open: By appointment.
Admission: Free.
Administration: National Park Service.

THE OLD CATHEDRAL

The square upon which the old Cathedral stands was set aside for religious purposes when the town was founded. Since 1770 a church has stood here, the present building since 1834, with few changes in its exterior. In a wing at the rear are exhibits portraying the history of early St. Louis.

THE OLD COURTHOUSE

The Old Courthouse, overlooking the river, was begun in 1839, but the rapid growth of the community soon made enlargement necessary. By 1864 it was com-

The Old Rock House.

pleted, with a tall new dome, and was used by St. Louis County and the city for eighty-five years. Dred Scott first appeared here to defend his status as a freeman. The exterior and parts of the interior are being restored to their appearance as of 1870. Dioramas recreating the early days are housed in this building, the headquarters of the Memorial.

How to reach: At Broadway and Market Streets.
Open: Weekdays, 9:00 A.M. to 4:30 P.M.; Sundays, 1:30 P.M. to 5:00 P.M.
Admission: Free.
Administration: The National Park Service.

THE EUGENE FIELD HOUSE

Eugene Field, the children's poet, was born in this house on South Broadway, September 3, 1850, and lived here until he was six years old. The house was one of twelve connected brick buildings called Walsh's Row, built in 1845. In the mid-century lawyers, doctors and merchants lived in similar row houses within

The Eugene Field House. Roswell M. Field, one of Dred Scott's lawyers, moved here shortly before his first son, Eugene, was born.

walking distance of the riverfront business district.

Eventually the neighborhood declined and the house was virtually abandoned. Through interested citizens, school children and the Board of Education, on whose property the house stands, the house was saved when the rest of Walsh's Row was torn down, restored and opened to the public in 1936.

————

How to reach: 634 South Broadway.
Open: Daily, 10:00 A.M. to 5:00 P.M., except Mondays and the first Tuesday of each month.
Admission: Free.
Administration: Board of Education of the City of St. Louis.

CAMPBELL HOUSE

Robert Campbell, fabulous fur trader who had made a fortune at a trading post he built at Fort William (later Fort Laramie) in the 1820's and 1830's, bought this house (built in 1851) in 1854. He and his wife spared no expense in decorating and furnishing the house in the ornate Victorian style of the time. Because their three bachelor sons wanted it to remain just as their mother had furnished it—she died in 1881 —it is probably one of the most characteristically Victorian houses in the United States. Though the house was restored in 1942, nearly every item in it belonged to the Campbells. Most of the furniture came from Philadelphia, but some probably was bought in Dublin, Ireland. The life of Campbell, a Presbyterian from Northern Ireland, had been described in several books, including Washington Irving's *Adventures of Captain Bonneville* and Bernard DeVoto's *Across the Wide Missouri.*

————

How to reach: Southwest corner of Fifteenth and Locust Streets.
Open: Weekdays, 10:30 A.M. to 5:00 P.M.; Sundays, 1:00 P.M. to 5:00 P.M.
Admission: 50¢; children, 10¢.
Administration: The Campbell House Foundation.

HARDSCRABBLE HOUSE

Just outside St. Louis is the cabin in which Ulysses S. Grant and his wife lived from 1854 to 1860. It is on the 281-acre Grant's Farm, once owned by Grant and now an estate owned by August A. Busch, Jr., head of Anheuser-Busch and of the St. Louis Cardinals.

Those were sad, bad years for Grant. In 1848 he had married Julia Dent of St. Louis, but army duties required him to be separated from his wife; he drank too much and was forced to resign from the army in 1854. He returned to St. Louis to live in this house, which he called Hardscrabble. He tried to work the farm but was a failure as a farmer, then as a salesman and later as a clerk. Then history in the form of the Civil War knocked on his door.

The double parlor of the Campbell House.

Hardscrabble House had been dismantled and moved several times when August A. Busch, Sr., who had already acquired Grant's Farm and had developed it as a magnificent estate, bought the house, moved it back to the farm and restored it.

————

How to reach: U. S. Route 30.
Open: By appointment.
Admission: Free.
Administration: August A. Busch, Jr.

Hardscrabble House.

Fort Osage

SIBLEY (JACKSON COUNTY), MO.

Blockhouse No. 1, Missouri River in background.

THE FIRST outpost of the United States in the Louisiana Purchase territory was built in 1808 by William Clark, joint commander of the Lewis and Clark expedition, on the Missouri River about twenty-four miles east of the mouth of the Kansas River. The purpose of Fort Osage was twofold: to serve notice on the Spanish, the British and the Indians that the United States would protect its new territory, and to establish friendly relations with the Indians by providing a trading post. The fort consists of the main blockhouse (No. 1), other blockhouses, officers' quarters, soldiers' quarters, the factory, or Indian trading house, and other structures. The U. S. factor (trader) at the fort was George C. Sibley, from whom the town takes its name. The fort played an important and useful role in western affairs until 1822, when Congress discontinued the system of government factories. Blockhouse No. 1 and the factory have been restored; other parts of Fort Osage have been partially restored.

How to reach: U. S. Route 24, on County Road 2E.
Open: Daily
Admission: Free.
Administration: Native Sons of Kansas City, Mo.

The factory (Indian trading house).

Factor's dining room.

Panorama of the Restoration. In the immediate foreground is the Woodruff House, which includes the original printing plant of the Arkansas Gazette. Governor Conway's home is at extreme right, the Noland home at the left.

Arkansas Territorial Capitol

LITTLE ROCK, ARK.

SET IN THE heart of downtown Little Rock, like a rural country seat, is a group of thirteen mellow brick and frame buildings connected by shady brick paths. This is the Arkansas Territorial Capitol Restoration as it looked in 1820 when Little Rock was the new capital of the Arkansas Territory, a portion of the Louisiana Purchase lands. This civic center, with its capitol building, office, tavern, homes, stables and print shop (the Arkansas *Gazette,* oldest newspaper west of the Mississippi), grew up near the boat landing on the Arkansas River. The *petit roche* from which the city gets its name was the first rock to be seen by the early French explorers on their journey up the Mississippi and Arkansas Rivers from the Gulf in 1722 and a landmark for the pioneers opening up the South and West.

The Territorial Capitol, in which the Territorial Legislature met for the last time in 1835, was built in 1820 of large hand-hewn oak logs covered with cypress siding. Here were quarters for the legislators (sometimes three in a bed), a tavern room, the governor's office and the Council, or Senate, Room. The adjoining houses, with outside kitchens and well-houses, are comfortably furnished. Entertained here were such visitors as Washington Irving, Sam Houston, Davy Crockett and John James Audubon (there are two original Audubon prints made in Arkansas in the governor's house).

With the passage of time these old buildings were built over and added onto but none was torn down. Spurred by Mrs. James Fairfax Loughborough, who helped to rescue the houses, a State Commission stripped away the layers of additions to make the restoration as authentic as possible. The work was completed in 1941.

How to reach: Via U. S. Routes 65, 67, 70. East Third and Cumberland Streets.

Open: Tuesday through Saturday, 9:30 A.M. to 5:00 P.M.; Sundays and Mondays, 1:00 P.M. to 5:00 P.M.

Admission: 30¢; children, 10¢.

Administration: Territorial Capitol Commission of the State of Arkansas.

The Noland House.

Monteigne.

Natchez
The Pilgrimage City
NATCHEZ, MISS.

THIS IS the romantic ante-bellum city which re-creates the glory of lovely plantation homes, magnificent mansions, the most exquisite taste and a charmingly mannered way of life. It was a stroke of genius for Natchezites to establish the annual Pilgrimage. It started in 1931, is held every year during the month of March and it gets bigger and better every year because the admission fees for the Pilgrimage, which is sponsored jointly by the Pilgrimage Garden Club and the Natchez Garden Club, are used not only for maintenance but also for further restoration. I have made the Pilgrimage a number of times, and while the tableaux and spirituals, the ladies in costume and the Confederate Ball are not exactly within the province of this book, I must say that they all contribute to an unquestioned achievement: the genuine revival of a time past.

I described Natchez as an ante-bellum city. That's because its great houses were built before The War between the States and its golden era was in that time. The city, named for the Natchez Indians, was founded by the French in 1716, as Fort Rosalie. It has been under four flags. The French ceded it to the English, who lost it to the Spanish, and it became part of the United States in 1798. From then on, until the war, Natchez had its greatest prosperity. Situated on a bluff over the Mississippi River, in the heart of a rich agricultural area, it became a vital trading, marketing, shipping and processing center for cotton and other farm products on the one hand and domestic and imported manufactured products on the other. With success and wealth the city became a cultural center also, and many homes in the fine style were built, always in magnificent settings of handsomely landscaped gardens, or beautiful gardens or both. Quite a number of the mansions stand today, preserved or restored to their ante-bellum appearance. All of them may be visited during March, the Pilgrimage month, when there is a complete tour of thirty houses which takes three days. Some of the houses are open also during other months of the year, but during the Pilgrimage month, all thirty houses may be seen only in their regular turn on the tours.

These are the houses:

Rosalie, south end of Broadway (1820-1823), Georgian style. Owned by Mississippi Society, Daughters of the American Revolution. Open daily, 9:00 A.M. to 1:00 P.M., 2:00 P.M. to 5:00 P.M. Admission, $1.00; children, 50¢

Stanton Hall.

Hope Farm.

The Elms (1783). Belongs to Natchez Spanish era. Of special note are hand-turned bannisters on upper galleries, hand-wrought iron strap hinges on blinds, curved iron staircase. Open daily, 9:00 A.M. to 5:00 P.M. Admission, 60¢.

Hawthorne (1814). Open October 1 to June 1. Admission, 60¢.

Longwood, Lower Woodville Road. Octagonal house, Moorish in feeling, unfinished as it was in 1861 when the call to arms was sounded. Open daily, 9:00 A.M. to 5:00 P.M. Admission, 60¢

Gloucester (1798-1804). Occupied by Winthrop Sargent, first territorial governor of Mississippi Territory. Georgian architecture. Door has exquisite fanlights and heavy inner bars. Dining room octagonal, fine china and rare silver of period, crystal chandelier. Open only during Pilgrimage.

Monteigne (1855). Famous for beautiful grounds, century-old live oaks and gardens which include superb roses, camellia japonicas, azaleas. Open only on special occasions. Admission, $1.00.

D'Evereux (1840), not open to visitors.

Monmouth (1818), one of the most famous houses in Natchez. Adam woodwork. Not open to visitors.

Hope Farm (1774-1789), front part built by an early Spanish governor. Owned by Mr. and Mrs. Balfour Miller. Mrs. Miller is the originator of the Natchez Pilgrimage. Open daily, 9:00 A.M. to 5:00 P.M. Admission, $1.00.

Dunleith (1847). Open daily, 9:00 A.M. to 5:00 P.M. Admission, 60¢.

Arlington (1816), at east end of Main Street. Present owner is Mrs. Hubert Barnum. Open daily, 9:00 A.M. to 5:00 P.M. Admission, $1.20.

The Burn (1832), not open to visitors.

Airlie (before 1790), not open to visitors.

Connelly's Tavern (before 1795) on Ellicott's Hill, once a famous Natchez Trace inn. Open daily, 9:00 A.M. to 5:00 P.M. Admission, 60¢.

Cherokee. Dining room.

Stanton Hall (1846-51) occupies an entire block on High Street, between Pearl and Commerce. One of the most palatial ante-bellum houses, it is owned by the Pilgrimage Garden Club, which uses it as a clubhouse. Open daily, 9:00 A.M. to 5:00 P.M. Admission, $1.00.

Holly Hedges (1796), not open to the public.

Oakland (about 1835). Open daily, 9:00 A.M. to 5:00 P.M. Admission, $1.00.

Green Leaves (before 1812). Open daily, 9:00 A.M. to 2:00 P.M. Admission, $1.00.

Mount Repose (1824), not open to the public.

Lansdowne (1852). Open daily, 9:00 A.M. to 5:00 P.M. Admission, 75¢.

Twin Oaks (1812-13), not open to the public.

Elmscourt (1810), famous as "The House of a Thousand

Candles." Open daily, 9:00 A.M. to 5:00 P.M. Admission, 60¢.

Elgin Plantation (1812), not open to the public.

Melrose (1845), with famous Natchez landscape painted by Audubon in the 1820's. Open daily, 9:00 A.M. to 1:00 P.M., except Sundays and holidays. Admission, $1.20.

Linden (1785-90), on Melrose Avenue. Open daily, 9:00 A.M. to 2:00 P.M. Admission, 65¢.

Richmond (1784-1832-1860), not open to public.

The Briers (1812). Jefferson Davis, President of the Confederacy, was married in the drawing room to Varina Howell,

"The Rose of Mississippi." One of the best-loved Confederate shrines. Open daily, 9:00 A.M. to 1:00 P.M., 3:00 P.M. to 5:00 P.M. Admission, $1.20.

The Parsonage (1840), not open to the public.

Bontura (1796), only house of eighteenth-century Spanish-Creole type left in Natchez. Home of Don José Bontura who began his career as tavern-keeper of notorious Natchez-under-the-Hill in the 1820's. Stephen Foster, Mark Twain and others were entertained here. Not open to the public.

Cherokee (1794), on High Street. Open daily, October 1 to May 15. Admission, $1.00.

Richmond. Double dining room.

Bontura.

Melrose. Double drawing room.

Connelly's Tavern.

Cherokee. Lower or basement room.

Hope Farm Bedroom.

Stanton Hall.
Dining room.

*Jackson Square. (Left to right) Cabildo, St. Louis Cathedral,
Presbytere, Pontalba Apartments.*

New Orleans

America's Old-World Capital

NEW ORLEANS, LA.

NEW ORLEANS has more names than any other
city in the country. It's the Crescent City because it's on a crescent-shaped bend of the Mississippi;
it's the Mardi Gras City because of its fabulous carni-
val held each year before Lent, ending on Shrove Tuesday (Mardi Gras); it's the Creole City because it
represents the culture of the Creoles, Americans of
Spanish or French descent; it's been called Paris in
America, but Spain in America would be more like it
—and still not right; it's been called "America's most
interesting city" and maybe that *is* right.

New Orleans was founded in 1718 by the French
explorer, Sieur de Bienville, who named the settlement
after the Duke of Orleans. In 1762 the area was ceded
to Spain and in 1803, as part of the Louisiana Purchase, it came under the American flag. It is a lively
and prosperous metropolis now, a combination of the
old and the modern. But it is the Old City—the Vieux
Carré, or French Quarter—that we are most interested
in. That is the original New Orleans, centering on
Jackson Square, formerly the Place D'Armes. It was

A typical example of the lacy iron balcony, so ubiquitous in the French Quarter. This building is at Saint Peter Street and Rue Royale.

named, of course, for Andrew Jackson, hero of the Battle of New Orleans.

My first unofficial guide to New Orleans was the late Dorothy Dix, the *Advice to the Lovelorn* writer. It was through her that I came to know the spirit and quality of the streets and shops of the Quarter. I've walked up and down Royal Street (Rue Royale) which was then and still is the main street. I found my own way to Bourbon Street which is the night-life cafe and bar street and that has an appeal too, but it is not so very different from many others. Later, Lyle Saxon showed and told me more of the charm of that exciting, sophisticated city that, with New York and San Francisco, is one of the three great cosmopolitan centers of the United States.

One of the most famous churches in the country, *St. Louis Cathedral,* faces Jackson Square. Built in 1794, it was remodeled in 1851 and in 1916. The *Cabildo,* the oldest part of which was built in 1795, was the headquarters of the Spanish governor and a great focal point of historic events. It was here that the Louisiana Territory was formally transferred by France to the United States. The Cabildo now houses a museum which is open daily from 9:00 A.M. to 5:00 P.M. without charge.

The *Absinthe House* on Bourbon Street, favorite of Jean Pierre Lafitte, is probably the most famous in the Vieux Carré. It now houses a bar. Other well-known old buildings in the Old City are the *Pontalba Apartments,* the oldest apartment building in the country, the *Presbytere, Madame John's Legacy,* etc. But it is the Quarter itself rather than the buildings that show the old French, Spanish and Creole past living today.

How to reach: Via U. S. Routes 11, 51, 90.

Pirates' Alley, New Orleans' informal art center, à la the Left Bank of Paris.

The Cabildo. It was named for the Illustrious Council of Cabildo, for which the building was constructed. Begun in 1795, it was completed in 1799. It was used as the City Hall for years, with courtrooms, prisoners' cells, etc. The most popular item in the Cabildo is the cell in which the famous pirate Jean Lafitte was supposed to have been imprisoned. It is now filled with all sorts of Lafitte guns, swords, pieces of eight and documents.

The Absinthe House, on Bourbon and Bienville Streets. The streetcar named "Desire" is now a bus.

Orleans Street, looking toward the rear of St. Louis Cathedral. Here is another example of the famous Creole ironwork, as well as a view of the Vieux Carre's unique architecture, which also is called Creole. The balconies, along with the patios, are distinctive features.

The Acadian Country

ST. MARTINVILLE, LA.

THE CAJUNS of Louisiana are descendants of the exiled Acadians, who were deported from Nova Scotia by the British in the 1750's and 1760's. It was only in the Louisiana country that the French nationals were welcomed. In the other colonies the violent anti-French feeling caused all the many boatloads of uprooted families to be turned away. But in Louisiana in the bayou country they found refuge, and in 1765 the first of a steady stream of Acadians established the community, on the Bayou Teche, known as St. Martinville. They engaged in farming and cattle-raising, as they had done in the Grand Pré district, and preserved their traditions, languages and customs. Just outside the town is the Longfellow-Evangeline State Park. The grave of Evangeline (Emmeline Labiche) is in an old cemetery near the Catholic Church, established in 1765. In these places, as in the typical Acadian planter's home called the Acadian House Museum, exhibits of the old Acadian way of life may be seen.

How to reach: On State Route 31.

The little wall shrine in the Acadian House Museum showing the "prie-dieu," hand-hewn cradle and spinning wheel.

Oakley Plantation House

AUDUBON MEMORIAL PARK

ST. FRANCISVILLE, LA.

IN THIS plantation home John J. Audubon painted his *Birds of America*. Some of the originals and many copies of the Audubon paintings may be seen here. Built in 1799 of early Louisiana and West Indian-influence architecture, it remained the property of the same family from 1799 to 1947, when it was sold to the Louisiana State Parks and Recreation Commission. Now part of Audubon Memorial State Park, it has been restored with furnishings of its vital period, 1790-1830. The garden has been restored by the Garden Club of America.

How to reach: On State Route 323.
Open: Daily, 9:00 A.M. to 5:00 P.M.
Admission: 50¢; children, free.
Administration: Louisiana State Parks and Recreation Commission.

Oakley Plantation House.

Sam Houston Memorial

Home of "The Raven"

HUNTSVILLE, TEXAS

The Sam Houston Home, designed and built by Sam Houston in 1847.

SAM HOUSTON, great statesman and famous soldier, was one of the most dramatic figures in our history. Born in Virginia, he moved with his family to Tennessee when he was fourteen. A year later he ran off to live for three years with a tribe of Cherokee Indians, who named him "Co-lonnah," "The Raven." Later he fought under Andrew Jackson, then studied law, went into politics, was elected to Congress, and in 1827 became Governor of Tennessee. In 1829 he married Eliza Allen, but after a few weeks the marriage was dissolved and he resigned the governorship, all for reasons unknown.

In 1832 he went to Texas and soon achieved prominence and importance. He was chosen commander-in-chief of the Texas army, in 1835 led the fight of the Texans for independence from Mexico and defeated Santa Anna in the Battle of San Jacinto in 1836. Texas became a republic and Sam Houston its first president. He married Margaret Lea in 1840, and in the next twenty years was a Congressman, U. S. Senator and then Governor of Texas. But he fought against slavery and against secession, thereby alienating most of Texas, and in 1861 he was deposed as governor. When in 1863 he was asked once again to be a candidate for that office, he declined. Soon thereafter, in July, he died at the Steamboat House.

He was six and a half feet tall, a handsome figure, made all the more striking by the fine clothes and the unusual costumes he affected (Indian garb, leopard-skin weskit, etc.).

At Huntsville, besides the Museum and the two main houses, there are also his kitchen, law office and carriage house, and in addition a 15-acre park.

How to reach: On Route 75.
Open: Daily in summer months. Other seasons, Sundays and throughout the week on request.
Admission: Free.
Administration: Sam Houston State Teachers College.

The Steamboat House, designed to suggest a Mississippi River steamboat. Built in 1858, it was occupied by Houston 1861-63.

Sam Houston slept here. The walnut fourposter is covered by a wedding quilt given the Houstons by Mrs. Houston's mother.

The Alamo

"Remember the Alamo!"

SAN ANTONIO, TEXAS

THIS FAMOUS fort was originally a church, part of the Mission San Antonio de Padua, established by the Franciscan Fathers in 1716. In 1718 it was renamed for the Spanish viceroy and called San Antonio de Valero. The church was begun in 1744, completed in 1761. But in 1793 San Antonio de Valero was secularized and the Fathers left it. A few years later the Mission was occupied by a company of Mexican soldiers from a town called "Pueblo de San José y Santiago del Alamo" and soon the Mission was known as The Alamo.

The historic siege, in which the Texans fought to the very end, lasted from February 23 to March 6, 1836. None of the one hundred eighty-odd Texans resisting the Mexican Army surrendered or tried to escape. They fired their guns until their ammunition was gone, then used them as clubs, or used their fists. But there were 1,600 Mexicans and the odds were too great. All or almost all of the defenders were killed.

Whether there were six or five or no survivors does not matter. What is important is that the heroic fight inspired the Texans and speeded their winning of independence. And "Remember the Alamo" has been a rallying cry for all Americans ever since. No one has ever called Santa Anna "Victor of the Alamo" and yet stars shine on the martyr defenders—Colonel Travis and his valiant men. Among the heroes who fought Santa Anna and who died in the Alamo were Lt. Colonel W. B. Travis, the commander; James Bowie, of Bowie knife fame; James Bonham and Davy Crockett, who had arrived with seventeen staunch Tennesseans.

How to reach: Via U. S. Routes 81, 87, 90. On Alamo Street, in the heart of the city.
Open: Daily, 9:00 A.M. to 5:00 P.M.; Sundays, 10:00 A.M. to 5:00 P.M.
Admission: Free.
Administration: Owned by the State of Texas, maintained by the Daughters of the Republic of Texas.

The Alamo arcade.

San José Mission

SAN ANTONIO, TEXAS

SAN JOSÉ, called "Queen of all the Missions in New Spain," is a National Historic Site. Founded by the Franciscan Fathers in 1720, it is one of the most important, historically and architecturally, of the many missions that stud the Spanish-influenced Southwest. It has probably more features of interest to visitors than any other mission—its south "rose window" notable for its superlative stone-carving, the Indian homes in the enclosure, the soldiers' barracks, the granary and other buildings and articles just as they were in the Spanish days.

How to reach: On U. S. Route 281.
Open: Weekdays, 9:00 A.M. to 6:00 P.M.; Sundays, 12 M. to 6:00 P.M.
Admission: 35¢; children, 15¢.
Administration: San José Mission Operations Board.

Judge Roy Bean's Court

LANGTRY, TEXAS

A POPULAR reminder of the rip-roaring days, when law was made on the run and order was what the local big shot decided, is the fabulous Judge Roy Bean's Court with its Jersey Lilly Saloon annex named, like the town, after Lily Langtry. She was Roy Bean's favorite actress but he couldn't spell her first name right. Bean proclaimed himself "The Law West of the Pecos" and he made it stick. Stories of his off-hand and informal hearings, sometimes held within the sanctity of the bar, are now firmly entrenched in our folklore. Yet except for the hilarious humor and comic oratory, Judge Roy Bean had many counterparts all over the Wild West and Southwest.

How to reach: Just off Route 90.
Open: Daily, 9:00 A.M. to 6:00 P.M.
Admission: Free.
Administration: State of Texas.

Eisenhower Home

ABILENE, KANSAS

ABILENE has had a colorful role in American history, and many Americans will remember its glory as the cattle capital of the country back in the 1870's when Wild Bill Hickok was marshal. That was when it was headquarters of the old Kansas Pacific Railroad and northern end of the Chisholm Trail. When the railroad moved further west, the city calmed down, and when the Eisenhower family lived here, Abilene was an average Kansas city and the house, built in the 1870's, was a simple middle-class home, like thousands of others. This boyhood home of President Eisenhower has been preserved actually as it was in his mother's time and left entirely without changes. Adjoining it is the Eisenhower Museum with two thousand Eisenhower items on display.

How to reach: On U. S. Route 40.
Open: Weekdays, 9:00 A.M. to 5:00 P.M.; Sundays, 1:00 P.M. to 5:00 P.M.
Admission: No fee for the home, small charge for the Museum.
Administration: Eisenhower Foundation.

Fort Leavenworth

LEAVENWORTH, KANSAS

THE MOST historic army fort in the West is Leavenworth, established in 1827. For many years it was a symbol of the nation's strength and a haven for scouts, traders and travelers to the far west. Leavenworth was an important station on the Pony Express and terminus for many stagecoach lines and many wagon trains headed west. Leavenworth figured in many Indian battles, and you can see in the Leavenworth Museum many vehicles, household and other items of pioneer days. But Leavenworth's oldest historic structure is the Old Stone Wall. It was built in 1827 when Colonel Leavenworth, after whom the fort is named, made a first temporary camp here. The colonel and his men threw up a rough stone wall as a protection against possible Indian raids. Later it was loop-holed and appeared approximately as shown in the picture. It was preserved and restored through the efforts of the Captain Jesse Leavenworth Chapter of the D.A.R.

The Old Stone Wall, original wall of Cantonment Leavenworth, seen behind statue of Ulysses S. Grant.

How to reach: Via State Route 92.

The Gordon Stockade and the Way Museum

CUSTER, SOUTH DAKOTA

IN THE Black Hills of South Dakota, in and near the town of Custer, are two historic preservations identified with the first settlers in the region. The Gordon Stockade, built on French Creek, about two-and-a-half miles from Custer, was built by the first group of prospectors (led by John Gordon) who came to the Black Hills in the winter of 1874-75 in search of gold. They were trespassers, acting in contravention of military orders and in danger of attack from the Sioux Indians. To protect themselves they built this stockade (restored) and several log cabins, like the restored ones shown. It was a well-planned and well-constructed settlement but ill-starred. Very little gold was found, and in April of 1875 the stockade was abandoned when a troop of U. S. cavalry arrived to drive the trespassing Gordon party out of the Black Hills.

A small log cabin, now called the Way Museum, is the original structure, built in 1875. It houses many items pertaining to the history of General Custer as well as a number of items of local historic interest, including guns, pictures, newspaper clippings and minerals. On the main street of Custer, across from the courthouse, it is open to the public without charge from 8:00 A.M. to 8:00 P.M.

How to reach: On U. S. Routes 16 and 85 alternate.

(Left to right) *Ruins of officers' quarters, "Old Bedlam," officers' quarters E and F and the sutler's store, erected in 1849, 1852 and 1884.*

Fort Laramie

Historic Fur Trade and Military Post

FORT LARAMIE, WYOMING

FOR FORTY-ODD years—from 1834 to 1876—Fort Laramie, an immortal name in American history, played a key role in the conquest of the West. On the old Oregon Trail, it is at the junction of the Laramie and North Platte Rivers. That was a favorite camping spot for scouts, trail-blazers and fur-traders as long ago as 1821. The first fort, called Fort William, was built in 1834 by fur-traders William Sublette and Robert Campbell. Eventually the powerful American Fur Company acquired the post and in 1841 built a new fort called Fort John on the Laramie, commonly called Fort Laramie. In 1849 the army acquired it as a military post to protect emigrants migrating westward. In 1850 more than 55,000 emigrants are said to have stopped here on the overland trek. When, in 1851, the Indians were alarmed by the growing invasion of their territory, a conference, at which ten thousand Sioux, Cheyenne and other Indians gathered, resulted in an agreement whereby the government was to pay $50,000 annually and the Indians were to let the wagon trains pass. But fighting and trouble with the Indians continued for many years, climaxed by the annihilation of Custer's command at the nearby Little Bighorn in 1876. Eventually the Indians were subdued, and with the establishment of the railroads, Fort Laramie ceased to be the crucial strong point of government authority and power, and in 1890 Laramie was abandoned. But its historic importance was recognized and in 1938 it was established as a national monument and restoration was begun of the remains of the twenty-one structures still standing. "Old Bedlam," the first army building, is the most important of those partially or wholly restored. Other famous Americans identified with Laramie, besides those already mentioned, are Kit Carson, Jim Bridger, Buffalo Bill, John C. Fremont, Chief Red Cloud and John "Portugee" Phillips.

How to reach: On U. S. Route 26.
Open: All year.
Admission: Free.
Administration: National Park Service.

The Healy House and the Dexter Cabin
LEADVILLE, COLORADO

Healy House and Dexter Cabin.

ALL OVER the western states there are little "pioneer museums," "restored" ghost towns and mining villages. Many of them are privately owned and are without any real authenticity except perhaps for a few old rifles and some dusty old posters. But there are some genuine preservations and restorations that do present an accurate picture of a way of life in a past era. One of the most interesting of these, maintained by the State Historical Society, is at Leadville, Colorado's fabulous old mining town.

Gold was discovered in this area of Colorado in April, 1860, and by fall ten thousand people had arrived. When the gold had been exhausted five years later, geologists discovered that the black boulders which had been hampering the gold mining were carbonate of lead, containing much silver. By 1878 the Little Pittsburgh and the New Discovery mines were in operation. Later, the gold mine known as the Little Jonny was opened and was a constant producer from 1893 until recently.

Healy House was built in 1878 by August R. Meyer, a mining engineer who established the first reduction and ore sampling works in the Leadville district. Later the house was sold, another floor added, and it became a rooming house. Diamond-dust mirrors in hand-carved rosewood frames, a parlor set that arrived by ox-cart from Boston, an 1879 sewing machine inlaid with mother-of-pearl, portraits of early pioneers and costumes are among the many items preserved at Healy House in tribute to the great Colorado mining era of the eighties and nineties.

James V. Dexter, a pioneer and one of the early millionaires of Colorado, built a log cabin, in 1879, for his comfort when visiting Leadville to attend to his various business interests. Rough-hewn on the outside, the cabin was furnished inside with a lavish hand, the floor being alternate strips of black walnut and maple.

How to reach: On U. S. Route 24. 912 Harrison Avenue.
Open: June 1 to October 1, daily, 9:00 A.M. to 5:00 P.M.
Admission: Free. Guide service is available.
Administration: State Historical Society of Colorado.

Front room of the Dexter Cabin.

Lion House

"MOUNT VERNON OF THE MORMONS"

SALT LAKE CITY, UTAH

UNLESS you have studied the philosophy of the Church of Jesus Christ of Latter-Day Saints (the Mormon Church), you cannot appreciate the deep sincerity of Brigham Young and his followers. I learned this lesson back in 1932 when I was lecturing in Salt Lake City. I made a statement about the Mormons—I forget just what it was—which was immediately picked up by the Church. The next day I was taken on a tour of the administration buildings and the Brigham Young houses, and when I left I was a much more understanding and a far wiser man.

Salt Lake City was founded in 1847 when Brigham Young and his followers established a Mormon settlement here. It flourished and became the most successful religious community in the country, and Utah, originally called Deseret, is among the most prosperous states in the Union.

The Lion House was built 1855-56 as a residence for Brigham Young and his family—but not all his family. More than twelve wives never lived in the Lion House at one time, but they did live in harmony, because they were motivated by a deep religious belief which included the practice of plural marriage, permitted to about three per cent of the male population. The practice was abolished in 1890 and has never been sanctioned since then. The Lion House is now used as a social center, but a number of the rooms have been restored to their appearance in Brigham Young's day, and many of his and his family's personal belongings may be seen there.

I think the Prayer Parlor is the most interesting of these rooms. Every evening at 7:00 P.M. Brigham Young,

South Temple entrance of the Lion House, showing above the entrance the lion that gives the home its name.

after lighting a candle in his Bee-Hive House room, would walk to the parlor in the Lion House, through the narrow hallway connecting the two houses. There he would take the prayer bell and ring it three times, and the entire family would assemble in the room. Then, usually, he would discuss the events and topics of the day. And later all would join in singing old time ballads, popular favorites, or religious songs. The ten oldest girls, called the "Big Ten," were permitted to entertain young men in the parlor on Sunday evenings—but all together, and with the lamps lit.

How to reach: On U. S. Routes 40, 89, 91. On South Temple Street.
Open: Daily, 10:00 A.M. to 4:00 P.M.
Admission: Free.
Administration: Young Women's Mutual Improvement Association.

Adjoining the Lion House are other Brigham Young houses, including his offices and the *Bee-Hive House,* built in 1855 as a home for Brigham Young. It served as the official residence of the President of the Church until 1916. Since 1920 it has served as a girls' home but a number of the rooms are restored and maintained as in Brigham Young's time.

The Lion House.

Brigham Young's offices (left) and the Bee Hive House (right).

Old Santa Fe
Oldest Capital In the United States
SANTA FE, NEW MEXICO

THERE is much to be said for the claim that New Mexico is "where history began in America." More than five centuries before Columbus, the Indians had established here an impressive civilization, and for three hundred years had a golden age of pueblo construction, some ruins of which may still be seen. Later examples are still standing, still in use by the Indians—at Taos and at other places.

The first white men to travel through the country were Cabeza de Vaca and his companions in 1536. Their reports of riches and gold caused Coronado's bloody expedition of conquest in 1540 and the establishment of the area as Spanish territory. In 1598 a band of colonists settled at San Gabriel, but in 1610 the viceroy moved the capital to its present site and called the new city La Villa Real de Santa Fe de San Francisco—Sante Fe for short. For more than three

Palace of the Governors.

hundred years Santa Fe has served as a capital—for Spain, for Mexico and for New Mexico. As always, the padres were not far behind the trail-blazers, and the Franciscan missionaries were soon active, establishing

This adobe structure, across the way from the San Miguel Mission in Santa Fe, is said to be the oldest house in the United States.

The Mission of San Miguel de Santa Fe, oldest in the United States. Founded in 1621, it is now in the charge of the Christian Brothers.

churches, converting the Indians and doing much to bring culture and education to the area. All over New Mexico you can see today the preservations of the churches they built and the evidence of their great work.

The Palace of the Governors was built 1610-12 on the site of an Indian pueblo. The oldest public building in the United States, it is now the Museum of New Mexico. It is open, without charge, weekdays, 9:00 A.M. to 12:00 M. and 1:00 P.M. to 5:00 P.M.; Sundays and holidays, 2:00 P.M. to 4:00 P.M. It is maintained by the Historical Society of New Mexico.

The largest of the early New Mexico missions is the San Estevan Mission on top of the Rock in Acoma, the city in the sky. One of the paintings in this mission, "St. Joseph and the Christ Child," was involved in a great dispute between the Acoma and Laguna Indians, decided in the earliest important case of the New Mexico courts.

———

How to reach: Via U. S. Routes 64, 84, 85.

The Pueblo in Taos, in northern New Mexico. (Kit Carson lies buried in the village of Taos.) Women are shown replastering the adobe walls which rise to five stories. The men, seen below, are in ceremonial regalia preparing for a ritualistic dance.

Mission
San Xavier del Bac

TUCSON, ARIZONA

IN THE Papago Indian reservation, nine miles south of Tucson, is probably the most beautiful Spanish mission in the United States, notable for its carvings and its murals. The present Church of San Xavier was built 1783-97. The mission at Bac was established some time before 1700, by the famous Father Eusebio Francisco Kino, as one of the chain of missions in Arizona and the present state of Sonora in Mexico, which included the Tumacacori Mission some forty miles away. San Xavier, now church and school for the Indians of the Tucson area, is open to the public, without charge, every day except Sunday.

How to reach: Via U. S. Routes 80, 89.

Pipe Spring National Monument

NEAR FREDONIA, ARIZONA

THERE is a "Winsor Castle" in the United States, built in 1870 by Bishop Anson P. Winsor of the Mormon Church. As early as 1856 Jacob Hamblin, sent out by Brigham Young to explore the country and to make peace with the Indians, camped here and reported on the riches of the territory. The Mormons, under Brigham Young, acquired the Whitmore-McIntyre estate, sent out Bishop Winsor, who built the red sandstone fort over the spring and cared for the "Church herd of cattle." This oasis-fort is now part of the Pipe Spring National Monument.

How to reach: Via U. S. Route 89.
Open: Daily, 8:00 A.M. to 5:00 P.M.
Admission: Free.
Administration: National Park Service.

Tombstone

TOMBSTONE, ARIZONA

TOMBSTONE was one of the great Wild West towns in the early 1880's, a rip-roaring, lawless, gun-fighting, gambling-hell center for all the prospectors, miners, cowhands and lone wolves between El Paso and San Francisco. It was then the largest city between those two points. In the annals of the West it is probably best remembered for the famous gun-fight between Wyatt Earp and his brothers and the Clanton gang at the O.K. Corral.

Tombstone boomed in 1878 when Ed Schieffelin made a lucky strike and found a rich vein of silver there. But after a few years the mines were flooded and Tombstone became almost a ghost town. Several years ago the town embarked on a project to restore its historic houses and landmarks, including the *Bird Cage Theatre, Schieffelin Hall,* etc.

How to reach: On U. S. Route 80.
Open: Daily.
Admission: Various fees.
Administration: Tombstone Chamber of Commerce.

Old Moduc stage in front of the office of the Tombstone *Epitaph.*

Virginia City

VIRGINIA CITY, NEVADA

ANOTHER rip-roaring mining-camp boom-town, famous in the Wild West days, was Virginia City. For a story-book place, for a razzle-dazzle remnant of a once-great metropolis of the West, for a look at millionaires' castles falling apart, their windows like vacant eyes staring down a 200-mile canyon, one should see Virginia City, "Queen of the Comstock," twenty miles up the mountain from Reno.

This 6,250-foot-high locale pulses with history. It was the heart-beat of America, that pumped gold and silver from its mines to build the nation—palaces on Nob Hill and Fifth Avenue, railroads, industrial empires, and skyscrapers. Its riches helped the North win the Civil War. Its Comstock lode was probably the largest body of precious ore ever discovered. But eventually the metal ran out, and so did the people—

Desk used by Mark Twain, 1863-67, when he was editor of the Territorial Enterprise.

leaving their homes, churches, stores and graveyards as ghostly reminders. Its once-elegant mansions recall past grandeur, while the saloons—Bucket of Blood, Brass Rail, Delta, Silver Stone, Crystal—are colorful reminders of the fast-paced, rowdy frontier days.

The *Territorial Enterprise,* the first newspaper in Nevada, was established in 1858 at Mormon Station and moved to Virginia City in 1860. It became one of the most celebrated newspapers of the West, with many famous writers on its staff from time to time, including Samuel Clemens, who first used the pen name of Mark Twain while working here. Publication was suspended in 1916, but it was re-established in 1952 by Lucius Beebe and Charles Clegg, and is still published.

Piper's Opera House, fabulous in the nineteenth century, was one of the most famous in the country. Many of the theatre's greatest stars appeared here—Modjeska, Edwin Booth, Maude Adams, Buffalo Bill, Lily Langtry—and received enormous salaries. David Belasco was stage manager in the early days. Outstanding architectural features are the suspended balcony, the spring dance floor and the rake, or sloping stage. This is the structure built by John Piper in 1885.

Interior of Piper's Opera House.

How to reach: Via U. S. Route 395 and State Route 17.
Open: Piper's Opera House, April to November.
Admission: 25¢; children under 10, free.

The Delta saloon (left) *and the Crystal bar* (right), *showing the elaborate glass chandelier.*
The Crystal was noted also for its wonderful mechanical piano, not shown here.

Sutter's Mill and Sutter's Fort

The Gold Discovery Memorials

COLOMA, CALIF. AND SACRAMENTO, CALIF.

THE ACTUAL discovery of gold in California was made by James W. Marshall on January 24, 1848, in the tailrace of *Sutter's Mill*. The town of Coloma grew up there and now a State Park at the site is open to visitors 9:00 A.M. to 4:00 P.M. daily. But apart from two stores—one a museum and one the State Park office—the remaining old buildings are dilapidated and contain nothing.

In my opinion, the real beginning of the gold rush was at *Sutter's Fort* fifty miles away, in what is now Sacramento. That's where in 1839 John A. Sutter established a fort that became a famous trading post, focal point of California's growth to greatness. The building was of adobe bricks and it became the goal and rallying point of explorers and pioneers in the 1840's. John C. Fremont and Kit Carson were there in 1844. The settlement grew and as part of his trading and building activities Sutter decided to build a sawmill on the American fork of the Sacramento River. It was in the course of the construction that gold was discovered and the gold rush was touched off. The fort was acquired by the State in 1891, was restored and preserved as a State Historical Monument. Of the original fort, the two-story central building of adobe and oak remains. A museum contains firearms, costumes, vehicles and many other items of the Sutter period.

How to reach: The fort is at 2701 L Street, Sacramento.
Open: Daily, 10:00 A.M. to 5:00 P.M.
Admission: Free.
Administration: State Division of Beaches and Parks.

A view of Sutter's Fort showing in the center the old barracks, the original adobe structure.

The California Missions

"The Camino Real"

SAN DIEGO TO SONOMA, CALIF.

San Antonio de Padua at Jolon.

SPREAD out along some six hundred miles of California's southern coast is the fabulous chain of missions which constitutes one of the most interesting historical preservations of the country. Regardless of the importance of these missions, the influence of the Franciscan Fathers who founded and conducted them, and their impact on American history and culture, this largest single segment of America's living past always had and continues to have a world of romantic appeal to Americans.

There are twenty-one missions and they are on El Camino Real (The Royal Road), or King's Highway, which extends from San Diego, the Harbor of the Sun, through Los Angeles and San Francisco, to Sonoma, the Valley of the Seven Moons. Their history goes back to 1769 when Father Junipero Serra and Don Gaspar de Portola arrived in San Diego. Father Serra was head of the Franciscan missionaries who had been directed to Christianize the Indians. Portola was the governor of Alta California. He established El Camino Real and played an important role in the history of

California as well as in the development of the missions. Father Serra established the first mission, *San Diego del Alcala,* on July 16, 1769, hardly more than two weeks after he had arrived there. (It was here that the first palm and olive trees were planted.) The next year the second mission, *San Carlos Borromeo,* was established at Monterey and that mission was Serra's headquarters until the mission was moved to Carmel in 1771. Father Serra is buried at Carmel. The other missions are:

San Antonio de Padua, near Jolon, 1771, one of the largest of the missions, substantially restored.

San Gabriel Arcangel, near Alhambra, 1771. One of the finest examples of mission architecture.

San Luis Obispo de Tolosa, San Luis Obispo, 1772. Church is restored and there is a museum containing Serra's vestments and other early articles.

San Francisco de Asis (Mission Dolores), San Francisco, 1776, the oldest building in San Francisco.

San Juan Capistrano, San Juan Capistrano, 1775. This is probably the best known of the missions, given added fame by its swallows which are supposed to return there in great

Santa Barbara Mission.

droves on St. Joseph's Day, March 19, and leave again on October 23. That's probably folklore, but with some basis of fact.

Santa Clara de Asis, Santa Clara, 1777, on the campus of Santa Clara University. Notable for its bells.

San Buenaventura, Ventura, 1782. Notable for its grounds and its museum.

Santa Barbara, Santa Barbara, 1786. Called the "Queen of the Missions," it is probably the best preserved.

La Purisima Concepcion, Lompoc, 1787, rebuilt 1813. Three major buildings are restored.

Santa Cruz, Santa Cruz, 1791, a reproduction, not the original.

Nuestra Senora de la Soledad, Soledad, 1791, being restored.

San Jose de Guadalupe, near San Jose, 1797. Only original building preserved is an adobe house.

San Juan Bautista, San Juan Bautista, 1797, the largest of the missions. All the buildings, built 1790s-1860s, are substantially preserved.

San Miguel, San Miguel, 1797. Notable for its arches and its murals.

San Fernando Rey de Espana, near San Fernando, 1797. Church and other buildings have been completely restored.

Oak- and bronze-bound hymnal in Santa Clara Mission.

Mission San Fernando.

San Luis Rey de Francia, near Oceanside, 1798. Called also "Old Mission" and "King of the Missions." Restored, it is now used as a House of Studies for aspirants to the Franciscan order.

Santa Ynez, Solvang, 1804. Completely restored, it is one of the most attractive of the missions.

San Rafael Arcangel, San Rafael, 1817. Monastery, chapel and other buildings have been reproduced.

San Francisco Solano de Sonoma, Sonoma, 1823, the last and most northerly of the missions.

Mexico seized the church property in California, as elsewhere, in 1832 and the missions deteriorated to ruins. But the property was later returned to the church and for the most part, except as indicated, the missions have been, to a considerable degree, restored. El Camino Real itself is now restored as U. S. Highway 101.

The architecture and layout of all the missions are essentially similar, quite naturally, since the functions of the missions, the cultural influence, the materials and labor skills at hand were pretty much the same in the 600-mile and roughly 50-year spread. It was in the main Spanish-Moorish style, with a dash of Mexican, and adobe construction with thatch and later tile roofs.

Most Americans think of San Juan Capistrano when anyone mentions the California missions—because of the swallows. But I believe that the sarcophagus of Father Junipero Serra, in the Carmel mission, San Carlos Borromeo, attracts the most visitors. I am told that he may be canonized soon, and then the Carmel mission will be one of the great sacred Catholic shrines of the country.

The missions were planned to be a day's journey apart from south to north. Their order is San Diego, San Luis Rey, San Juan Capistrano, San Gabriel Arcangel, San Fernando, San Buenaventura, Santa Barbara, Santa Ynez, La Purisima, San Luis Obispo, San Miguel, San Antonio de Padua, Nuestra Senora de la Soledad, San Carlos de Borromeo, San Juan Bautista, Santa Cruz, Santa Clara, San Jose de Guadalupe, San Francisco (Dolores), San Rafael, San Francisco Solano de Sonoma.

How to reach: Most are on or near U. S. Route 101.
Open: Almost all are open during the usual visiting hours.
Admission: Most are free, a few charge a small fee, 35¢ or so.
Administration: Various, chiefly the Franciscan Fathers, but also Fathers of the Society of Jesus, Claretian Fathers, State Historical Monument, etc.

The altar, Mission San Miguel Arcangel.

Santa Ynez Mission.

Compo Santo and bell tower, Mission San Luis Rey de Francia. This was one of the largest of the missions, and at one time some 3000 converted Indians lived within its walls. It is also one of the most beautiful, notable for its high ceilings and its Indian decoration.

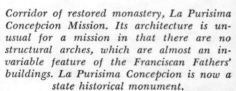

Corridor of restored monastery, La Purisima Concepcion Mission. Its architecture is unusual for a mission in that there are no structural arches, which are almost an invariable feature of the Franciscan Fathers' buildings. La Purisima Concepcion is now a state historical monument.

The assay furnace room of the Wells Fargo building. Restored.

The Wells Fargo building and warehouse (1854). Restored.

Columbia Historic State Park
Memorial to the Mother Lode
COLUMBIA, CALIF.

THE BEST of old-time California mining towns is at Columbia in the Mother Lode area which runs through eight counties: Mariposa, Tuolumne, Calaveras, Amador, El Dorado, Placer, Nevada, Sierra. There are lots of rebuilt or "restored" mining towns in that section, but the best preserved is Columbia, "gem of the southern mines," which is characteristic of the Mother Lode towns. Booming in the days of the great rush, Columbia was quite orderly though full of excitement. Its history began in 1849 when the first mines were dug, but by 1860 mining and business were on the decline. Yet Columbia never quite became a ghost town. Now a state park, a number of its buildings have been restored.

How to reach: On State Route 49.
Open: 8:00 A.M. to 5:00 P.M.
Admission: Free.
Administration: State Division of Beaches and Parks.

Fort Ross

CAZADERO, CALIF.

THIS IS the farthest penetration south of the Russians who were active in California early in the 1800's. It was built in 1812 by the Russian American Fur Trading Company and was occupied as a center for otter hunting, agricultural activities and a supply post for Alaska. It was sold in 1841 to Captain Sutter and the last of the Russians left in 1844. It is now a State Historical Monument and a number of buildings have been restored, including a Russian Orthodox chapel, Commander's House and blockhouses, one of which is shown.

How to reach: On Route 1.
Open: Daily 9:00 A.M. to 5:00 P.M., except holidays.
Admission: Free.
Administration: State Division of Beaches and Parks.

McLoughlin House

OREGON CITY, OREGON

DR. JOHN McLOUGHLIN, chief factor and superintendent of the Columbia department of the Hudson's Bay Company, built this frame house 1845-46. That was the time when fur trading in the Oregon country was declining and permanent settlers were coming in. Dr. McLoughlin was a great and important figure in those pioneer days. He helped many of the early settlers with advice, guidance, seeds and provisions. He sent supplies to the starving immigrants at The Dalles and protected them from the Indians. Dr. McLoughlin lived in this house until his death in 1857. Eventually it fell into disrepair but was saved from destruction by the McLoughlin Memorial Association which, with the aid of the city, moved the house to its present site in McLoughlin Park. It is now restored essentially to its original condition.

———

How to reach: On Routes 99E and 43. At 7th and Center Streets.
Open: 10:00 A.M. to 5:00 P.M. in summer, 10:00 A.M. to 4:00 P.M. in winter, except Mondays.
Admission: 25¢; children, 10¢.
Administration: McLoughlin Memorial Association and the Municipality of Oregon City, by arrangement with National Park Service.

Hudson's Bay Company desk used by McLoughlin.

Old Fort Nisqually

TACOMA, WASH.

THIS WAS the first outpost of the Hudson's Bay Company on the North Pacific coast, established in 1833 by four men sent here by Dr. John McLoughlin. Archibald McDonald was in charge and he was the first factor. The first fort was destroyed and a new one built nearby in 1843. The United States bought the property in 1867, and in 1934 the two remaining buildings were moved to Point Defiance Park by the Young Men's Business Club of Tacoma. There the stockade and other elements of the old fort were rebuilt, following the old specifications, and it is now open to the public. The two original buildings are the old *Granary*, built in 1843, the oldest building still standing in Washington, and the *Factor's House*. This was the main building, where visitors were entertained and the factor's family lived in royal style, attended by Indian, Chinese, French Canadian and Hawaiian servants. It is now a museum of pioneer and Indian days.

How to reach: Via U. S. Routes 99 and 410.
Open: 8:00 A.M. to dark.
Admission: Free.
Administration: Metropolitan Park District of Tacoma.

The old Granary.

The porch of the Factor's House. The Indian war canoe is a reproduction.

Directory of
National Historic Preservations

Directory of
National Historic Preservations

Directory of
National Historic Preservations

This listing, as full as possible though not a complete one, is based on a thorough canvass and check of the available information.

Apart from the name and location of the restoration or preservation, four elements of information are given in concise form, with abbreviations: *Period, Historic Interest, Admission Hours and Fees.* Under *Period* the century or approximate part of the century is given. Under *Historic Interest,* there are three classifications to indicate whether the place is notable because it shows an earlier way of life, is of historic importance because of an event or personality, or is notable for its beauty or architectural importance. Under *Admission Hours and Fees,* the information is approximate. There are so many variations in these factors, as demonstrated in the full descriptions in the body of the book, that to provide exact details would require more space for each listing than all the other information combined. Therefore, the general indications, as listed in the key below, are used. But the prospective visitor to any of these places is advised to check the possibility that the historic house, though open at the usual times, may be closed Tuesday afternoons or Monday mornings, or something like that.

KEY TO ABBREVIATIONS: Abbreviations are used for these elements of information:

1. Approximate Period with Century

  E = Early
  M = Middle
  L = Late

2. Historic Interest

  A = Architectural
  W = Way of Life
  H = Historic Event or Personality

3. Admission Hours and Fees

  App. = By appointment
  U = Usual hours
  SS = Saturdays and Sundays only
  S = Special—one day a week or one day a year
      Usual abbreviations for days of the week and months.
  X = Free
  Z = Nominal fee, under $1.00

ALABAMA

Birmingham
  Arlington Historical Shrine
    Described

Forkland
  Rosemount
    Described

Montgomery
  First White House of Confederacy
    E19; H; UZ

Tuscumbia
  Helen Keller Shrine
    Described

University
  Gorgas Home
  University Campus
    E19; W; UX

ARIZONA

near Fredonia
  Pipe Spring National Monument
    Described

Prescott
  Sharlot Hall Museum & Old Governor's Mansion
    M19; W; UZ

Tombstone
  Birdcage Theatre
    Described

Tucson
  San Xavier Mission
    Described

Tumacacori
  Mission of San José de Tumacacori
    L18; A; UZ

Yarnell
  Shrine of St. Joseph of the Mountains and Outdoor Way of the Cross
    20; W; UX

ARKANSAS

Fort Smith
  Old Commissary Building
    E19; A; UZ

Arkansas (*continued*)

Little Rock
  Arkansas Territorial Capitol
    Described
  Old State House
    E19; A; UX

CALIFORNIA

Benicia
  Old State Capitol Building
    707 First St.
    M19; H; UX

Buena Park
  Knott's Ghost Town
    M19; W; UX

California Missions
  Described

Cazadero
  Fort Ross
    Described

Coloma
  Gold Discovery Site State Park
    Described

Columbia
  Columbia Historic State Park
    Described

Inglewood
  La Casa de la Centinela
    7634 Midfield, L. A.
    E19; A; App.X

Lebec
  Fort Tejon Historical Monument
    M19; H; UX

near Modesto
  Pierce A. Miller's California Ranch Collection of Old Transportation
    Route 1, Box 1856
    19-20; H; OZ

Monterey
  California's First Theatre
    M19; H; UX

Pacific Palisades
  Will Rogers Home
    20; W; UZ

Sacramento
  Sutter's Fort
    Described

St. Helena
  Old Bale Mill
    St. Helena Highway
    M19; H; UX

San José
  Winchester Mystery House
    439 Winchester Rd.
    L19; A; UZ

Santa Rosa
  Luther Burbank's Home and Gardens
    204 Santa Rosa Ave.
    L19; A; UX
  Church Built of One Tree
    Ross & B Sts.
    M19; H; UX

Sonoma
  Wine Cellars of Count Agoston Haraszthy
    Old Winery Rd.
    M19; H; UX

Susanville
  Roop's Fort
    N. Weatherlow St.
    M19; H; UX

Weaverville
  Chinese Joss House
    Main Street & Oregon
    M19; W; UZ

Whittier
  Pio Pico Mansion
    6003 Pioneer Blvd.
    M19; A; UX

COLORADO

Central City
  Opera House, etc.
    M19; W; UZ

Fort Collins
  Fort Collins Pioneer Museum
    219 Peterson St.
    19; W; UX

La Junta
  Bent's Fort Museum
    Third & Santa Fe
    19; W; UX

Leadville
  Healy House and Dexter Cabin
    Described

CONNECTICUT

Bridgeport
  Barnum Museum
    804 Main St.
    19; H; UX

Clinton
  Stanton House
    E. Clinton Green
    18; H; UX

East Haddam
  Gillette Castle State Park
    20; A; Je-O; UZ

East Lyme
  Thomas Lee House
    M17; H; UZ

Essex
  Pratt House
    20 West Ave.
    E18; H; UZ

Farmington
  Farmington Museum (Stanley Whitman House)
    M17; A; UZ
  Hill-Stead Museum
    19; A; App.Z

Greenwich
  Putnam Cottage
    Post Road
    L17; H; M,Th-Sat; UX

Guilford
  Henry Whitfield House
    Described
  Hyland House
    Described

Hartford
Mark Twain Library and Memorial Commission
351 Farmington Ave.
L19; A; UZ
Second State House
800 Main St.
L18; A; UX

Lebanon
Jonathan Trumbull House
E18; H; UZ

Litchfield
Tapping Reeve House and Law School
Described

Madison
Nathaniel Allis House
Post Road
E18; A; UZ

Milford
Eells-Stow House
34 High St.
M17; A; App.X

Mystic
Mystic Seaport
Described
Pequotsepos Manor
Pequotsepos Ave.
E18; A; UZ

New Haven
Pardee-Morris House
325 Lighthouse Rd.
L17; A; UZ

New London
Nathan Hale School House
Bulkeley Sq. & Huntington St.
M18; H; UZ
Shaw Mansion
Bank and Blinman Sts.
M18; H; UX

Norfolk
Church of Christ Meeting House
Route 44
E19; A; UX

Norwich
Stone House
42 Rockwell St.
E19; A; Wed.X
Nathaniel Backus House
42 Rockwell St.
M18; A; Wed.X

Stratford
Judson House
967 Academy Hill
E18; A; App.Z

Wallingford
Nehemiah Royce House
538 North Main St.
L17; A; UZ

Wethersfield
Webb House
Described

Windsor
Fyler House
96 Palisado Ave.
M17; A; UZ

Winsted
Solomon's Temple
225 Prospect St.
E19; A; UZ

Woodbury
Glebe House
Described

DELAWARE

Dover
Various. Write to Friends of Old Dover, Box 44, for information concerning Old Dover Days in May.

New Castle
Amstel House
Fourth & Delaware Sts.
18; A; UZ
Various. For information concerning "A Day in Old New Castle" in May, write to Chairman, Immanuel Parish House.

Odessa
Various. Community Center Assn., Odessa Day, second Sun. in May.

Wilmington
Eleutherian Mills-Hagley Foundation
Brandywine Creek
19; H; UX
Holy Trinity (Old Swedes) Church
Described
Old Town Hall
6th & Market Sts.
L18; A; UX

Winterthur
Henry Francis du Pont Winterthur Museum
Described

DISTRICT OF COLUMBIA

Anderson House
2118 Massachusetts Ave., N.W.
20; A; UX

Episcopal Christ Church
620 G Street, S.E.
E19; A; UX

The Octagon
1741 New York Ave., N.W.
E19; A; UX

White House
Described

Joaquin Miller Cabin
Described

Pierce Mill
Described

Ford's Theater
511 Tenth St., N.W.
M19; H; UZ

House Where Lincoln Died
516 Tenth St., N.W.
M19; H; UZ

[215]

FLORIDA

Apopka
The Lodge
M19; H; App.X
Dry Tortugas
Fort Jefferson
M19; H; App.X

Ellenton
Gamble Mansion
M19; W; UZ

Fernandina Beach
Fort Clinch & Museum
P.O.B. 524
M19; H; UZ

Fort George Island
Fort George
18-19; W; UX

Fort Myers
Thomas Edison Winter Home
L19; A; U, $1

Key West
East Martello Tower
Roosevelt Blvd.
(Atlantic Side)
M19; H; UZ

Mandarin
Stowe Home & Church
L19; H; UZ

Miami
Villa Vizcaya
Described

North Miami Beach
Monastery of San Bernado de Sacramenia
M12; A; U, $1.30

Ormond Beach
John Bunch Sugar Mill Ruins
1 mi. n. Tomoka State Park
E19; A; UX

Rattlesnake Island
Fort Matanzas National Monument
Ocean Shore Blvd., Anastasia Island
M16-E18; H; UX

St. Augustine
Described

Sarasota
John and Mable Ringling Residence
20; A; U, $1.50

White Springs
Stephen Foster Memorial
19; H; UX

GEORGIA

Atlanta
Burns Cottage of Atlanta
988 Alloway Pl.
20; W; UX
Rhodes Memorial Hall
1516 Peachtree
E20; H; UX
The Wren's Nest
1050 Gordon St., S.W.
L19; W; UZ

Jonesboro
Fair of 1850
19; W; U, $1

Louisville
Old Slave Market
M18; A; UX

Macon
Sidney Lanier Cottage
935 High St.
E19; A; App.X

Midway
Midway Church
Described

Savannah
Described

Sea Island
St. Simons
Described

Warm Springs
Little White House
Described

ILLINOIS

Bement
Bryant Cottage
M19; H; UX

Cahokia
Cahokia Court House
E18; H; UX

near Charleston
Lincoln Log Cabin
E19; H; UX

Chicago
Hull House
800 So. Halsted St.
M19; W; App.X

Decatur
Lincoln Log Courthouse
Fairview Park
E19; H; UX

Evanston
Rest Cottage
1728 Chicago Ave.
E19; H; UX

Fort Gage
Pierre Menard Home
Fort Kaskaskia State Park
E19; H; UX

Fort Massac State Park
Fort Massac
Massac County
M18; H; UX

Galena
Grant Home
Described

Galesburg
Birthplace of Carl Sandburg
331 East Third St.
M19; H; Sun, 3-5, App.X

Henry County
Old Colony Church
Bishop Hill State Park
M19; W; UX

Petersburg
New Salem
Described

Prairie du Rocher
Fort Chartres
Randolph County
E18; H; UX

Metamora
Metamora Court House
M18; H; UX

Mt. Pulaski
Mt. Pulaski Court House
M19; H; UX

Quincy
Historical Building of Quincy
and Adams County
425 South 12 St.
E19; H; UX

Rock Island
Fort Armstrong
Blockhouse
E19; H; UX

Salem
William Jennings Bryan Birth-
place
408 South Broadway
M19; H; UX
Bryan-Bennett Library
404 South Broadway
E20; H; UX

Springfield
Lincoln Home
Described

Vandalia
Vandalia State House
E19; H; UX

INDIANA

Corydon
The Corydon Capitol
E19; H; UX

Crawfordsville
Lane Place
212 South Water St.
M19; H; UZ

Fort Wayne
The Swinney Homestead
1424 Swinney Court
M19; A; UX

Fountain City
Levi Coffin House
E19; H; C

Geneva
Limberlost State Memorial
L19; W; UZ

Greenfield
James Whitcomb Riley Home
Described

Indianapolis
James Whitcomb Riley House
Described

Lincoln City
Nancy Hanks Lincoln
State Memorial
H; UX

Madison
James F. D. Lanier Home
Described

New Harmony
Described

Newburgh
Old Stone House
E19; A; C

Richmond
Earlham Hall
Earlham College
M19; A; UX
Julia M. Gaar Wayne County
Historical Museum
N. "A" at 11 St.
M19; H; UX

Rockport
Lincoln Pioneer Village
Described

Rome City
The Gene Stratton Porter State
Memorial
E20; W; UZ

South Bend
Log Chapel
Old College
Notre Dame
E19; W; UX

Spring Mill State Park
Spring Mill Village
Described

Vincennes
Harrison Mansion
Described
Territorial Capitol
Described

IOWA

Iowa City
Plum Grove
727 Switzer Ave.
M19; H; UX

Pella
Pella Historical Museum
810 Washington St.
M19; H; S
The Scholte Home
734 Washington St.
M19; W; S

West Branch
Birthplace of Herbert Hoover
Described

KANSAS

Abilene
Eisenhower Museum & Boyhood
Home
Described

Council Grove
Kaw Mission Museum
500 North Mission St.
M19; H; UX

Dodge City
Beeson Museum
19; W; UZ

Fort Leavenworth
Described

KENTUCKY

Anchorage
George Caldwell Home
M19; A; U, $1

Barbourville
Dr. Thomas Walther State Shrine
Route 2, Box 196
M18; H; UX

near Bardstown
My Old Kentucky Home
Described

Bardstown
Farmington
Described

Bourbon City
Cane Ridge Meeting House
L18; H; UX

Danville
McDowell House
Described

near Danville
Isaac Shelby Memorial,
Traveler's Rest
L18; H; UX

Frankfort
Liberty Hall
Old State House

Greensburg
The Old Stone Court House
Jane Todd Crawford
Memorial Library
18-19; H; UX

Harrodsburg
Old Fort Harrod
Described

near Henderson
John James Audubon Memorial
Museum
19; A; UX

Hodgenville
Lincoln's Birthplace Cabin
Described

La Grange
Rob Morris Memorial
Described

Lexington
Ashland
Described

near Lexington
Hillandale
Muir Station Pike
L18; W; UZ

near London
Levi Jackson Wilderness
Road State Park
E19; W; UX

near Louisville
The Locust
Pewee Valley
E19; W; UZ
O'Bannon
E19; A; U, $1

near Mt. Olivet
Blue Lick Battlefield
State Park
L18; H; UX

Paris
Duncan Tavern
Described

Pewee Valley
The Beeches
E20; W; UX

near Springfield
Lincoln Homestead
L18; H; UX

near Stanford
William Whitley House
Described

Tompkinsville
Old Mulkey Meeting House
Blacktopped Rd.
E19; W; UX

Washington
Federal Hill
L18-19; H; UZ
Albert Sidney Johnston Home
L18; H; UZ

Winchester
Clark Mansion
High School Campus
E19; H; UX

LOUISIANA

near Franklin
Oaklawn Manor
E19; W; U, $1

near Jackson
Asphodel Plantation
E19; A; App. $1.50

Napoleonville
Madewood
M19; A; App. $1

New Orleans
Various Houses
Described

St. Francisville
Oakley Plantation House
Described

St. Martinville
Described

MAINE

Augusta
Blaine House
Described
Fort Western
M18; H; UX
State Capitol
Described

Brunswick
Harriet Beecher Stowe House
63 Federal St.
E19; H; UX

Columbia Falls
Ruggles House
E19; A; UZ

Ellsworth
Colonel Black Mansion
Described

MARYLAND

Gorham
Baxter House
L18; A; Summers: Wed. &
Sat. X

Kennebunk
The Brick Store Museum
E19; A; UX

Kittery Point
Lady Pepperrell Mansion
Described

Machias
Burnham Tavern
M18; A; Tues. & Wed. Z

Pemaquid Beach
Fort William Henry
L17; H; UZ

Portland
Tate House
Stroudwater
LM18; A; UZ
Wadsworth-Longfellow House
Described

Searsport
Penobscot Marine Museum
M19; A; UX

Skowhegan
History House
Elm St.
E19; A; M,W,F.X

South Berwick
Sarah Orne Jewett House
101 Portland St.
L18; H; UZ

Thomaston
Montpelier
High St.
L18; A; UZ

Waterville
William Redington House
64 Silver St.
E19; A; UX

Baltimore
*The Baltimore Catholic Cathe-
dral*
Cathedral & Mulberry Sts.
E19; A; UX
*Fort McHenry National Monu-
ment and Historic Shrine*
L18; H; UZ
Peale Museum
Described
Poe House
Described
Star-Spangled Banner Flag House
844 East Pratt St.
L18; H; UX

Beachville
Manor of Coren Waleys Cross
M17; A; U, $1

Easton
The Anchorage
E18; A; S
Wye House
M17; A; S

Fort Washington
Fort Washington
E19; H; UX

Frederick
Barbara Fritchie House
156 W. Patrick St.
A; UZ
Rose Hill Manor
L18; H; UX

Great Falls
Great Falls Tavern
Described

Hagerstown
Jonathan Hager House
Described

Leonardtown
Tudor Hall
M18; A; UX

Princess Anne
Washington Hotel
L18; A; UX

Towson
Hampton National Historic Site
L18; W; UZ

MASSACHUSETTS

Amesbury
*Mary Baker Eddy Historical
House*
Described
Whittier Home
Described

Amherst
Nehemiah Strong House
Amity & N. Prospect Sts.
M18; A; Je-O,Tu,Th,F.Z

Andover
Deacon Amos Blanchard House
97 Main St.
L19; W; UZ

Arlington
The Jason Russell House
L18; W; UZ

Barnstable
Crocker Tavern
M18; A; M,Th,Sat.Z

Beverly
The Old John Balch House
Balch & Cabot Sts.
E17; W; UZ
Cabot House
117 Cabot St.
L18; A; UZ
Hale House
39 Hale St.
L17; A; UZ

Boston
Faneuil Hall
Described
First Church in Boston
Described
*Isabella Stewart Gardner Mu-
seum*
280 the Fenway
E18; A; Je-S,UZ

Massachusetts (*continued*)
Boston (*continued*)
  King's Chapel
    M18; A; UX
  Old North Church
    Described
  Paul Revere House
    Described
  Old South Meeting House
    Washington & Milk Sts.
    L18; A; UZ
  Harrison Gray Otis House
    141 Cambridge St.
    L18; A; UZ
Bourne
  Aptucxet Trading Post
    Described
Brewster
  Stoney Brook Mill
    Described
Brookline
  Edward Devotion House
    347 Harvard St.
    L17; W; App.Z
  Longyear Foundation
    120 Seaver St.
    L19; W; UX
Cambridge
  Cooper-Frost-Austin House
    21 Linnaean St.
    M17; A; Je-O,M,Th,F.;
    N-My,M,Th.Z
Chatham
  The Old Atwood House
    Stage Harbor Road
    M18; W; W,F.Z
Concord
  Antiquarian House
    Described
  Emerson House
    Described
  Old Manse
    Described
  Orchard House
    Described
  The Wayside
    Described

Cummington
  William Cullen Bryant Homestead
    E19; W; M,W,F.Z
Dalton
  Crane Museum
    M19; W; UX
Danvers
  Judge Samuel Holten House
    171 Holten St.
    M17; W; App.Z
  Rebecca Nurse House
    149 Pine St.
    L17; W; Je-O,U;App.Z
Danversport
  Samuel Fowler House
    166 High St.
    E19; W; W,S,App.Z
Dedham
  Fairbanks House
    511 East St.
    E17; A; My-N,UZ
Deerfield
  Various Buildings
    Described
Dorchester
  Clapp House
    195 Boston St.
    E19; W; App.X
  Phineas Upham House
    255 Upham St., Melrose
    E18; H; UZ
Duxbury
  John Alden House
    Described
Edgartown
  Squire Thomas Cooke House
    Cooke St.
    M18; W; UX
Gloucester
  James Babson Cooperage Shop
    M17; W; UX
  "Beauport"
    18; A; U, $1

Hammond Museum
  20; A; UZ
Sargent-Murray-Gilman-Hough House
  49 Middle St.
  M18; W; UZ
Hadley
  Farm Museum
    65 South Middle St.
    L18; W; SS X
Hanover Centre
  Samuel Stetson House
    Route 139
    L17; W; U,App.Z
Harvard
  Fruitlands Museum
    L18; W; UZ
Haverhill
  The Buttonwoods
    240 Water St.
    E19; A; T,Th,Sa,Z
  John Ward House
    240 Water St.
    M17; W; T,Th,Sa.Z
  Whittier's Birthplace
    Route 110
    L17; H; UZ
Hingham
  Samuel Lincoln House
    North St.
    M18; W; MZ
  Old Ordinary
    Lincoln St.
    M17; A; Je-Au,UZ
  Old Ship Meetinghouse
    L17; W; UX
Ipswich
  Emerson-Howard House
    41 Turkey Shore Road
    M17; W; M-Th.Z
  Lakeman-Johnson House
    16 East St.
    W; T,Th,Sa.Z
  Preston-Foster House
    6 Water St.
    M17; W; UZ

Thomas Franklin Waters Memorial
　　40 South Main St.
　　L18; W; UZ
John Whipple House
　　53 South Main St.
　　M17; W; UZ

Kingston
Bradford House
　　L17; A; Je-S,UZ

Longmeadow
Colton House
　　Longmeadow St.
　　E18; W; M,W.App.Z

Lowell
Whistler House
　　243 Worthen St.
　　E19; A; UX

Lynn
Mary Baker Eddy Residence
Lynn Historical Society House
　　125 Green St.
　　M19; A; UX

Marblehead
Abbott Hall
　　Washington St.
　　L17; A; UX
General Glover House
　　L19; A; UX
Hooper-Parker House
　　181 Washington St.
　　L18; W; M,W,F.Z
Jeremiah Lee Mansion
　　161 Washington St.
　　M18; A; UZ

Marshfield
Historic Winslow House
　　17-18; A; UZ

Medford
Royall House
　　Main & George Sts.
　　E18; A; My-S,UZ
Peter Tufts House
　　350 Riverside Ave.
　　L17; A; Je-O,M,Th,F.;
　　N-My,M,Th.Z

Nantucket and Martha's Vineyard
Aptucxet Trading Post
　　See Bourne
Jethro Coffin House
　　Described
The Squire Thomas Cooke House
　　See Edgartown
The Stoney Brook Mill
　　Described
The 1721 House
　　Described
Town Square
　　Described

New Bedford
Jonathan Bourne Whaling Museum
　　Rogers Building, and Wood Addition
　　18 Johnny Cake Hill
　　19-20; W; UZ

Newbury
Tristram Coffin House
　　High Rd.
　　M17; A; M,W,F;App.Z
Short House
　　33 High Rd.
　　E18; W; M,W,F;App.Z
Swett-Illsley House
　　4-6 High Road
　　L17; W; UX

Newburyport
Pettingill-Fowler House
　　High and Winter Sts.
　　L18; A; UZ

North Oxford
The Clara Barton Birthplace
　　E19; H; UX

Old Deerfield
Various Houses
　　Described

Plymouth
Various Houses
　　Described

Provincetown
Church of the Redeemer, Universalist
　　238 Commercial St.
　　M19; W; Summer, UX
Provincetown Historical Museum
　　230 Commercial St.
　　L19; A; UZ

Quincy
Various Houses
　　Described

Rockport
Old Castle
　　Castle Lane, Pigeon Cove
　　L17; A; Summer, SSX
Old Tavern
　　12 Main St.
　　L18; A; UX

Rowley
Chaplin-Clark House
　　Haverhill St.
　　L17; W; App.Z
Platts-Bradstreet House
　　Main St.
　　L17; W; App.Z

Salem
Various Houses
　　Described

Saugus
Saugus Ironworks Restoration and Various Houses
　　Described

Scituate
Cudworth House and Barn Museum
　　First Parish Rd.
　　E18; W; Summer, UX

South Hadley
Joseph Allen Skinner Museum
　　35 Woodbridge St.
　　M19; A; UX

South Orleans
Cape Cod House
　　Described

Massachusetts (*continued*)
South Sudbury
Longfellow's Wayside Inn
L17; A; UZ

Springfield
Alexander House
284 State St.
E19; W; App.
William Pynchon Memorial Building
18-19; W; UX

Stockbridge
Mission House Museum
Main St.
M18; A; UZ

Sturbridge
Old Sturbridge Village
Described

Swampscott
Mary Baker Eddy Historical House
23 Paradise Rd.
M19; W; UZ
John Humphrey House
99 Paradise Rd.
E17; A; UX

Taunton
Old Colony Historical Hall
66 Church Green
M19; A; UZ

Topsfield
Parson Capen House
L17; A; My-O, UZ

Townsend Harbor
Conant House
E18; A; M,W,F., App.Z
Spaulding Cooperage Shop
M19; W; M,W,F., App.Z
Spaulding Grist Mill
M19; W; M,W,F., App.Z

Waltham
Gore Place
252 Gore St.
E19; W; UZ

Lyman House
Lyman St.
L18; A; Wed-Sat. Z

Watertown
Abraham Browne House
562 Main St.
L17; W; UZ

Wenham
Claflin-Richards House
Main St.
M17; A; UX

Westfield
Grandmother's Garden
Smith Ave.
A; UX

Weston
Smith Tavern
M18; A; UX

West Springfield
Storrowton Village
18; W; UX

Williamstown
West College
Williams College Campus
L18; A; UX

Worcester
The John Woodman Higgins Armory, Inc.
100 Barber Ave.
16; A; UX
Worcester Historical Society Building
39 Salisbury St.
L19; A; UX

Yarmouth
Col. John Thacher House
Hallett St.
L17; W; UZ

Yarmouthport
Winslow-Crocker House
L18; A; App.Z

MICHIGAN

Ann Arbor
Nichols Arboretum
Geddes Ave.
20; A; UX

Bloomfield Hills
Cranbrook House
A; My-O,UZ

Copper Harbor
Fort Wilkins
M19; H; UX

Dearborn
Greenfield Village
Described

Detroit
Palmer Park Log Cabin
Woodward Ave. & Six Mile Rd.
18; W; UX

near Grayling
Hartwick Pines Lumberman's Museum
Hartwick Pines State Park
20; W; UX

Lansing
Michigan Historical Museum
505 N. Washington Ave.
20; A; UZ

Mackinaw Island
J. J. Astor House
E19; A; UZ
Fort Mackinaw
L18; H; UX

Mackinaw City
Fort Michillimackinac
M18; H; UX

Owosso
Curwood Castle
604 John St.
20; A; UX

Saginaw
Schuch Hotel
M19; W; UX

MINNESOTA

Brown's Valley
Sam Brown Monument
M19; H; UX

Little Falls
Charles Lindbergh Park
20; A; UX

Mendota
Sibley House
E19; A; UZ

MISSISSIPPI

Bay St. Louis
Darwood on the Jordan
20; A; U, $1

Biloxi
Beauvoir
M19; H; U, $1
*Biloxi Lighthouse and other
Buildings*
M19; A

Holly Springs
Grey Gables
E19; A; App.Z

Jackson
Governor's Mansion
M19; A; UX

Natchez
Pilgrimage
Described

Pascagoula
Spanish Fort & Museum
E18; A; UZ

Port Gibson
*First Presbyterian Church
Church & Walnut Sts.*
A; UX

Sandy Hook
John Ford Home
L18; H; UZ

Vicksburg
Old Courthouse Museum
M19; A; UZ

Woodville
Rosemont
E19; H; UZ

MISSOURI

Diamond
*George Washington Carver
House*
E19; H; UX

Hannibal
Mark Twain Boyhood Home
Described

Kansas City
*Kansas City Museum
3218 Gladstone Blvd.*
E20; A; UX

Old Sibley
Fort Osage
Described

St. Genevieve
Trading post, houses, church
Described

St. Joseph
St. Joseph Museum
L19; A; UX

St. Louis
Campbell House
Described
Eugene Field House
Described
Grant's Cabin
Described
Jefferson National Exp. Mem.
Described

MONTANA

St. Ignatius
St. Ignatius Mission
W; UX

NEBRASKA

Bellevue
*The Pioneer Log Cabin
1805 Hancock*
M19; W; Su.Z

Hastings
House of Yesterday
20; A; UX

Nebraska City
Arbor Lodge Mansion
M19-E20; A; UZ

NEVADA

Carson City
The Bliss Mansion
M19; A; UZ
King Home
M19; A; UZ
Matt Rinckle House
L19; A; UZ

Genoa
Genoa Fort & Stockade Museum
M19; W; UX

near Gering
*Scotts Bluff National Monument
Museum
Scotts Bluff*
20; A; UX

Reno
Bowers Mansion
M19; A

Virginia City
Piper's Opera House
Described
Territorial Enterprise
Described
The Delta Saloon
Described
The Crystal Bar
Described

NEW HAMPSHIRE

Amherst
Horace Greeley Birthplace
Horace Greeley Rd.
L18; H; S

Concord
Franklin Pierce House
52 South Main St.
M19; H; UZ

Cornish
Saint-Gaudens Memorial
P. O. Windsor, Vt.
E19; H; UZ

Dover
Dam Garrison
182-192 Central Ave.
L17; A; UX
Hale House
182-192 Central Ave.
E19; A; UX
Woodman House
182-192 Central Ave.
E19; A; UX

Exeter
Cincinnati Memorial Hall
Governor's Lane
E18; A; UX
Gilman House
Front & Elm Sts.
M18; A; UX

Franklin
Daniel Webster Birthplace
Described

Hanover
Dartmouth Hall
L18; A; App.X

Hillsboro
Franklin Pierce Homestead
E19; H; UZ

Manchester
Stark House
1070 Canal St.
E18; H; App.X

New Ipswich
Barrett House (Forest Hall)
Main St.
E19; A; UZ

Newport
South Congregational Church
62 South Main St.
E19; W; UX

Peterborough
Goyette Museum of Americana
Elm St.
A; Je-O,UZ

Portsmouth
Various Houses
Described

Rumney Village
Mary Baker Eddy Historical
House
M19; W; UZ

Wolfeboro
Clark House
South Main St.
L18; W; UX

NEW JERSEY

Bordentown
Clara Barton School
Crosswicks and Burlington Sts.
M18; H; UX

Burlington
James Fenimore Cooper Birth-
place
457 High St.
L18; A; App.X
James Lawrence House
459 South High St.
L18; H; UX
Revel House
8 East Pearl St.
L17; W; App.X

Caldwell
Grover Cleveland Birthplace
207 Bloomfield Ave.
E19; H; UZ

Camden
Charles S. Boyer Memorial Hall
("Pomona Hall" or "Joseph
Cooper Jr. House")
Euclid Ave. & Park Blvd.
E18; W; UX
Walt Whitman House
328 Mickle St.
L19; H; UZ

Elizabeth
Boudinot Mansion
("Boxwood Hall")
1073 East Jersey St.
M18; W; UX

Englishtown
Englishtown Inn
E18; H; UX

Freehold
John Craig House
E18; H; UX
Hankinson Mansion
M18; H; UX
Old Tennent Church
M18; W; UX
St. Peter's Church
Throckmorton & Main Sts.
L18; W; UX

Greenwich
Richard Wood Mansion
L18; A; UZ

Haddonfield
Haddonfield Historical Society
231 Kings Highway East
E19; A; UX
Indian King Tavern
233 Kings Highway East
M18; H; UZ

Hancock's Bridge
Hancock House
E18; H; UZ

Hoboken
Castle Stevens
Stevens Institute of Technol-
ogy
M19; A; App.X

Matawan
Burrowes House
E18; H

Middletown
Marlpit Hall
L17; A; UX

Morristown
Schuyler-Hamilton House
Described
Ford Mansion
Described
Historical Museum
Described
Wick House
Described

Mt. Holly
The John Woolman Memorial
99 Branch St.
M18; W; UX

New Brunswick
Buccleuch Mansion
College Ave. & George St.
E18; W; UX
Henry Guest House
M18; W; UX
Wood Lawn
E19; W; UX

North Hackensack
Zabriskie Steuben House
M18; H; UX

Paterson
Lambert Castle
L19; A; SS.X,Jl-Au,UX
Garret Mtn. Reservation
L19; A; UX

Plainfield
Nathaniel Drake House
602 West Front St.
M18; H; UZ

Princeton
Nassau Hall
Described

Ringwood
Ringwood Manor State Park
Museum
(Ryerson House, Hewitt Mansion)
Ringwood Manor State Park
L18; A; UX

Rocky Hill
Berrian Mansion
(Rockingham)
Rocky Hill
E18; H; UZ

Salem
Alexander Grant House
81-83 Market St.
E18; A; App.X

near Sandy Hook
Navesink Lighthouse
M19; A

Shrewsbury
The Allen House
M17; W
Christ Church
M18; A; UX
Friends' Meeting House
E19; W; UX

Somers Point
Somers Mansion
Shore Rd. & Circle
E18; A; UZ

Somerville
Old Dutch Parsonage
Washington Place
M18; A; UZ
Wallace House
Washington Place
L18; H; UZ

Titusville
McKonkey Ferry House
(Johnson House)
State Park
M18; H; UZ

Trenton
Old Barracks
South Willow St.
M18; H; UZ
Old Masonic Lodge House
South Willow & Lafayette Sts.
L18; A; UX
William Trent House
Described

Wayne Township
Dey Mansion
Preakness Valley Park
M18; H; UZ

Woodbury
John Lawrence House
58 North Broad St.
M18; A; UZ

near Woodbury
Whitall Mansion
Fort Mercer
M18; H; UZ

NEW MEXICO

Acoma
Old Acoma
E17; W; UZ

Albuquerque
Ernie Pyle Memorial Branch
Library
900 Girard Boulevard, S.E.
20; W; UX

San Felipe de Neri
Old Town Plaza
E18; A; UX

Moriarty
Longhorn Ranch Museum of the
Old West
19; A; UZ

New Laguna
Mission of San José de Laguna
L17; W; UX

Santa Fe
Palace of the Governors
Described

New Mexico *(continued)*
Santa Fe *(continued)*
Mission San Miguel
Described
Old House
Described

Taos Pueblo
Described

NEW YORK CITY

City Hall
E19; A; UX (C temp.)
Cooper Union
Described
Dyckman House
Broadway at 204th St.
L18; W; UX
Federal Hall
Wall & Nassau Sts.
E18; H; UX
Fraunces Tavern
Described
Frick Collection
Described
Gracie Mansion
88th St. at East River
L18; A; UX
Roger Morris-Jumel Mansion
Described
Poe Cottage
Poe Park, Fordham
E19; W; UX
Theodore Roosevelt House
28 East 20th St.
M19; H; UX
Abigail Adams Smith House
421 East 61st St.
L18; A; UX
Van Cortlandt House
Described

NEW YORK STATE

Albany
Joseph Henry Memorial
Academy Park
E19; A; UX

Schuyler Mansion
Described
Alexandria Bay
Boldt Castle
Heart Island
20; A; UX
Amsterdam
Guy Park
West Main St.
M18; A; UX
Canandaigua
Granger Homestead
295 North Main St.
E19; A; UX
Centerport
Vanderbilt Museum
Little Neck Rd.
20; A; UZ
Constableville
Constable Hall
A; Je-N,UZ
Cooperstown
Baseball Hall of Fame
Described
Doubleday Field
Described
Farmers Museum
Described
Fenimore House
Described
East Hampton
Home Sweet Home
Described
Old Hook Mill
Described
Elmira
Mark Twain Study
Described
Flushing
Bowne House
Described
Friends' Meeting House
Described
Fort Johnson
Old Fort Johnson
M18; A; UX

Goshen
Hall of Fame of the Trotter
240 Main St.
20; A; UX
Huntington
Huntington Historical Society
High Street & New York Ave.
M18; A; UZ
Hyde Park
Hyde Park
Described
Vanderbilt Mansion
Described
Irvington
Sunnyside
Described
Jamaica
King Mansion
150 St. & Jamaica Ave.
M18; A; UX
Johnstown
Johnson Hall
18; A; UX
Kingston
Old Stone House
L17; A; UX
Senate House
Described
near Lake Placid
John Brown's Farm
M19; H; UX
Lawrence
Rock Hall
Broadway at Lawrence Ave.
M18; A; UZ
Little Falls
General Herkimer Home
Described
near Monroe
Old Museum Village of Smith's
Clove
20; W; UZ
Mt. McGregor
Grant Cottage
M18; H; UX

Newburgh
Hasbrouck House
Described

New Paltz
Various Houses
Described

New Rochelle
Thomas Paine Cottage
North & Paine Ave.
L18; H; UX

near North Hudson
Frontier Town
19; A; UZ

North Tarrytown
Philipse Castle
Described

Oswego
Old Fort Ontario
M18; H; UX

Oyster Bay
Home of Mrs. Theodore F.
Humphrey
East Main St.
M17; A
Reginald P. Rose House
Mill River Rd.
18; A
Raynham Hall
West Main St.
M18; A
Sagamore Hill
Described

near Oneida Lake
Fort Brewerton
M18; H; UX

Palmyra
Joseph Smith Home
E19; A; UX

Plattsburgh
Kent-DeLord House Museum
17 Cumberland Ave.
L18; W; UZ

Poughkeepsie
Clinton House
549 Main St.
M18; A; UX

near Remsen
Steuben Log Cabin
L18; A; UX

Rensselaer
Fort Crailo
Described

Rochester
Eastman House
Described

Saranac Lake
Stevenson Memorial Cottage
M19; H; UZ

Saratoga Springs
The Casino
Congress Park
M19; A; UZ

Scarsdale
Wayside Cottage
1039 Post Rd.
E18; W; App.X

Schoharie
Old Stone Fort Museum
N. Main St.
L18; A; Ap-N,X

Schuylerville
General Philip Schuyler House
L18; H; Je-S,UZ

South Huntington
Walt Whitman Birthplace
246 Walt Whitman Rd.
E19; H; UZ

Staatsburg
Ogden Mills Home
A; UZ

Syracuse
French Fort
M17; H; UX
Salt Museum
W; UX

Ticonderoga
Fort Mount Hope
M18; H; UX
Fort Ticonderoga
M18; H; My.-N, U, $1

near Vail's Gate
Knox Headquarters
M18; A; UX

Yonkers
Philipse Manor
Described

NORTH CAROLINA

Aberdeen
Old Bethesda Church
L18; W; UX

Asheboro
Central Hotel
E19; A; UX

near Asheville
Richmond Hill
PO; 19; A

Asheville
Biltmore House and Gardens
Described
Biltmore Industries
Described
Stuart Nye Silver Shop
940 Tunnel Rd.
20; A; UX
Thomas Wolfe Memorial
48 Spruce St.
20; H; UZ

Bath
Glebe House
M18; A; UX
Marsh House
M18; A; UX
St. Thomas Episcopal Church
E18; A; UX

Beaufort
Davis House
A; UX

North Carolina (*continued*)
Beaufort (*continued*)
   Duncan House
    Front Street
    L18; A
   Hammock House
    E18; W
   Masonic Lodge
    A; UX
   Odd Fellows Home
    Turner St.
    E19; A; UX

near Blowing Rock
   Cone Mansion
    Moses H. Cone Memorial Park
    E20; A; UX

Burnsville
   Nu-Wray Inn
    E19; A; UX

Buxton
   Cape Hatteras Lighthouse
    L18; H; Th-M, X

Chapel Hill
   Old East Building
    University Campus
    L18; A
   South Building
    University Campus
    L18; A

Charlotte
   Hezekiah Alexander House
    L18; A
   William Phips Home
    722 N. Tryon St.
    M19; H

Cherokee
   Oconaluftee Indian Village
    Described

Clemmons
   Mount Pleasant Methodist
   Church
    William & Kate B. Reynolds
    Memorial Park
    E19; A; UX

near Columbia
   Somerset
    Pettigrew State Park
    E19; A; UX
Durham
   Bennett Place
    M19; H; UX
near Durham
   Duke Homestead
    Described
   Fairntosh Plantation
    E19; W; UX
Edenton
   Various Houses
    18; A
Fayetteville
   First Presbyterian Church
    Bow Street
    E19; A; UX
   Mackethan House
    Cool Spring Street & Cool
    Spring Lane
    L18; A; UX
   Market House
    L18; H; UX
   Masonic Lodge
    Mason Street
    L18; A; UX
   Woman's Club
    225 Dick St.
    E19; A; UX
Flat Rock
   Woodfield's Inn
    PO; M19; A; UX
Halifax
   Constitution House
    M18; H; UX
   Colonial Gaol
    E18; H; UX
   Davie Home
    L18; A; UX
   Halifax County Free Public Library
    M18; A; UX
Hertford
   Perquimans Courthouse
    E18; H; UX

High Point
   Allen Jay House
    Box 1551
    L18; W; App.X
   Springfield Museum of Old Domestic Arts
    Box 1551
    M19; A; App.X

Hillsboro
   American Legion Building
    L18; A; UX
   Ayr Mount
    L18; A; UX
   Colonial Inn
    L18; H; UX
   Dickson House
    M18; H; UX
   Masonic Lodge
    E19; A; UX
   Presbyterian Church
    E19; A; UX

Lenoir
   Fort Defiance
    L18; H; UX

Littleton
   Old Ordinary Tavern
    L18; A; UX

Manteo
   Fort Raleigh
    L16; H; UX

Morehead City
   Fort Macon
    E19; H; UX

Murfreesboro
   Freeman House
    L18; A; UX

New Bern
   Gaston Hotel
    M19; W; UX
   Presbyterian Church
    New Street
    E19; A; UX
   Stanly-Green-Winfield House
    Pollock St. at Hancock
    M19; A; UX

Tryon Palace
  200 George Street
    M18; H; UZ
John Wright Stanly Home
  New Street near Middle
    L18; H; UX
Penland
  The Weavers Cabin
    20; A; UX
  Edward F. Worst Craft House
    20; A; UX
Raleigh
  Christ Episcopal Church
    Edenton & Wilmington
      M19; A; UX
  Christ Church Rectory
    E19; A; UX
  Andrew Johnson Birthplace
    State College Campus
      E19; A; UX
  Joel Lane House (Wakefield)
    728 W. Hargett St.
      M18; A; UX
Salisbury
  Old Stone House
    L18; A; UX
Shiloh
  Baptist Church
    E18; A; UX
Southern Pines
  Shaw House
    L19; A; UX
Wilmington
  Cornwallis House
    226 Market St.
      L18; H; UX
  Governor Dudley House
    Front and Nun Sts.
      E19; A; UX
  St. James Church
    Third & Market Sts.
      M18; H; UX
  St. John's Tavern
    E19; A; UX
near Wilmington
  Orton Plantation
    E18; A; UX

Winston-Salem
  Various Houses
    Described
  Wachovia Museum and other
    Houses
    Described

NORTH DAKOTA

Abercrombie
  Fort Abercrombie
    M19; H; UX
Fort Rice
  Fort Rice Historic Site
    M19; H; UX
Medora
  Chateau De Mores
    L19; A; UZ

OHIO

Chillicothe
  Adena
    Described
Cincinnati
  The Taft Museum
    316 Pike St.
      E19; A; UX
Cleveland
  Dunham Tavern
Dayton
  Wright House
    Described
  Patterson Memorial Center
    Described
  Pioneer House
    Described
Gambier
  Old Kenyon
    Kenyon College Campus
      E19; A; UX
  Bexley Hall
    Kenyon College Campus
      E19; A; UX

Kirtland
  Kirtland Temple
    E19; W; UX
Lebanon
  Glendower Warren County Museum
    seum
      E19; A; UZ
Marietta
  Campus Martins, land office
    Described
Marion
  President Harding Home
    380 Mt. Vernon Ave.
      L19; H; UZ
Massillon
  The Massillon Museum
    212 Lincoln Way East
      E19; A; UX
Mentor
  President James A. Garfield
    Home
    1059 Mentor Avenue
      L19; H; UZ
Mercer County
  Fort Recovery
    L18; H; UX
Milan
  Thomas Edison Birthplace
    Described
North Bend
  Benjamin Harrison Home
    M19; H; UX
New Philadelphia
  Schoenbrunn Village
    Described
Point Pleasant
  Grant Birthplace
    Described
Unionville
  Shandy Hall
    E19; W; UX
Upper Sandusky
  The Wyandot Mission Church
    E19; W; UX

Ohio (*continued*)
Zoar
Zoar Village
Described

OKLAHOMA

Claremore
Will Rogers Memorial Museum
20; W; UX
Fort Gibson
E19; H; UX

OREGON

Canyon City
Grant County Museum & Historical Bldg.
20; A; My-O, UZ

Newberg
Herbert Hoover Boyhood Home
19; H; UX

Oregon City
McLoughlin House
Described

PENNSYLVANIA

Altoona
Baker Mansion
3502 Baker Boulevard
M19; A; SSX

Ambridge
Old Economy Harmony Society

near Baumstown
Daniel Boone Homestead
Described

Bethlehem
The Gemeinhaus
M18; W; UX
The Sisters' House
M18; W; UX
The Bell House
M18; W; UX
Colonial Hall
M18; W; UX

The Old Chapel
M18; W; UX
The Widows' House
M18; W; UX
Central Church
E19; W; UX

near Birdsboro
Hopewell Village
Described

Boalsburg
Boal Mansion
L18; A; UZ
Christopher Columbus Family Chapel
16; A; UZ

Chester
Old Colonial Court House
Market St. bet. 4th & 5th Sts.
E18; H; UX

Danville
Montgomery House
1 Bloom St.
L18; A; W,App.X

Ephrata
Ephrata Cloister
Described

Erie
Wayne Blockhouse
3rd & Ash
L19; A; Je-S,UX
The Flagship Niagara
State St.
E19; H; UX
Old Customs House
M19; A; UX

Germantown
Several Houses
Described

Gettysburg
Jennie Wade Museum
546 Baltimore St.
E19; H; UX

Hanover
Shrine of the Sacred Heart
L18; A; UX

Harmony
Grace Reformed Church
On the Square
E19; W; UX

near Harmony
Mennonite Church
E19; W; App.X

Hershey
Derry Presbyterian Church
M18; W; UX

Lancaster
Wheatland, Home of James Buchanan
M19; A; UZ

Lima
John J. Tyler Mansion House & Arboretum
M18; A; UX

Lititz
Old Moravian House
M18; A; App.X

Mercersberg
Buchanan Cabin
Mercersburg Academy
L18; H; UX

near Morrisville
Pennsbury Manor
Described

Nazareth
Gray Cottage
M18; W; UX
Nazareth Hall
Center St.
L18; W; UX
Nazareth Moravian Church
M19; W; UX
Whitefield House
East Center St.
M18; W; App.Z.

Philadelphia
Various Homes
Described

Pittsburgh
Fort Pitt Block House
Point Park
M18; H; UX

Pottstown
Potts Grove
M18; A; UX

Prospect Park
John Morton House
Described

Scottdale
Historical House of the West-moreland-Fayette Historical So-ciety
M19; A; My-N,SS or App.X
Museum of the Westmoreland-Fayette Historical Society
M19; A; My-N,SS or App.X

State College
Old Main
University Park
M19; A; UX

Stroudsburg
Stroud Community House
9th & Main Sts.
L18; A; App.X

Sunbury
Fort Augusta
1150 North Front St.
M18; H; UX

Titusville
Drake Well Memorial Park & Museum
Described

Towanda
French Azilum, Inc.
L18; W; UZ

near Uniontown
Fort Necessity
M18; H; UX

Valley Forge
Washington Headquarters
Described

Washington Crossing
Thompson-Neely House
Described

Waterford
Amos Judson House
First & Walnut Sts.
E19; A; UX

RHODE ISLAND

Anthony
General Nathanael Greene Homestead
48 Taft St.
M18; H; W,SSX

Johnston
Clemence-Irons House
L17; A; UZ

Lincoln
Eleazer Arnold House
449 Great Rd.
L17; A; UZ

Newport
Various Houses
Described

Pawtucket
Old Slater Mill
Described

Providence
Various Houses
Described

Saunderstown
Gilbert Stuart Birthplace
Described

Wickford
Old Narragansett Church
E18; A; UX
Smith's Castle
E17; A; UZ

SOUTH CAROLINA

Beaufort
Hepworth-Pringle House
214 New St.
E18; A; S

Charleston
Various Houses
Described

Clemson
Fort Hill, Home of John C. Calhoun
Described
Woodrow Wilson Memorial Mu-seum
1705 Hampton St.
M19; H; UX

McClellanville
Hampton Plantation
E18; A; U, $2

TENNESSEE

Columbia
Ancestral Home of James K. Polk
Described

Greeneville
Andrew Johnson National Monu-ment
M19; H; UX

Knoxville
Governor Blount Mansion
Described

near Nashville
Belle Meade Mansion
Described

Nashville
The Hermitage
Described
Fort Nashborough
L18; W; UX

Smyrna
Home of Sam Davis
E19; H; UZ

TEXAS

Huntsville
Sam Houston Home
Described

Texas *(continued)*
San Antonio
The Alamo
Described
San José
Described

UTAH

Brigham City
Box Elder Tabernacle
200-300 S. Main St.
L19; W; UX, App.

Fillmore
State House Museum
M19; H; UX

Salt Lake City
Bee Hive House
Described
Lion House
Described
Brigham Young's Offices and
Other Houses
Described

VERMONT

Bennington
First Congregational Church
E19; W; UX

Dummerston
Naulakha, Rudyard Kipling's
Vermont Home
R.F.D. 1, Brattleboro
L19; H; UZ

Middlebury
Sheldon Museum
E19; A; UZ

Orleans
Old Stone House (Athenian Hall)
E19; A; U, $1

Plymouth
Birthplace of Calvin Coolidge
M19; H; UX

Sharon
Joseph Smith Memorial Cottage
20; W; UX

St. Johnsbury
St. Johnsbury Athenaeum
L19; A; UX

Shelburne
Shelburne Museum
Described

Weston
Farrar-Mansur House
L18; A; UZ
Vermont Guild of Oldtime
Crafts and Industries
L18; W; UX

VIRGINIA

Abingdon
Barter Theatre of Virginia
E19; A; U, $1.80

Alexandria
Gadsby's Tavern
M18; H; UZ
Carlyle House
121 N. Fairfax
M18; A; UZ
Christ Church
M18; H; UX
Old Presbyterian Meeting House
L18; H; UX
Stabler-Leadbeater Apothecary
107 S. Fairfax
M18; W; UX

Appomattox
Appomattox Court House
Described

Arlington
Lee Mansion Memorial
Described

Charles City
Berkeley Plantation
Described
Shirley Plantation
E18; A; U, $1
Westover, Home of William Byrd
PO; E18; A; U, $1

Charlottesville
Ash Lawn
Described
Michie Tavern
Described
Monticello
Described

Culpeper
Greenwood
M18; A; UX
Redwood
M18; A; UX
Salubria
M18; A; UX
Shackelford House
M19; A; UX
The Horseshoe
M18; A; UX
Liberty Hall
E18; A; UX
Del Rae
M18; A; UX
Greenville
M19; A; UX
Level Green
E18; A; UX
Val Verde
M19; A; UX
St. Stephen's Church
E19; A; UX
Little Fork Church
L18; A; UX

Fredericksburg
Ferry Farm
E18; H; UX
Stonewall Jackson Shrine
Described
Kenmore
1201 Washington Ave.
M18; H; UX
Fredericksburg Lodge No. 4, AF
& AM
Princess Anne St. & Hanover
E19; H; UZ
Hugh Mercer Apothecary Shop
Described

[232]

James Monroe Law Office & Museum
Described
Rising Sun Tavern
1306 Caroline St.
M18; H; UZ
Mary Ball Washington House
Described

Jamestown Island
Jamestown Excavation
Described

King George County
Marmion
Comorn Post Office
L17; A; UZ

Lexington
Robert E. Lee Chapel
Described

Lorton
Gunston Hall
Described
Pohick Church
Described

Luray
Luray Museum
213 West Main St.
E19; A; UZ

Lynchburg
Miller-Claytor House
L18; A; App.X

Mount Vernon
George Washington's Home
Described
Woodlawn Plantation
Described

Norfolk
St. Paul's Episcopal Church and Parish House
E18; A; UX

Petersburg
Centre Hill Mansion Museum
E19; A; UX

Richmond
The Lee House
707 E. Franklin St.
M19; A; UZ
The Poe Shrine
1916 East Main St.
L17; A; UZ
White House of the Confederacy
12th & Clay Sts.
E19; H; UZ
Wickham-Valentine House and Various Houses
Described
Wilton
Described

Smithfield
Old Court House
M18; H; UX
Old Fort Boykin
E17; H; UX
St. Luke's (The Old Brick Church)
Isle of Wight County
E17; A; UX

Spring Grove
Brandon Plantation
E17; A; U, $1.50
Upper Brandon Plantation
E17; A; U, $1

Stafford
Aquia Church
M18; A; Je-S, UX

Staunton
Woodrow Wilson Birthplace
Described

Surry
Rolfe Property
M17; A; UZ

Westmoreland County
Stratford Hall Plantation
Described
Wakefield, George Washington Birthplace
Described

Williamsburg
Colonial Williamsburg
Described

Winchester
George Washington's Office
M18; H; UZ

Yorktown
Moore House
E18; H; UZ

WASHINGTON

Olympia
State Capitol Historical Museum
20; A; UX

Port Townsend
Alexander's Blockhouse
M19; A; UX

San Juan Island
British Blockhouse
M19; A; UX

Tacoma
Old Fort Nisqually
Described

Fort Vancouver
Fort Vancouver National Monument
M19; A; UX

Walla Walla
Whitman Mission Building Ruins
E19; A; UX

near Yakima
Fort Simcoe
M18; A; UX

WEST VIRGINIA

Ansted
Halfway House Tavern
M18; A; UX

Bethany
Alexander Campbell House

West Virginia (*continued*)
Charles Town
  The Washington Homes of Jefferson County
    Described

Fayette County
  Old Half Way House
    M18; A; UZ

Lewisburg
  Old Stone Church
    L18; A; UX

New Gap Mills
  Methodist Church
    L18; A; UX

Point Pleasant
  Mansion House
    Main Street at Tu-Endie-Wei Park
    L18; A; UX

Wheeling
  Oglebay Park Mansion House
    Described
  Shepherd Hall
    Described

WISCONSIN

near Belmont
  First Capitol Building
    First Capitol State Park
    E19; H; UX

Beloit
  Rasey House
    517 Prospect St.
    M19; A; UZ

Cassville
  Stonefield State Farm & Craft Museum
    Nelson Dewey State Park
    M19; A; UZ

Eau Claire
  Paul Bunyan Camp
    Carson Park
    20; A; UX

Green Bay
  The Howard Hospital Museum
    402 N. Chestnut Ave.
    E19; H; UZ
  Roi-Portier-Tank Cottage
    Tank Park
    L18; A; UZ

Greenbush
  Old Wade House
    M19; A; UZ

Janesville
  Lincoln Tallman House
    440 N. Jackson St.
    M19; A; UZ

Kohler
  Waelderhaus
    Described

Milton
  The Milton House
    M19; A; UZ

Mineral Point
  Cornish Miners' Homes
    Described

Mt. Horab
  Little Norway
    19; W; My-N, UZ

Neenah
  Doty Cabin
    Lincoln St.
    M19; H; UX

Portage
  Agency House
    E19; A; UZ
  Surgeon's Quarters, Fort Winnebago
    E19; H; UZ

Prairie du Chien
  Brisbois House
    325 N. Water St.
    E19; A; UZ
  Villa Louis
    M19; A; UX

Ripon
  Little White School House
    M19; H; UX

Wauwatosa
  The Lowell Damon House
    M19; A; Su.X

Watertown
  The Octagon House
    919 Charles St.
    M19; A; UZ

WYOMING

Fort Laramie
  Fort Laramie
    Described

Moose
  Homestead cabin of William D. Menor
    Grand Teton National Park
    L19; A; UX